Joseph Tom Burgess

Historic Warwickshire

Its Legendary Lore, Traditionary Stories, and Romantic Episodes

Joseph Tom Burgess

Historic Warwickshire
Its Legendary Lore, Traditionary Stories, and Romantic Episodes

ISBN/EAN: 9783337021412

Printed in Europe, USA, Canada, Australia, Japan

Cover: Foto ©ninafisch / pixelio.de

More available books at **www.hansebooks.com**

HISTORIC WARWICKSHIRE:

ITS LEGENDARY LORE, TRADITIONARY STORIES, AND ROMANTIC EPISODES.

BY

J. TOM BURGESS,

AUTHOR OF "OLD ENGLISH WILD FLOWERS," "THE LAST BATTLE OF THE ROSES," "LEGENDS OF THE DALCASSIANS," ETC., ETC.

With Numerous Illustrations.

LONDON:
SIMPKIN, MARSHALL, AND CO.
WARWICK: H. T. COOKE AND SON.
LEAMINGTON: WIPPELL, CARTWRIGHT, CUNNEW, DEW, AND SIMMONS.
BIRMINGHAM: CORNISH. COVENTRY: CURTIS. RUGBY: BILLINGTON.
ALCESTER: WRIGHT. STRATFORD: ADAMS, PALMER, AND REEVE.
TAMWORTH: THOMPSON.

LONDON:
PRINTED BY W. H. AND L. COLLINGRIDGE,
ALDERSGATE STREET, E.C.

TO

LIEUT.-GEN. FRANCIS HUGH GEORGE SEYMOUR,

THE MOST HONOURABLE

THE MARQUIS OF HERTFORD,

THE REPRESENTATIVE OF THE ELDER BRANCH OF THE

ANCIENT LORDS OF ARROW,

This Volume,

EMBODYING THE LEGENDS, TRADITIONS, AND

ROMANCES OF WARWICKSHIRE,

IS MOST RESPECTFULLY DEDICATED BY

THE AUTHOR.

PREFACE.

During the past eight years I have been busily engaged in collecting materials for an historical description of Warwickshire, which should be at once exhaustive, portable, and exact, yet published at a price which would bring it within the means of every class of the community. With this view I have visited nearly every parish in the county, and have consulted all the known available documents relating to the past and present history of the county; yet now, to keep even lingering faith to those kind friends who so early encouraged me with their approval and subscriptions, I have issued this volume full of the knowledge of its shortcomings and knowing that it represents but the fringe and tassels of history. I felt, however, that these legendary stories—the myths and traditions of the past—would perhaps create a wider interest than a drier but more connected narrative of the events which have been interwoven with the shire of Warwick. Some of the episodes here briefly related are known to all, some are fresh and new, some are presented with newer facts and under a different guise, and others will dispel a widespread belief in the fables of history. There are some well-known romantic incidents I have purposely omitted; there are others I have foreborne to touch upon, because of the paucity and uncertainty of the materials. The defence of Venusius, the Traitor's Ford at Wichford, the Soldier's Bank at Willey, the parson-chaplain of Spernal, the princely pleasures of Kenilworth are amongst these omissions. There are some little scraps of folk lore and superstitions which have come to my knowledge since this volume has been in the printer's hands. During this brief period, the discovery of the plaque at the bottom of the Macer Bowl at Harbledown, near Canterbury, has thrown some light on the legend of Guy of Warwick, for the knight there slaying the dragon bears the arms of Beauchamp, and in all probability is intended for Guy Beauchamp, and the dragon for Piers Gaveston. It is of an earlier date than any known MSS. of the legend, for we must not forget that the statue of Guy's Cliffe bears the arms of the family of Arden.

I have avoided, as far as possible, advancing any theory

as to the origin of the many legends embodied in this volume. It is the first time that an attempt has been made to gather these strange stories and to divide the mythical from the historical, and I have preferred rather to collect, abridge, and cull the most interesting of the many romantic stories connected with the county of Warwick than to speculate on their origin. If I, by so doing, have aroused a feeling of interest in the history of this great Midland shire, I shall be well repaid, and may at no distant period appeal to my many friends and readers on behalf of a more general, more abstruse, but more original "Ancient History of Warwickshire," as well as of the new borough of Royal Leamington Spa.

I had intended, and indeed have prepared, a long list of names and derivations relating to the earlier history of the shire, as well as a glossary of Warwickshire words, but this has grown from a few pages to the extent of a volume.

I have been indebted to many books and to many friends for the facts embodied herein. My thanks are especially due to Sir Thomas Duffus Hardy, the late Dr. O'Callaghan, Messrs. Evelyn Philip Shirley, J. Staunton, M. H. Bloxam, Joseph Burtt, S. Timmins, Edward Scriven, Thomas Beasley, J. R. Planché, Walter de Gray Birch, James Parker, Thomas Gibbs, W. G. Fretton, J. W. Kirshaw, J. Cove Jones, and R. H. Hobbes, for many courtesies and assistance in this labour of love.

J. TOM BURGESS.

GRASSBROOKE, LEAMINGTON, 1876.

CONTENTS.

LEGENDS AND TRADITIONS.

ROMANTIC AND HISTORIC EPISODES.

ILLUSTRATIONS.

THE

Legends and Traditions

OF

WARWICKSHIRE.

HISTORIC WARWICKSHIRE.

The Legends and Mythical Lore.

> "O hallowed memories of the past,
> Ye legends old and fair,
> Still be your light upon us cast,
> Your music on the air.
>
> In vain shall man deny
> Or bid your mission cease,
> While stars yet prophesy
> Of love, and hope, and peace."

THE bards of the Gaels—the fathers of the land—sang in forest and in temple the glories of the past. The young were incited to emulate the deeds of heroes, and receive their reward in the land of the blest. The gleemen of Woden and of Thor, the scalds of the north, took up the strain, and in the famed days of chivalry the romancer and the troubadour threw a poetic glamour over the glories of the knightly deeds of baron and squire. In song, in story, and in legend many of these remnants of mythical lore have come down to us, and have been preserved in the memories of the people; thus

> "The intelligible forms of ancient poets,
> The fair humanities of old religion,

B

> **The power, the beauty, and the majesty**
> **That had their haunts in dale or piny mountain,**
> **Or forest, by slow stream, or pebbly spring,**
> **Or chasms and wat'ry depths "**

have been preserved, and though "they live no longer in the faith of reason, still the heart doth need a language," still the old instinct survives, and we do not cease to love the lore which our fathers loved, mythical and fabulous though it may be.

The mind easily grasps what it can see, and when ideas are wedded to familiar objects they are easily retained, and we unconsciously clothe our hero-Guys with all the attributes of heroism and our Godivas with the perfection of goodness and of charity. Give these embodiments of love, of valour, and of beauty a local habitation, and we have a key to the charm which the novelist and the poet throw round the objects they describe. They people each bosky wood, each lane, headland, or verdant dell with personages and attributes which, if not ideal, are idealized embodiments of what they ought to be.

Fabulous though many of these old wives' tales and fireside stories may be, they contain a germ of truth and life amid their poetic and mythical surroundings. We find them continually intermixed with undoubted facts, and are related day by day as literal truth. We cannot, therefore, wonder at their being preserved in monkish chronicles, or even in the ponderous pages of Dugdale. It might be asked why these pieces of legendary lore should be preserved. They are but the dust of the past—mere fables, full of improbable incident. They have deceived people long enough. Let them be forgotten. Let them perish. But in the economy of nature nothing is valueless. The refuse of a town fertilizes the fields; from nauseous coal tar the chemist produces bright dyes and transparent wax candles; and even now it is proposed to utilize the much abused scoriæ of the furnaces and engines. We should not, therefore, despise what seems meaningless, for the dirty pebble may conceal the diamond. Even if they are but fables—

> "Fable is Love's world,
> His home, his birthplace;
> Delightedly dwells he among fays and talismans,
> And spirits, and delightedly believes divinity,
> Being himself divine."

There is a witching character about some of these old stories which affects the imagination, and they linger for ages. There is a story told of an ancient tumulus—of which there are many in Warwickshire—that it was haunted by the spirit of a warrior clad in glistening armour. Not that any one had seen the spirit, but the memory of it remained. During a fit of antiquarian research the tumulus was opened, and on the ground, beneath the superincumbent earth, there lay the figure of a warrior of old, with the remains of his armour. Here popular tradition had preserved the memory of an event which must have come down through many ages. In other instances, however, the original story has been lost, and has been supplemented by another from some accidental resemblance, or from the association with some later event within the memory of the people whose ancestors resided in that part of the country. Thus, in the neighbourhood of Edgehill, anything which is observed of an unusual character is referred to the fight there. The people who erected those singular stone circles and monuments in different parts of the country have passed away and are forgotten. Historians know but little about them; the common people have forgotten their object. Their origin is lost in the dim past. Hence we find traditional stories relating to them, evolved only out of what Carlyle would call "the inner consciousness of the people;" yet frequently their names embody their original designation, though changed and adapted to the newer thought and the later ideas. These old names frequently guide the etymologist to some long-forgotten battle field, ancient temple, or lonely tomb. Hartshill and Yarningale have been pointed out as instances of this. Brailes indicates an outwork, and here are fortifications, the outwork of the greater fortifications on the Edge hills. Donnilee, the ancient name of Beaudesert, would imply the place of the fort. The Roman station of Bennones evidently alludes to its site at the top of the hill, as Manduesedum shows that it was the seat of the stone; and in its modern name, Mancetter, we have literally the stone camp, the British prefix being added to the Saxon castra. There is scarcely a parish in Warwickshire which does not possess a field or hillock known as the Castle Hill or field, though we know that no castle in the mediæval sense of the term ever stood there. The name points to the older tongue, when the *cæsail* stone fort, or fortified dwelling of the old inhabitants, stood on the spot. There is one of these fields close to the scene of the legend of the bell at Whitnash. There are two castle sites at Fillongley, one the modern moated, fortified dwelling, the other belonging to the older time and people, and is a good example of these ancient dwellings. Frequently, however, as at Allesley, the older mound has been adapted to the more modern purpose. Warwick and Tamworth mounds are probably other instances. Readers of history know the part the Frisians took in the invasion of England. Curiously enough on the Fosse way on either side of the Roman camp at Chesterton there are two Friz hills. The one in Radford parish, near the spot where the Great Western railway crosses the Fosse, is called Frizmore. Its top, like a similar but smaller mound near Ufton, shows signs of sinking or of excavation. They may be denuded hills, but they seem like large barrows. At Frizhill, near Combrooke, there are distinct tumuli in Bowshot-Wood. These tumuli are close to where the six mile station from Chesterton would be placed.

On the Edge hills, close to where the Red Horse is cut,

is the Sunrising, and curiously enough the only derivation suggested of Tysoe is Tighsollas—the house of the sun or the house of light. The Celtic *tigh*, pronounced *ty* or *tee*, is found in Coventry. Dugdale says this is derived from Covent-tre—the house of the convent. Others affirm that there was a tree before the convent, and the town took its name from this obviously mythical tree. In Co-van-tigh we have the house of the holy woman. A French writer derives it from *cowen*, bright, and *tigh*, a house. On the Fosse way, near where it joins the Watling Street way, is Cloudsley Bush. There was once a tumulus here, with a bush or tree on the summit. This has been pronounced to be a corruption of Claudius, a commander of a Roman cohort, whose grave it was said to be.

These are some of the many old and modern names, which show obvious signs of corruption and yet the germs of truth.

Amongst the many fables which remain to us which show signs of belonging to ancient superstitions are those relating to birds. There are some who see in Gaydon the "hill of the goose," and it is a favourite spot for breeding geese now. The goose was a favourite and holy bird, and almost within sight of this hill, says the story, the legend of St. Werburgh and the geese took place. St. Werburgh was a saintly virgin, who resided not far from the Warwickshire borders on the Northamptonshire side. On one occasion a neighbour complained that his crops had been injured by the wild geese, and besought the aid of St. Werburgh. The saint commanded the geese to appear, and after some remonstrances the wise birds promised to leave and never trouble the land again. After a brief confinement the birds were released, but, instead of proceeding on their way, they hovered round the forbidden fields uttering plaintive cries. Again was complaint made to St. Werburgh, who, on inquiring the reason, found that one of the geese had been taken away, and the rest of the flock refused to leave without their lost companion. The missing goose had been in the meantime cooked and eaten, but St. Werburgh was equal to any emergency, and like a good saint she restored the goose to its companions, and, though it had been eaten, gave it back the life it had lost, and then the flock disappeared and troubled the land no longer.

In this fabulous narrative we see the remnant of an old superstition lingering in spite of the life and teachings of St. Werburgh; though in this story of the geese we find them displaced from the high and holy position they had before occupied, and sent off to trouble the people and the land no longer. The gallant and pious Æthelfleda, Lady of Mercia, founded the Abbey of Chester, and dedicated it to this Mercian saint, and on one of the stalls this story may be found portrayed by the art of the carver in wood.

There is one legend that is mentioned by Shakespeare which is yet preserved in the memory of the old inhabitants of his native shire. Hamlet, speaking of that gracious time commemorative of our Saviour's birth, alludes to the crowing cock, and says:—

"This bird of dawning singeth all night long,
And then they say no spirit can walk abroad;
The nights are wholesome; then no planets strike,
No fairy takes, nor witch hath power to charm,
So hallow'd and so gracious is the time."

The belief is yet general in the power of the cock to foretell events, and in many a country homestead you may yet hear sage remarks on the cock crowing at unusual times, and thus foretelling, like an oracle, births, deaths, and unusual occurrences.

Though, perhaps, at the present time, not one in a thousand remembers the pretty legend of the social robin acquiring his ruddy vest by his loving attention to our Saviour's wounds on the cross, there is a universal regard felt for the pert and impudent homely bird which is associated with the reverent feeling once felt for him. You frequently hear

"Remember that robins and wrens
Are God Almighty's cocks and hens."

They are, therefore, to be preserved and cherished, in remembrance of the forgotten legend which gave them almost a sacred character.

Whilst some of these mythical stories are confined to special localities, others are so common and general as to be almost universal. Amongst these is the belief in the existence of subterranean ways. Wherever an abbey stood, or an old castle existed, there we find this belief. There is a notable instance in the general belief of a subterranean passage existing between Kenilworth Castle and Coventry, though no one has ever seen it. This story evidently derives its origin from the fact that Simon de Montfort, when he received a grant of Kenilworth Castle, cut the broad highway through the woods to Coventry, which still exists. By this he freed the road from the predations of robbers and rendered travelling safe.

On the high road between Stratford-on-Avon and Alcester, just beyond the fifth milestone, where the road from Haseler to Temple Grafton crosses it, is what appears to be an immense barrow; the wooded knoll of Rollswood rises behind, and is cut by a green field or two from a remarkable conical hill, called Alcock's Arbour. It is in the parish of Haseler and hamlet of Upton, and adjoins the hills of Oversley. The neighbourhood is interesting, from its proximity to the Roman station of Alauna—the Alenas of Ptolemy—which, from certain expressions, was thought to have been an advanced post of the Dobuni into the forest land. This is hardly probable, though there are indications of an early camp, called Dane's Bank, in Coughton Park, not far from the British road known as the Ridgeway, to the north-west of Alcester.

Alcock's Arbour is, from its singular and apparently artificial form, a striking object in the landscape. The legend attached to this hill is given by Dugdale in these terms :—

"Southwards from Haseler (but within the same parish) is a coppice wood, and in it a notable hill, which is of such a steep and equal ascent from every side as if it had been artifically made, so that it is a very eminent mark over all that part of the country, and by the common people called Alcock's Arbour ; towards the foot whereof is a hole, now almost filled up, having been the entrance into a cave, as the inhabitants report. Of which cave there is an old, curious story, that passes for current amongst the people of the adjacent town, viz., that one Alcock, a great robber, used to lodge therein, and having got much money by that course of life, hid it in an iron-bound chest, whereunto were three keys : which chest they say is still there, but guarded by a cock that continually sits upon it. And that on a time an Oxford scholar came thither with a key that opened two of the locks, but as he was attempting to open the third the cock seized on him ; to all which they add, that if bone of the party who set the cock there could be brought he would yield the chest. But leaving this fable to those that fancy such things, I come to a place not far from it called Grove Hill, whence issueth a very pleasant spring, which anciently bore the name of Cald-well, being remarkable for an hermitage that stood close by it, and at the foundation of Alcester Priory, by Ralph Boteler, of Overbury, in King Stephen's time, was by him given thereto."

The hill itself, I believe, has never been explored. It belongs to Sir William Throckmorton, and would amply repay research. The legend is almost, if not entirely unknown in the immediate neighbourhood. There is a somewhat similar story told in connection with "The Mound," on the south of the Fen Lane near Lindley Hall, but the robber in this case was said to be Dick Turpin.

There are some curious covered ways—deep roads—apparently constructed to provide for the marching of a body of men unperceived through the country. There is a remarkable one near Bensford Bridge, apparently in connection with the great earthworks of Brinklow. There is another which runs by the side of Wixford church to Oversley road; and a very curious one in the immediate vicinity of Kent's moat, a large but irregular earthwork near Yardley, but just within the county boundary.

The Chesterton ghost was for many years the talk of the country-side, so much so, that when the ghost appeared to one of the inhabitants of Harbury on Thursday night, May 1, 1755, the Rev. Richard Jago, the poet of

Edgehill, who was then vicar of Harbury, thought it necessary to preach a sermon on the occasion on the Sunday following. The sermon was printed and is now scarce. The reverend poet took for his text Luke xvi. 31, and considered briefly the causes of impenitence, as well as in the case of extraordinary warnings as under the general laws of providence and grace.

The story of One-handed Boughton is firmly believed in and around Lawford and Rugby. Lawford Hall, prior to its being taken down in 1784, was the scene of a ghostly legend of one of the Boughton family, who lived in the time of good Queen Bess, known to fame as the One-handed Boughton. For some reason or other the bed-chamber of this worthy was reported to be haunted, and many people tried to sleep in it, but in vain. This One-handed had a fashion of riding about the country in a coach and six, to the great disgust of the sober inhabitants of the neighbourhood. At length a body of neighbouring clergymen met, and managed to put the purturbed spirit into a phial, which they threw into a neighbouring marl pit. It is alleged that the father of Sir Theodosius believed in the ghost, and that when his neighbour, Sir Francis Skipwith, wished to see if there were any fish in the pond, he objected, saying that his ancestor, One-handed Boughton, rested there and should not be disturbed. So great was this belief, that it was with the utmost difficulty that workmen were obtained to pull down the hall. This ghost story has been recently revived, and made the subject of a Christmas story, but the writer forgot to add that at the time the story was laid the hall did not exist. The pond has since been drained, and the bottle containing the spirit of One-handed Boughton is now in the possession of his descendant, Mr. Boughton Leigh, of Brownsover.

The remembrance of One-handed Boughton has descended until our own day. Mr. Matthew Bloxam states that he had in his time conversed with old men, who, if they had not seen that personage themselves, had heard from others who had seen him. One old gentleman named Wolfe, who died three or four years ago at the age of nearly a hundred years, remembered when a child, at King's Newnham, sitting by his mother's side, when a man ran in breathless and said, "I have just seen One-handed Boughton. I saw him coming and opened the gate for him, but he flew over it in a carriage and six." Another old gentleman, Mr. John Watts, who died eleven or twelve years ago in his ninety-third year, was formerly an old and respected inhabitant of Rugby. He said he knew a man who always professed to have seen One-handed Boughton. Mr. Watts was with him one day, when he pointed to a distance and said, "There is One-handed Boughton." Whether this man had the gift of second-sight it is impossible to say, but Mr. Watts declared that, staring with all his eyes, *he* could not see him.

There are traditions, which are more in the nature of prophecy, associated with wells and streams. Between Barby Wood and Dunchurch there is a little stream called Rainsbrook, which meanders through the valley, innocent of evil as the stream at which Jacques saw the wounded deer. Yet this quiet brook is the theme of an old tradition, that a great battle is to be fought in its neighbourhood, and its pure limpid stream is to flow with blood. At this battle, which is probably a memory of a past event, three kings are to be present, and their horses will be held by a miller with three thumbs. Amongst the legends of the lone country side, those connected with wells are the most common. Many wells were sanctified, and dedicated to various saints, and in many instances miraculous virtues were attributed to them. The well of St. Keene, immortalized by Southey, is a familiar instance. There are a number of ornamental wells in Warwickshire, notably in the south-western portion of the country. On the extreme east, adjoining the Watling Street way, there is a well called Sketchley Well, which is supposed to have the power of sharpening the wits of those who taste of its waters. It is quite a common remark to a witty man that "he had been to Sketchley." The fact of the well being now enclosed may perhaps account for the lack of wit now observed in the locality. There was formerly an ancient well by the side of the Whitnash brook, to the south of the footway from Whitnash to Radford, and concerning which this curious legend is told :—That the ancient inhabitants, when removing their bell from the ancient church to its present site, brought it to this holy well to be freshly consecrated. In doing this it fell into the water and gradually disappeared. The country people who wish to know coming events, cast stones into the well at night, and in the morning their questions are answered by the sounding of the bell. The site is now drained, but the little stream of water which flows into the Whitnash brook is still believed to be possessed of healing power, and people come from great distances to procure the water. There is a remarkable well near Berkswell churchyard, and another at Burton Dassett, which appear to have been used for the purposes of baptism and immersion.

In Sutton Coldfield Park there is a spring long known as Rowton Well. It was once in repute as a medicinal water, but its virtue as such has long since disappeared. It is now pure and cold enough, famed only by Charles Barker in his poem on Sutton Park.

> " In Nuthurst's windings would you stray,
> Or o'er wild heath and length'ning way
> That leads to Rowton Well?
> Pellucid fount! what annual scores
> Thy stream to cleanliness restores,
> The scribbled post may tell!
> How many Smiths and Joneses came,
> And left to thee their votive name;
> How many more had done the same
> Only they could not spell."

Amongst the folk lore of Warwickshire there is a wide-spread idea, not only that the county is the centre of England, but different localities are specially distinguished. Near Leamington, on the Lillington road, there is an oak tree standing by the side of the road on an elevated mound, which is universally called the centre of England. At Meriden, the cross there is stated to be the exact spot, though it has been moved in the memory of man. The Roman centre of England, and which is nearer the real centre than any other spot known, is situated on high ground between the counties of Leicester and Warwick, where the Watling Street and the Fosse ways cross each other. This spot, known as High Cross, is near the Roman station of Bennones, known to the Saxons as Cleaycestre. There are the shattered remains of a pillar standing in a garden there, on the site of an ancient tumulus. The pillar was erected in obedience to the following order of Quarter Sessions :—

"A.D. 1711, 10 Anna.—At the Easter Sessions some Warwickshire Justices at High Cross, 'in order to have hands sett up there for direction of passengers, according to the statute in that case made and provided,' this conference ended in a recommendation 'that there should be something memoriable built in stone at a place called High Cross, between the two countyes of Warwick and Leicester, as well to direct travellers in the great roades called Wattling Streete and Fosse, as also (for) that it was esteemed the centre of England, and that there should be allowed to the workmen that should finish the same forty pounds, viz., "forty pounds by each county," which, on the report of Sir William Boughton, Bart., and John Shuckburgh, Esq., two of Her Majesty's Justices of the Peace, was at the following Epiphany Sessions, 1711-12, ordered to be done."

There is a view of this cross in its perfect state in Stukeley's "Iter Curiosum" (Vol. i., p. 110). At present the inscription, which was written by Mr. George Greenway, a schoolmaster of Coventry, is barely legible. It was as follows:—

"Vicinarum provinciarum, Vervicencis scilicet et Leicestrensis, ornamenta, proceres patriciique, auspiciis illustrissimi Basilii Comitis de Denbigh, hanc columnam statuendam curaverunt, in gratam pariter et perpetuam memoriam jani tandem a Serenissima Anna clausi A.D. M.D.CC.XII."

Which is thus translated:—

"The noblemen and gentry, ornaments of the neighbouring counties of Warwick and Leicester, at the instance of the Right Honourable Basil Earl of Denbigh, have caused this pillar to be erected in grateful as well as perpetual remembrance of peace at last restored by her Majesty Queen Anne, in the year of our Lord 1712."

The inscription on the other side runs thus:—

"Si Veterum Romanorum vestigia quæras, hic cernas, viator. Hic enim celeberrimæ illorum viæ militares, sese mutuo secantes, ad extremos usque Britanniæ limites procurrunt: hic stativa sua habuerunt Vennones; et ad primum ab hinc lapidem castra sua; ad Stratam, et ad Fossum tumulum, Claudius quidem cohortis præfectus habuisse videtur."

Which may be thus rendered:—

"If traveller you search for the footsteps of the ancient Romans, here you may behold them, for here their most celebrated ways, crossing one another, extend to the utmost boundaries of Britain. Here the Vennones kept their quarters; and, at the distance of one mile from hence, Claudius, a certain commander of a cohort, seems to have had a camp towards the street, and towards the Fosse a tomb."

The ground here is so high, and the surrounding country so low and flat, that it is said fifty-seven churches may be seen from this spot without the help of a glass. Here stood one of the three Warwickshire beacons; the others were at Bickenhill and Burton Dasset. From hence you can obtain a view of the great Midland Vale, and the backbone of England, studded with trees, and decked with the flowers whose legend and story awaits you.

Legends and Stories of Plants and Flowers.

"They are flown,
Beautiful fictions of our fathers, wove
In Superstition's web, when Time was young
And fondly loved and cherished; they are flown
Before the wand of science! Hills and vales,
Mountains and moorlands, ye have lost
The enchantments, the delights, the visions, all
The elfin visions that so blessed the sight
In the past days romantic. Nought is heard
Now, in the leafy world, but earthly strains,
Voices, yet sweet, of breeze, and bird, and brook,
And waterfall; the day is silent else,
And night is strangely mute."

N. T. CARRINGTON.

THE ancient inhabitants of Warwickshire planted flowers over the remains of their dead, and many a flower thus planted yet blooms in silent sweetness over forgotten graves. Many beautiful and comparatively rare species may be found near these last resting places of the fathers, or nestling beneath the sheltered entrenchment of their ancient camps and homes. Not even yet is the old custom forgotten or neglected. In many a rural churchyard bright flowers may be found gracing the graves of the departed. Do not let us rudely blame the faith of those who plant these "stars of earth," for though in crowded city cemeteries fashion may rule even sentiment, yet in out-of-the-way nooks the old emblems have a meaning, and old customs linger in all their poetry of action and of thought. It is no new feeling that prompts the heart to strew sweet flowers over the dead. It was so in far off times, and many a flower was bedewed with holy tears as it lay on the breast of the departed. Many a wife now, as many a dame in mediæval times, says in her heart, with the Katherine of many troubles and sorrows—

> "When I am dead, good wench,
> Let me be used with honour; strew me o'er
> With *maiden flowers*, that all the world may know
> I was a chaste wife to my grave."

Shakespeare and Drayton allude to this custom; and in "Twelfth Night" we find an explanation of Katherine's wish, for in Act ii. Scene 4 the clown sings—

> "Come away, come away, Death,
> And in *sad cypress* let me be laid:
> Fly away, fly away, breath,
> I am slain by a fair, cruel maid.
> My stuck all with *yew*.
> O, prepare it,
> My part of death no one so true
> Did share it.
>
> Not a flower, not a flower sweet
> On my black coffin let there be strewn;
> Not a friend, not a friend greet
> My poor corpse where my bones shall be thrown;
> A thousand thousand sighs to save.
> Lay me, O, where
> Sad, true lover never find my grave
> To weep there."

Here we have the gloomy view of death's emblems, as opposed to maiden flowers. Though the yew was present in churchyards from an early period, it seems to have been preserved for its evergreen character, making it an emblem of immortality. Tamora, the Queen, in "Titus Andronicus," says, "They would bind me here unto the body of a dismal *yew*, and leave me to this miserable death."

How different are the flower-decked graves of Fidele and Juliet, which give us a glimpse of what Katherine wished for. In "Cymbeline," Arviragus says (Act iv. Scene 2), where Imogen swoons and is supposed to be dead

"With fairest flowers,
Whilst summer lasts, and I live here, Fidele,
I'll sweeten thy sad grave; thou shalt not lack
The flowers that's like thy face, *pale primrose*, nor
The *azured harebell*, like thy veins; no, nor
The *leaf of eglantine*, whom not to slander,
Outsweeten'd not thy breath; the ruddock would
With charitable bill (O, bill, sore shaming
Those rich left heirs that let their fathers lie
Without a monument) bring thee all this;
Yea, and furr'd moss beside, when flowers are none
To winter ground thy corse."

The same play affords us another instance of flower strewing (Act iv. Scene 2)—

GUIDERIUS. "We have done our obsequies; come, lay him down."
BELARIUS. "Here's a few flowers; but about midnight more.
The herbs that have on them cold dew o' the night

Are strewings fittest for graves. Upon their face
You were as flowers, now wither'd; even so
These herblets shall, which we upon you stow.
Come on, away; apart upon our knees:
The ground that gave them first has them again;
Their pleasure here is past, so is their pain."

Michael Drayton, in Rowland's song in praise of Beta, also alludes to the chaplet of flowers for the dead—

"Make her a goodly chaplet of azured cullumbine,
And wreath about her coronet with sweetest eglantine."

Shakespeare, too, in Pericles (Act iv. Scene 1). Marina, whilst strewing flowers over the grave of Thaisa, says:—

"No: I'll rob Tellus of her weed
To strew thy green with flowers; the yellows, blues,
The purple violets, and marigolds,
Shall, as a carpet, hang upon thy grave,
Whilst summer days do last. Ah me, poor maid,
Born in a tempest when my mother died,
This world to me is like a lasting storm,
Whirring me from my friends."

There is also an allusion to the bridal and funeral flowers in "Romeo and Juliet," and a "winding sheet was frequently taken out of lavender to be stuck with rosemary," for special flowers have their special uses. Some were truly herbs of grace, and these yet retain somewhat of there legendary fame and virtues. Rosemary is still the "herb o' remembrance." "Cheerful rosemarie," which Spencer calls "refreshing rosemarie," lingers yet in cottage gardens. Cultivated for its many uses, as well as for its sweet odour, it is the "herb o' remembrance;"

it forms an indispensable part of a lover's posy, like the garland woven by Dorcas in the " Winter's Tale"—

" Reverend sirs,—
For you there's rosemary and rue; these keep
Seeming and savour all the winter long;
Grace and remembrance be to you both."

And gentle Ophelia, in parting with Laertes, gives him this plant—

" There's rosemary, that's for remembrance;
Pray you, love, remember."

The rue was specially the "herb of grace"—the chaste herb. If rosemary improved the memory, rue improved the sight, and thus they embodied "grace and remembrance." There is perhaps no more affecting passage in history than the fate of the youthful queen of Richard II. The gardener, in alluding to her sorrows, gave expression to the popular ideas respecting this herb—

" Poor queen! so that thy state may be no worse,
I would my skill were subject to thy curse.
Here did she drop a [illegible]ar; here in this place
I'll set a bank of rue, sour herb of grace.
Rue, even for Ruth, here shortly shall be seen,
In the remembrance of a weeping queen."

The humble *viola tricolor*—the "pink o' my John" of the fields—the "pansy streaked with jet," has a home amongst Warwickshire legendary flowers.

" There is pansies,
That's for thoughts,"

says Ophelia, playing apparently upon *pensée*, and other poets have noticed the flower by the same name—

> "The pansie; O, that's for lover's thoughts—"

and hence we have the name "Heart's Ease." But pansies in "Midsummer Night's Dream" are called "Love in Idleness," and they supplied Oberon with the witching juice which, on touching the eyelids of the sleeping lovers, gave provoking contrary loves, and made Titania love the ass. There is a pretty legend which gives us the origin of the name of "Love in Idleness" to the "three faces under a hood," known also as "call me to you":—

> "It was at the noontide hour,
> A lady reposed in a bower,
> Where, shaded between
> The branches of green,
> Blossom'd and blush'd a fair flower;
> Not a pinion was moved, nor a breeze was heard,
> As with curious hand the lady stirr'd
> The leaves of this unknown flower.
>
> She saw in its cradling bloom
> A cherub, with folding plume,
> And a bow unstrung,
> And arrows were flung
> O'er the cup of this opening flower;
> And the lady fancied she mnch had need
> Of the light of his wak'ning eyes to read
> The name of this unknown flower.

> She placed it too near to her breast,
> And the cherub was charmed from his rest;
> Then he winged a dart
> At the lady's heart
> From the leaves of this treacherous flower.
> 'Ah, cruel child!' said the lady, 'I guess
> Too late that *Love in Idleness*
> Is the name of this unknown flower.'"

In a hundred instances in Shakespeare's plays we find this popular knowledge of plants and flowers recorded, and on every hand we have evidence of the influences of the flowers which bloomed by the wayside, in green meadows, and in woodland glades, on the minds of men. Whether these were only the memories of the past—of pagan rites and panthean worship—who can tell? or whether they merely embodied in an oral form the experience of country-bred boys transmitted from generation to generation.

In the "Tempest," Caliban threw some light on the past and present Warwickshire country life when he says to Trinculo—

> "I prithee let me bring thee where crabs grow,
> And I with my long nails will dig thee pig-nuts.
> Show thee a jay's nest, and instruct thee how
> To snare the nimble marmozet; I'll bring thee
> To clust'ring filberds, and sometimes I'll get thee
> Some scamels from the rock: wilt thou go with me?"

Warwickshire schoolboys still know where crabs grow, and can dig pig nuts, and in remote districts, particularly to the east of the county, you may still find the "roasted crab" "lurking in the gossip's bowl." The villagers still tread on the camomile, and the twigs of birch which Shakespeare alluded to are no longer used either to impress knowledge or to terrify little boys, though a "besum of birch" is, as of yore, an article of use and commerce. Cankers are to be found in every hedge, to be "as a rose to his grace," and many a village Rosalind has, within the year, had "burs" thrown on her in holiday foolery, and found "burs in her heart." Columbine—the thankless columbine—so freely used to colour the jellies of Prince Hal, after his pranks at Coventry, has been superseded in cookery, but yet holds a foremost place in village gardens, and has even found a native home in Warwickshire. Peonies figured till lately at shepherd's feasts; gorse still blooms, and therefore "kissing is still in fashion." The "speckled cowslip" flavours the rural home-made wine. Chestnuts are still "roasted at the farmer's fire." Medlars still bear their vulgar name. The marigold is still the "husbandman's dial." Everyone remembers Shakespeare's description of the poor apothecary of his time—

> "In tattered weeds, with overwhelming brows,
> *Culling of simples.*"

Many of these simples are yet sold by herb women.

> "Smell like Bucklersbury in simple time."

Drayton tells us what the simples were. He tells us that the apothecary

> "Choicely sorts his simples got abroad.
> Here finds he on an *oak* rheum purging *polypode*,
> And in some open place that to the sun doth lie
> He *fumitory* gets and *eyebright* for the eye;
> The *yarrow* wherewithal he stops the wound-made gore,
> The healing *tutsan* then, and *plantane* for a sore,
> And hardly them again he holy *vervain* finds,
> Which he about his head that hath the megrim binds;
> The wonder working *dill* he gets not far from these
> Which curious women use in many a nice disease;
> For them that are with newts, or snakes, or adders stung
> He seeketh out an herb called *adder's tongue*;
> As nature it ordained, its own like hurt to cure
> And sportive did herself to niceties inure.
> *Valerian* then he crops and purposely doth stamp
> To apply unto the place that haled with the cramp;
> As *centuary* to close the wideness of a wound:
> The belly hurt by birth, by *mugwort* to make sound.
> His *chickweed* cures the heat that in the face doth rise
> For physic some again he inwardly applies
> For comforting the spleen and liver, gets the juice
> Pale *horehound* which he holds of most especial use.
> So *saxifrage* is good and *hart's tongue* for the stone,
> With *agrimony*, and the herb we call *St. John*.
> To him that hath a flux, of *shepherd's purse* he gives,
> And *mouse ear* unto him whom some sharp rupture grieves.
> And for the labouring wretch that's troubled with a cough,
> Or stopping of the breath by phlegm, that's hard and tough
> *Campane* here he crops, approved wondrous good;
> As *comfrey* unto him that's bruised, spitting blood
> And from the falling ill, by *five leaf* doth restore,
> And melancholy cures by sovereign *hellebore*.
> Of these most useful herbs yet tell we but a few
> To those unnumbered sorts of simples here that grew."

The *plantain* is alluded to by Shakespeare, not only as a remedy for a sore, but as a preventative of poison; but amongst the twenty plants mentioned by Drayton, shepherd's purse and fumitory have only been specially alluded to by Shakespeare. Shepherd's purse is believed to have been the parmacety of Hotspur. Shakespeare, however, uses with masterly skill the names and uses of about seventy other flowers that are truly wild in Warwickshire, and about fifty other varieties of trees and flowers.

Amongst the legends connected with plants, perhaps the one most widely spread in the county, though its story is fast dying out, is that of the shriek of the mandrake (*Atropa mandragora*)—

> "Alack! alack! is it like that I
> So early waking, what with loathsome smells
> And shrieks, like *mandrakes* torn out of the earth,
> That living mortals, hearing them, run mad."

The mandrake belongs to the same order, *Solanaceæ*, as the potato and deadly nightshade. Its root is bifurcate, like an ill-grown, crooked carrot, and is supposed to bear some resemblance to the human figure. In fact, the popular superstition was that it was connected in some way with the germ of life, buried with some felon or murderer. To drag it from the earth was to invoke instant death, because when it was torn from the earth it shrieked or groaned. To hear its shriek meant madness, and as the plant possessed narcotic properties it was sought after, but a dog was employed to gather the root. A string was tied to the dog's tail and to the stem of the mandrake, and the unfortunate animal was whipped until the root was extracted. The persons who assisted filled their ears with pitch, so that they should not hear the groan.

In the second part of Henry VI. (Act iii. Scene 2) Suffolk says to Queen Margaret:—

> "Would curses kill as doth the *mandrake's* groan,
> I would invent as bitter searching terms
> As curse, as harsh, and horrible to hear."

But when the root was in the possession of man, it was valued for its many excellent properties.

Amongst the baleful herbs is placed the misletoe, and there is a prevalent legend that if, like other Christmas decorations, it is left in the house after Candlemas, it brings ill-luck. The quaking grass (*Briza*) has a similar legend attached to it, but the hateful *darnel* is frequently used for incantations. Each side is counted in order to know the probability of a wish, or the day on which the stranger will arrive.

The dwarf elder (*Sambucus ebulus*), is the danewort—the plant which is said only grows where the blood of a Dane has been spilt, so fœtid is its smell. This is the "stinking elder" of Shakespeare, not the black elder. Old poets and writers seem to have confounded the two. Shakespeare alludes to the prevalent legend that Judas hung himself on an elder tree in "Love's Labour Lost;"

and in the first "Vision of Piers Plowman" there is this reference to it :—

"That is the castel of care;
Whoso cometh thereundre
May banne that he born was,
To bodi or to soule,
Therein worryeth a wight
That wrong is y hate,
Tader of falsehede,
And founded it himselfe.
Adam and Eve
He egged to idle,
Counselled Kayen
To killen his brother;
Judas he japed
With Jewen silver,
And sithen on an elder,
Hanged himselve."

Whilst we have the danewort, we have also the more pleasant daneweed (*Eringum campestre*) which lurks here and there on the borderland of the Danegeld.

"We have the receipt for *fernseed*," says Gadshill to Chamberlain, "we walk invisible;" and this old legend still lingers among us. It is thought, because the seed of the fern is invisible, it must make the holder of it invisible also; but its magical power cannot be exercised unless it is gathered on the eve of St. John—the old festival of Bel-tane. Old writers on plants show that this superstition was by no means confined to Warwickshire.

The story of the *forget-me-not* has been variously told, but its Warwickshire version is not only romantic but historical. The incident and the legend connected therewith will be found at length amongst the traditionary stories in history. It is somewhat curious that the wager of battle at Gosford Green should have indirectly given rise to the use of two other historical flowers. During the time of Henry's grandson, the white and the red rose became the emblems of the opposing factions of the Houses of York and Lancaster, and there is preserved at Ettington the memory of those struggles in which the ancient family of Shirley took a prominent part, for so loyal were the Shirleys to the House of Lancaster, so firm adherents to the red rose, that even now it is fancifully said that the white rose fades and dies when near their ancestral home. The story is not an ancient one, but it has been pleasantly told by the distinguished antiquary, who is now the Lord of Ettington:—

"Faithful to the roses red
The Shirleys were, I ween;
And still where they were wont to tread
The roses red are seen.

Near Ettington, their Saxon seat,
The white rose scantly grows:
'Twould seem as if that ancient seat
Still recognized its foes.

'Was mindful still of Salop's field,
Where brave Hugh bit the dust,
Arrayed like king with royal shield—
In a righteous cause, we trust.

Still lingers there the memory
Of Ralph and his roses red,
When England's foremost chivalry
To Agincourt were led.

Those days are gone; but still a share
Of glory shall remain,
While roses sweetly scent the air,
And still their hue retain."

Ninety years after the wage of battle on Gosford Green, after the Wars of the Roses had deluged the country with blood and destroyed the mass of the old nobility, the border town of Atherstone was disturbed by the passage of armed bodies of men. The troops of Lord Stanley, the husband of the celebrated Margaret of Beaufort, had retreated along the Watling Street way, followed at a short interval by Sir William Stanley, who encamped in the immediate neighbourhood, on a spot now pointed out as Camp Fields. The mercenary troops of Henry Earl Richmond were following after, and, under the guidance of John Hardwick, a native of the neighbourhood of Leamington Hastings, chose the ground on which the battle of Bosworth Field was fought, on the 22nd of August, 1485, within sight of our county. Richard III., who fell there, was the last of the race of English kings who bore the name of Plantagenet, and bore the *planta genista*—the bonny broom—as their badge. With this battle ended the Wars of the Roses, and gave to the Tudors a new floral badge—a sprig of hawthorn

—in commemoration of the story that the crown of Richard was found concealed in a hawthorn bush, on a hill near Stoke Golding, and which is now known as Crown Hill. Thus three of the principal historical flowers of England are closely connected with Warwickshire and Warwickshire men. These are scarcely all, for the subject is an enticing one, for, like Dorcas, I can point to

> "Daffodils
> That come before the swallow dares, and take
> The winds of March with beauty; violets dim,
> But sweeter than the lids of Juno's eyes,
> Or Cytherea's breath; pale primroses,
> That die unmarried, ere they can behold
> Bright Phœbus in his strength, a malady
> Most incident to maids, bold oxlips, and
> The crown imperial; lilies of all kinds,
> The flower-de-luce being one! Of these I lack
> To make your garlands of."

These are the flowers that crown the hillsides and deck the valleys of the Heart of England. These the stories that human faith and human wishes have thrown over the wells and streams, and made poetry in prosaic places, and we find

> "The glorious dream of past eternities
> Running adown
> The long time avenues,
> Towards unknown futurities,
> Till he hath perused
> The chapter of its doom."

These form but the chaplet which adorns the land we are proud to call the "Heart of England."

"Such delight I found
To note in shrub and tree, in stone and flower,—
That intermixture of delicious hues,
Along so vast a surface, all at once,
In one impression, by connecting force
Of their own beauty, imaged in the heart."

From these poetic images let us turn to the land they are associated with, and see in loved Warwickshire the image of the "Heart of England."

HIGH CROSS
The Heart of England

The Heart of England.

"This song our shire of Warwick sounds
Revives old Arden's ancient bounds."

THE HEART OF ENGLAND! The very name is suggestive of all that is great and noble in a noble land. A thousand associations are connected with the name, and the history of a thousand years shows how many great men have been nurtured on its undulating breast, and what great deeds have been wrought on its bosom. It has been the nursing mother of poets and the cradle of heroes. On its fair fields the battles of liberty and freedom have been fought. The earliest records, which have come down to us through the mists of time, tell us that it was a frontier land—the southern frontier, held by the fierce tribes who inhabited the great forest land which extended from the river Avon to the estuary of the Dee, that forest whose

"Right hand touched Trent, the other Severn's side."

The memory of these early struggles and later contests appears to have lingered among the people, for when English people began to speak the Saxon tongue they called it by the distinctive name of Wæringawic—the bulwark of the Wiccii—and the chief town, the citadel of the dwellers by the river.

Who were the Huicci or Wiccii? Was this the old name of the original tribes of the Cornavii resumed after the last Roman legion had left the shores of Britain? or was it the name of a newer people who had learned in the Roman settlements the power of self-government, and extended their dominion from the Severn to the great Midland Vale? Whoever they were, Warwick was one of their camps or frontier posts, and gave its name to "that shire which we the 'heart of England' well may call."

The old trackway, which stretches in a nearly straight line from Dover to the Irish Sea, at its central point crosses the river Avon, and marks the "heart of England" on the adjacent hills. Along this trackway the students of Gaul went to the great Druidical seminaries of learning of the time at Mona and at Ierna—the Isles of Anglesea and Erin. Along this trackway the Roman troops advanced; their camps and settlements are to be seen on either hand. From this trackway the "heart of England" was first seen by strangers, and the way was called Gathelian—the road or way of the stranger.* This great road, which we know as the Watling Street, now forms for a long distance the eastern boundary of Warwickshire, separating

* Dr. Stukeley, "Iter Curiosum."

it from the sister county of Leicester. From this boundary the rivers and rivulets flow to the eastern as well as to the western seas, for it here traverses the depressed hillocks which form at this point the back bone of England. To the left of this road, where the setting sun casts its rays on hill and vale, may be seen the shire of Warwick.

It is a country of gentle undulations, soft flowing rivers, and well timbered vales. It stretches its angular form from the steep escarpments of the Oxfordshire oolite and the "dumpling hills" of Northants to where the still waters of the Tame empty themselves into the Trent; from the level expanse of the Leicestershire pastures to the rolling hills of Worcester and Gloucester, overhanging Severn's side.

Close to the point where the old Watling Street becomes the boundary of the historic shire, it crosses the little tortuous stream which here represents the midland Avon. This celebrated stream rises in the neighbourhood of Naseby, in the adjacent county of Northants, and flows for a few miles in a northerly direction to Welford, and then, taking a westerly direction, forms for a distance of eight miles the boundary between its native county and Leicestershire. It enters Warwickshire at Dowbridge, near the site of the ancient Roman station of Tripontium, in the parish of Catthorpe, and flows through the county in a south-westerly direction, receiving its great tributary, the Leam, in the neighbourhood of Warwick, and the lesser streams of the Swift at Bensford Bridge, near Rugby, the Sow near Stoneleigh, the Dene near Charlecote, the Stour near Stratford, and the Alne near Bedford. The course of the Avon marks the great natural division of the county. The southern open country is termed the Feldon, or champagne country. The northern bank is termed the Arden, or the woodland. The heights of Shuckburgh, Napton, Burton, and Brailes alone break the monotony of the plain of the Feldon, which rises in successive undulating billows to Hodnell, Gaydon, and Wellesbourne, and sinks to the foot of the Edge hills, on the Oxfordshire boundary. On the western side the country is far more broken and diversified; Ilmington and Ettington form a prominent feature in the landscape above the valley of the Stour. Many of these hill-tops were oolitic islands when the waters flowed on the liassic bed of the plain. Nothing could be more natural than that these elevated positions would be seized, even by the most barbarous tribes, as "points of vantage," and here we find the remains of the earliest settlements of the ancient inhabitants; and from them extensive views of the Feldon and of the distant heights which mark the Arden country can be obtained.

Across the Avon the scene changes; the country becomes more picturesque along its banks. Spurs of the keuper sandstone stretch here and there into the plain or skirt the river side, and form a natural boundary of considerable elevation. Here and there are giant trees, gaunt and grim, and hoary with age. The dwellers by the Leam side know nothing of the expansive views which meet the eye from Cave's inn, Willey or High Cross, or from the rocky edges of Hartshill and Oldbury, where the upheaval of the igneous greenstone has brought within reach of the inhabitants coal, clay, and other materials of manufacture. The tall chimnies and their smoky pennons show that industrious enterprise is not unknown on the east, though they are more numerous on the north-west, where plastic ware and textile fabrics give place now, as in ages past, to the workers in metal, whose metropolis is the "toy-shop of Europe"—the great "hardware village" of Birmingham. The extent and beauty of the "heart of England" can be seen also from the beacon hills of Dasset and the bluff fringe of the vale of the Red Horse. In the Arden land there are fine views from Corley, from Meriden, and from the wild promontory of Yarningale, as well as from Coplow and Welcombe and Snitterfield.

The hills and the valleys, the woods and the rivers yet speak to us in the tongue of the old fathers of the land. In the Avon we have the flowing water. In the river Anker we have the lesser Avon, and in the Alenus or Alne we recognise the forest river. The Arrow (*Arow*) yet maintains the rapid motion which gave it its name. In the Blythe we have the many branching stream and the Cole, the two-armed branch of the Blythe itself. The Stour is the flowing stream, and the Tame the pool-like waters.* In the Leam we have the contraction of Leamhain—the water of the elms—and the elm is even now known as the Warwickshire weed.

The hills of Arden are full of significance. In Hardresull, the old name of Hartshill, we have an aspirated form of the height of the sun. In Yarningale we have a softened local form of Ardengael—the height of the stranger—and through this name the low tumulus on its top was discovered. More obvious derivations are on every hand.

These uplands and plains not only speak the language of an ancient race, but are studded with the remains of past grandeur, strength, and power. The summits of the hills still bear traces of the barbarous tribes who stayed for a time the triumphant course of the legions of Imperial Rome. By their side are the camps of the ultimate conquerors, as silent and as desolate as the entrenchments of the conquered. The mediæval chieftains built stronger mansions if not more enduring. Warwick's embattled towers, Tamworth's keep, and Kenilworth's proud ruins attest the power of the old Norman barons no less than the minor fortresses and moated areas which stud

* See Bullet, "Mémoires sur la Langue Celtique." Vol. i.

the country side. On some of these the comfortable manor houses and pleasant half-timbered granges and mansions yet remain to attest the wealth and comfort of the yeomen and squires of the past.

The great religious establishments suppressed by Henry VIII. may be traced in bare ruins, or interspersed with more modern erections on the same site. At Polesworth, Merivale, Nuneaton, Coombe, Maxstoke, Wroxall, Kenilworth, Coventry, Stoneleigh, Pinley, and Henwood, and in many lesser establishments, the monuments of the religious zeal of the middle ages may be found in pleasant nooks by the side of still waters and flowery meads.

Many of these uplands and gentle vales have been bedewed with blood in historic times; they have witnessed struggles for liberty and aspirations for freedom as well as the cruel tortures of hard conquerors. The Conqueror's Norman troops ravaged the country on their way to quell the great revolt of the north. The records of Kenilworth and Warwick teem with accounts of civil strife, when kings and kings' sons strove for mastery, or the fierce barons tried to throw off the feudal yoke. The siege of Kenilworth is marked deep on the page of history. Warwickshire furnished large contingents of men, gallant knights, and able commanders for the French wars of the Plantagenet princes. Royal favourites found lynch law even amid the sweet beauty of Guy's Cliff.

Edward II. and Richard II. saw mournful days in Kenilworth's lordly keep, for the lord of the latter was Henry Bolingbroke, the first of the Lancaster line of our kings. In the wars of the Roses, which followed, the fields of Edgcote, Tewkesbury, and of Bosworth tell of the bloody struggle in many a sad page of history, to be repeated some 150 years later at Edgehill and at Naseby. But in all this, who can forget that prior to Simon de Montfort's defeat at Evesham, Warwickshire furnished the first speaker of the first English Parliament in the Lord of Beaudesert, Petrus de Montfort, a follower, but not a relative, of his namesake, the great Earl of Leicester; and the third speaker, William Trussell, was also a Warwickshire knight. Looking back, too, at the great Civil War, we remember that the cradle of constitutional freedom was stained with the first blood shed in the sanguinary struggles between parliamentary and kingly power. It requires no great stretch of imagination to picture Richard Baxter disturbed in his preaching at Alcester on that famous Sunday in October, 1642, and going forth to hear the distant boom of the cannon which told of King and Parliament being in hostile array in the very heart of the land. A hundred years later than this the troops of the Duke of Cumberland were encamped on Meriden Heath, adjoining Packington Park, to meet the wild Highlanders who were following the last Prince of the House of Stuart in his Quixotic attempt on the English throne.

It was but fitting, too, that the heart's core of England should be at once the cradle and the shrine of England's greatest poet. By the placid Avon William Shakespeare played when a boy. In the daisy-strewn meadows which skirt the river's brink he gathered inspiration and uttered his love story to no unwilling ears. Here, too, in the autumn of his days, and in the fulness of his fame and fortune, the bard of Avon sought the scenes of his childhood to live and to die. With him, when he died, was another son of mid-England, Michael Drayton, who threw the glamour of his verses over these fair scenes. Neither must it be forgotten that Sir Thomas Overbury received his first breath from the same nursing mother, and in this consecrated land of Arden, which has been peopled with ideal personages, Somerville and Jago sang of the chase and of the glories of this mid-English land.

The sons of this shire were not only men of song but men of action. Across these scenes have flitted men whose names are entwined with the history of the land, and not a few noble women have left their impress on the records of the shire. There yet remains the mounds on which the gallant daughter of Alfred erected her castles after the fierce Mercian kings had passed away. But there is some reason to think that nearly a thousand years before her "coigns of vantage" these mounds had been fortified by the allies of Cartismandua's rebellious subjects. At

Polesworth "pious Edith," the daughter of Egbert, the first English king, found a tomb in the religious house she had raised ; and who in thinking of mid England will fail to remember that here dwelt the fair and benevolent Lady Godiva, whose legendary story is enshrined in song, as her deeds are in the cartularies of monasteries and in the history of the eleventh century.

The names of De Montfort, of Arden, Beauchamp, Hugford, Shirley, Astley, Burdett, and Catesby are not dimmed by the later names of Throckmorton, Greville, Dudley, Leigh, Bracebridge, Conway, or Willoughby. Some of the old names have disappeared, but the Shirleys, the Chamberlains, the Comptons, the Shuckburghs, the Lucys, and the Throckmortons yet remain in possession of their ancestral seats, and though many of the old families have disappeared, their daughters have intermarried, and their estates have passed into the hands of those who bear another name, even though they are allied in blood with the original possessors, whose names are enshrined in history.

When we search the ancient records of this land we find the earliest events shrouded by the mists of ages. We can only pierce the gloom darkly. Here and there we can lift the veil and point to the material and indisputable evidence of past events. Others are entwined with fiction, changed by time or the ever varying disposition of men to make the past chime in with the present.

To this latter feeling we must ascribe the mythical character of many of the stories of past days which have come down to us, and whose obscurity we will try to pierce; rejecting that which is indisputably false, and revealing, as far as possible, the germs of truth hidden in these legends, stories, and episodes of bygone days.

REMAINS OF KENILWORTH PRIORY.

The Rollright Stones.

HOARY and grey, as if ten thousand tempests had furrowed its cheeks and blanched its rugged sides, the King Stone at Rollright, or Rollrich, remains in its gaunt and solemn solitude, the only stone monument of the prehistoric past within the old shire of Warwick. In the dim gloaming it seems to spread its arms as if to curse or bless the wayfarer who may traverse the ancient trackway which runs bleakly along the ridge of the high land, which here separates for a long distance Oxfordshire from Warwickshire. Within a hundred years it stood amongst well-defined barrows and ancient graves; these have disappeared by the operations of the busy agriculturist, but fortunately the King Stone yet remains. Eighty-three yards distant, but on the Oxfordshire side of the road, a clump of shattered fir trees mark the site of the stone circle of Rollright. These wrinkled, wizened stones have stood there for more than a thousand years we know; and, if the story of their origin is true, we may add ten centuries more to their age ere we reach that remote time when our forefathers gathered together the boulders and fragments

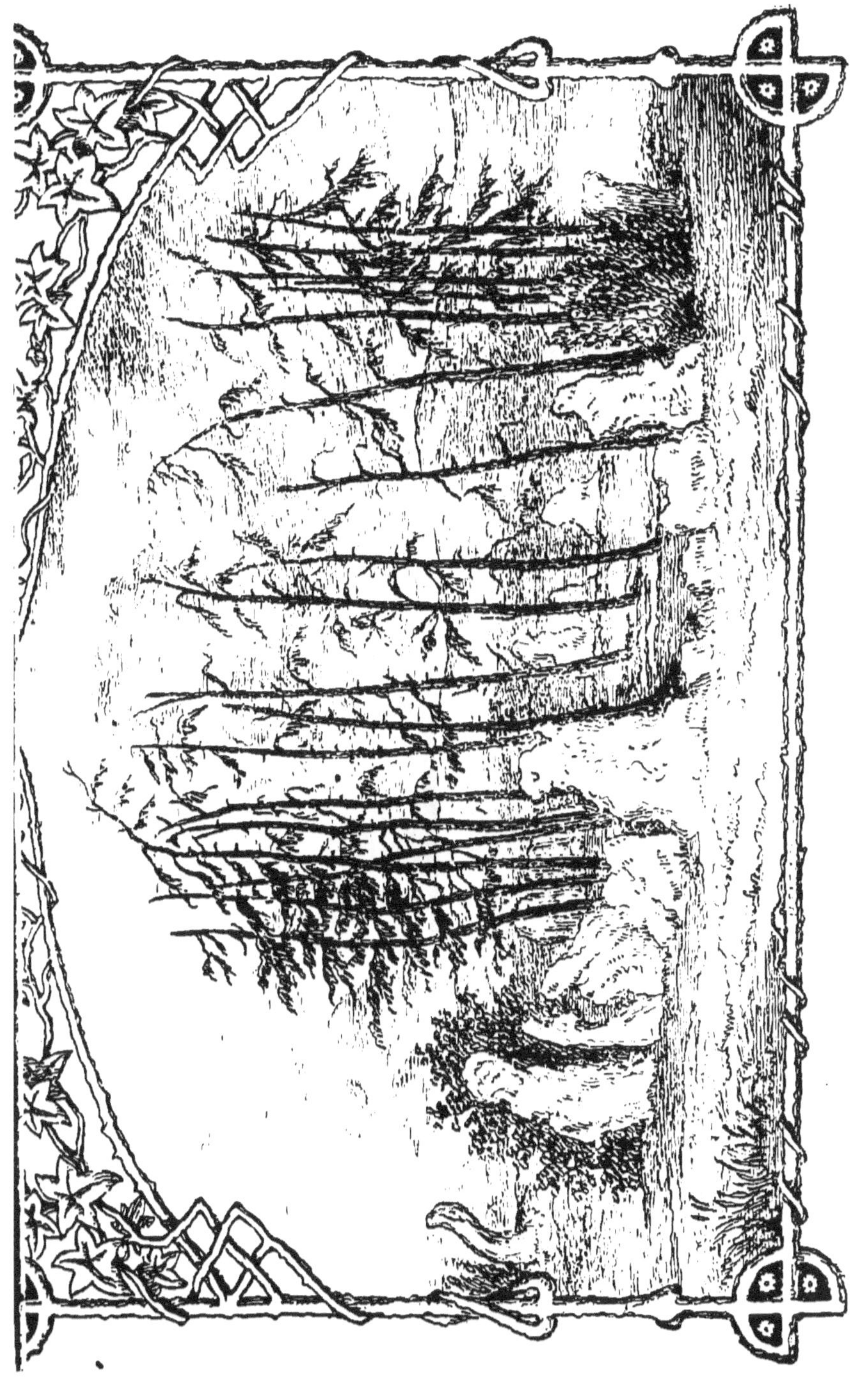

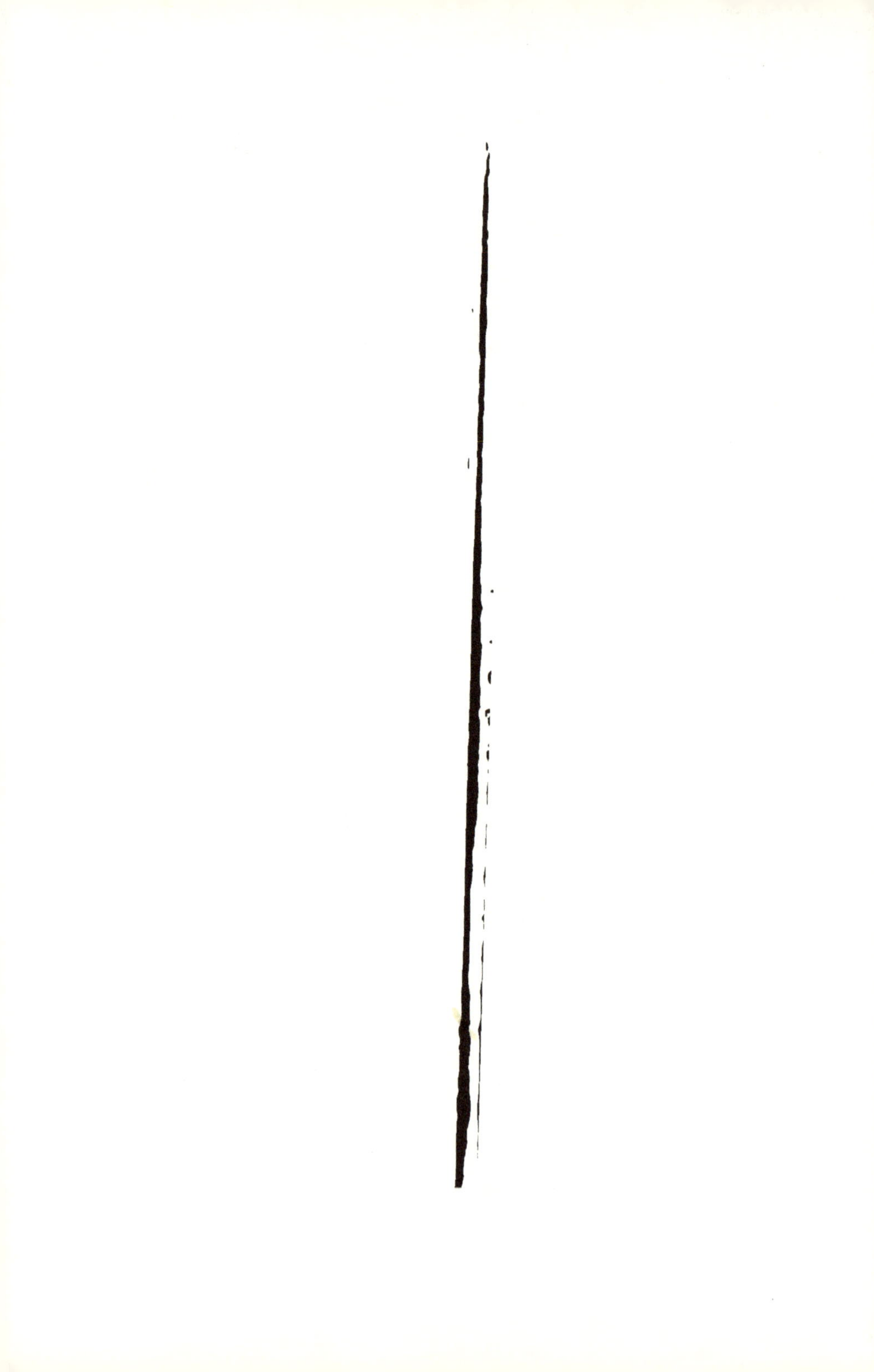

of the inferior oolite which were scattered about the old ridgeway and formed that curious circle of upright stone which now, furrowed and old, crown as of yore the summit of this lofty hill. Those who only know Warwickshire from its alluvial plain can form but little idea of the beauty of the scene. At the foot of the hill the grey tower of Long Compton church rises amid the sinuous line of houses which form the only street of the "town of the valley." * The road winds up the hill towards Weston Park on its way to Shipston, and beyond the wooded summit rise the swelling, lofty Broadway and Ilmington hills, studded with many a church tower, and tree-embosomed homestead; and beyond all, in clear weather, you may discern the serrated edge of Bromgrove Lickey. The view is bounded on the south by the Oxfordshire hills, crowned by the tower of the church of Stowe-in-the-Wold. The impressiveness of the scene is increased by the few splintered fir trees which wave their shattered and battered branches over the gaunt stones. To the right stands the King Stone, and a little to the left in the distance may be seen the huge dolmen or cistvaen known as the "Whispering Knights."

Around these stones the halo of romance has been thrown; but if we accept the truth of the axiom, that "tradition is the parent of history," we shall probably find the clue to the name of these stones, and why they

* *Coomb*, a valley; *ton*, a town.

were erected. The earliest known notice of these ancient remains is in a manuscript ascribed to the Venerable Bede, which is said to be preserved in the library of Benet College, Cambridge, and there the Rollright stones are described as the "second wonder of the kingdom"—Stonehenge being alluded to as the first. In a list of the wonders of Britain, given by Henry of Huntingdon, and written in the earlier part of the twelfth century, Stonehenge is given as the second wonder. There is a doubt as to the antiquity of the MSS. in question, and certainly the Rollright stones are not so numerous or so important as those at Avebury, in the county of Wilts. We have, however, many other testimonies as to the antiquity of the stones and the wonder they have excited amongst the people. In more than one of the old chronicles they are mentioned, and they are old enough to give their name to the parish in which they stand. There is a characteristic notice of these remains in a catalogue of strange wonders, printed by Hearne, under the title of "De Mirabilibus Britanniæ," as an appendix to "Robert of Gloucester." The notice is curious, and is at least five centuries old. It thus reads:—

"Sunt magni lapides in Oxenfordiensi pago, manu hominum quasi sub quadam connexione dispositi, set a quo tempore, vel a qua gente, vel ad quid memorandum vel signandum factum fuerit ignoratur. Ab incolis autem vocatur locus ille Rollendrych."

(There are great stones in Oxfordshire, seemingly placed

by the hand of man in a certain connected order, but at what time it was done, or by what people, or what it was intended to record or signify is not known. By the people there the place is called Rollendrych.)

None of the very early novices afford us any indications of the common name or of the legends which are now connected with the spot.

In the folio edition of Camden's "Britanniæ," published in 1607, there is an engraving of the stones, stated to have been then done "some time," which, though it bears some signs of truthfulness, when compared with the stones as they at present exist, is by no means to be relied on in all its details. Camden calls them "An ancient monument, a number of huge stones placed in a circle and called by the vulgar Rollrich Stones, and fancied to have been once men, changed by a strange metamorphosis into stones. They are shapeless, unequal, and by length of time much eaten and consumed. The highest of them, standing out of the circle and facing the east, is called 'The King,' because they fancy 'if that had once seen Long Compton it would have been King of England.' Five others adjoining are said to have been knights, and the rest common soldiers. I am apt to think it a memorial of some victory, perhaps erected by Rollo, who afterwards obtained the sovereignty of Normandy." This legend, thus alluded to as accounting for the origin of the stones, states, that when Rollo, the Dane, was about

THE ROLLRICH STONES.

to invade England, he was told by one of the good people or oracles he consulted that

> "When Long Compton you shall see,
> You shall King of England be."

A series of victories brought him and his army to the summit of the hill where the great Warwickshire Vale stretched out before them until it melted away into the primeval forest of Arden. The soldiers halted whilst their leader advanced towards the brow of the hill, from which Long Compton could be seen in the valley below. Ere he could reach the spot from whence the village could be discerned the good genius of the nation and of the native king turned him and his host into stone. The King Stone, situated within the boundary of Warwickshire, is said to have been Rollo himself, and the five stones standing about 390 yards due east of the circle are called the Whispering Knights. The circle itself represents the fabulous army.

Similar legends are current respecting many other stone circles which yet remain in Britain. The "Dance Maine," or "Dawn's Maên"—that is the stone's dance—near Penzance, is said to have been a number of merry maidens turned into stone for dancing on a Sunday. There are three large intersecting circles of upright stones near Liskeard, in Cornwall, termed the "Hurlers," which are stated by the inhabitants to have been formerly men, who were transformed into stones for hurling on a

Sunday. On the coast of the Bay of Galway are several dolmens or cromlechs, of which the people can give no account, save that they are "Bob and Joan's Beds," or small folds for sheep, to shelter them from the westerly breezes.

The influence of the legend may be traced in the following history of the stones from the pen of an Oxfordshire historian, who writes as if the legend embodied ascertained facts :—

"Upon the verge of our county, in the neighbourhood of Chipping Norton, is an ancient monument, to wit, certain huge stones placed in a circle—the common people call them Rollrich stones, and dream they were some time men, by a miraculous metamorphosis turned into hard stones. The highest of them all, which without the circle looketh into the earth, they call the King, because he should have been King of England (forsooth) if he had once seen Long Compton, a little town lying beneath, and which one may see if he go a few paces forward. Other five standing on the other side, touching as it were one another, they imagine to have been knights on horseback, and the rest of the army. These would, I verily think, seem to have been the monument of some victory, and happily erected by Rollo, the Dane, who afterwards conquered Normandy ; for what time he with his Danes troubled England with depredations. We read that the Danes joined battle with the English at Hook Norton, a place for no one thing more famous in old time than for the woful slaughter of the English in that foughten field under the reign of King Edward the Elder. That this monument might be erected by Rollo the Dane, or rather Norwegian, perhaps may be true, but by no means about the time of Edward the Elder; for though it be true enough he troubled England with depredations, yet that he made them in the days of King Alfred I think that all historians agree—Anno 807, according to Florilegus; but, according to Abbot Brompton, a much better author, in the year 975, near forty years before the slaughter of the English in King Edward's days. Therefore, much rather than so, should I think he erected them upon a second expedition he made into England, when he was called in by King Athelstan to assist him against some potent rebels that had taken arms against him, whom, having vanquished, he reduced to obedience to their prince, and perhaps, too, slain the designed king of them (who possibly might be persuaded to this rebellion upon a conditional prophesie of coming to that honour when he should see Long Compton), might erect this monument in memory of the fact: the great single stone for the intended king, the five stones by themselves for his principal captains, and the round for the mixt multitude slain in the battle, which is somewhat agreeable to the tradition concerning them."

The same writer further states:—"But if it happened the King fell in a foreign expedition by the hand of the enemy, the army presently got together a parcel of great stones, and set them in such a round, as well sometimes, perhaps, for the interment of the corps of the deceased king as the election of his successor. And this 'tis like they did, because they esteemed an election in such a *forum* a good addition of title; and, second, with all expedition, because, by the delay of such election too long, irreparable damages many times accrewed to the Republick thereupon."

The legend of the "King Stones" has been accepted as a fact by more than one Oxfordshire historian, though it is obvious that if the stones were known to, or mentioned by the Venerable Bede, this story, or indeed any connection of the circle with Rollo, the Dane, must be fabulous, and suggested only by a similarity of sound in the name.

There is extant a letter of Dr. Gale's to Dr. Stukeley, describing these stones, and it is curious to mark the difference of tone with which these two learned antiquarians speak of them. Dr. Gale thought them meagre, and hardly worthy of mention, beside the statelier monuments of Stonehenge, Avebury, and other similar remains. There were, in his opinion, neither tumuli or barrows in the neighbourhood. On the other hand, Dr. Stukeley, who saw the Rollright at a subsequent period, enters into a long disquisition respecting the origin and unit employed in the erection of this and similar structures, and this unit he traces to the Phœnician cubit.

He points out that the diameter of the circle is the same as Stonehenge, and he had no doubt whatever that the remains were Druidical, or that the circle was connected with the worship of the sun. Near the King Stone he describes a large tumulus, 60 feet long by 20 feet broad, which he named the "Barrow of the Archdruid." The Whispering Knights, in his time, surmounted another tumulus; and Godfrey Higgins, in his work on the Celtic Druids, mentions that tumuli and barrows abound. Stukeley thought the King Stone the remains of an avenue of approach, and derived the name from Rholdrwyg, the wheel or circle of the Druids, or from Roilig—in Erse, the church or temple of the Druids. Elsewhere we have seen that the Welsh derivations are hardly applicable to Warwickshire and the midland shires. The old terms are far more closely allied to the Gaelic branch of the Celtic language, and in Rollright or Rollrich, as it is spelt on the ordnance map, we find only a debased form of *Roithlean an Rign* (pronounced Royl*l*an Ree, giving the second *l* the sound of *y*), and we have the circle of the king—the common name being yet the King Stones. A writer in the *Gentleman's Magazine* suggests that the name is derived from *Rhol,* a circle or circular temple, and *ric,* of the region or kingdom. This is altogether untenable. The balance of probability is in favour of the King Stones. Those who believe that the circle was the necropolis of the neighbourhood—a burying-place of kings and chieftains—have this strong point in their favour: Roilig (having the same origin as relic) signifies a church or churchyard.

Of the circle itself a general impression will be obtained

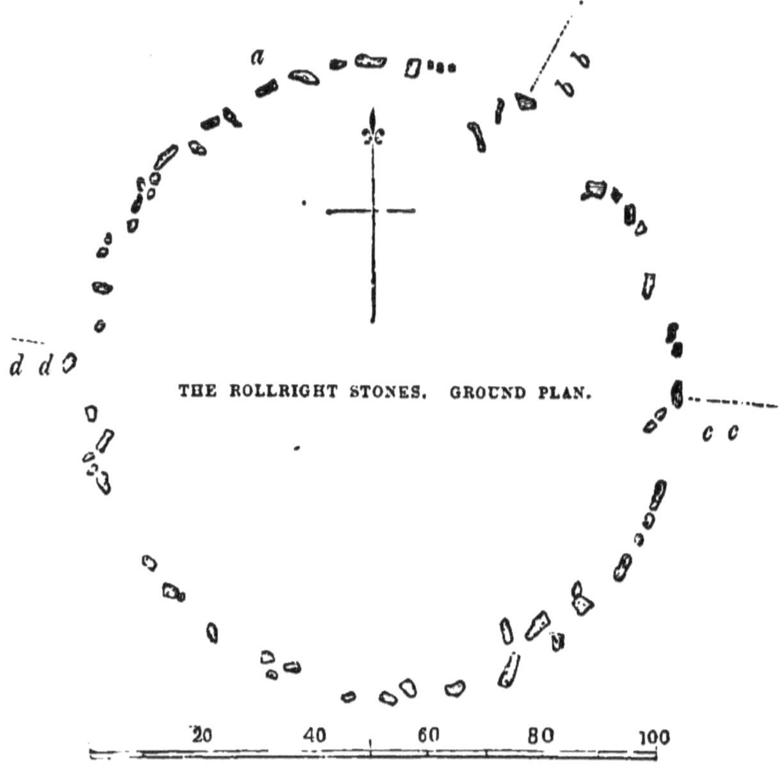

THE ROLLRIGHT STONES. GROUND PLAN.

from the view (sketched October 12, 1869) of its western aspect. Its diameter from north to south is 107 feet, and from east to west 104 feet.

Many of the stones are broken and partly hidden by the earth and the brushwood. In October, 1869, there were fifty-eight, of which thirty-two were upright. Originally there appears to have been about sixty stones placed close together, so as to form a close fence. The highest stone is marked *a* on the plan, and this stone is 7 feet 4 inches in height, and 3 feet 2 inches in breadth. It is easily distinguished in Camden's view (page 50). The average breadth of the stones is 15 inches.

The King Stone is 8 feet 6 inches in height, and 5 feet 3 inches in breadth, and stands 83 yards north-east of the circle, across the road in the direction marked (*b b*) on the plan. Another large stone formerly stood on a bank of earth 141 yards west of the circle, within the Warwickshire boundary, marked *d d*. On the eastern side, at a distance of 390 yards (*c c*), there are the five large stones, known as the Whispering Knights, which have been removed by the present tenant. The plan of these stones is subjoined, and their present appearance is well depicted in the accompanying illustration. The stones, as now exposed, show other stones driven in the ground around them to support the greater ones and keep them upright. The largest stone is 10 feet 10 inches in height, and as they stand together form a rude cell, or cistvaen, with an entrance on the west. Probably not one stone would have been left of this interesting monument, had not a dread of supernatural interference prevented this further desecration. A local tradition

FIVE KNIGHTS' PLAN.

asserts that a farmer once carried away one of the large stones of the Whispering Knights to make a bridge, but it so disturbed the man's rest, that he restored it to its former position. It took, says the local tradition, five horses to cart the stone away, but one sufficed to bring

THE WHISPERING KNIGHTS.

it back again. A gentleman, now living in Leamington, states that when young he saw an attempt made to upturn the King Stone, which has since been much mutilated by wanton mischief, but the attempt from some cause or other failed.

Who shall decide whether these grey stones, "corroded

like worm-eaten wood," as Dr. Stukeley remarks, "by the harsh jaws of time, and that much more than Stonehenge, was originally a temple to the sun, a crowning place of kings, or the sacred and hallowed repository of their bones?" Their pale, ragged, and broken lips return no answer. If they could do so, we should probably learn that they were all these.

Mr. Thomas Beesley, F C.S., of Banbury. in an interesting paper on this subject, and to whose courtesy I have been indebted for the plan and sketch of the Whispering Knights, is of opinion that the circle is the remains of the outer boundary of a burial barrow of the ancient Celts, who 2,000 years ago inhabited those parts of Europe where similar remains are still found. Sir Thomas Browne, in his "Urn Burial," especially points out analogous structures used by the ancient Danes and Norwegians, for, though there have been no remains found within the circle itself, though searched for by Mr. Ralph Sheldon in the 17th century, the neighbourhood itself has been rich in treasures, and probably a careful search would bring to light many more. Some 200 yards east of the King Stone, within the Warwickshire border, there is a bank running north and south, where the exposed soil is a darker colour than the surrounding earth, and covers the remains of many men and horses. Burnt stones and a few fragments of pottery are scattered about. East of this, about twelve skeletons were found a few years ago, and the head of one was noticed as pointing to the west. In the year 1836, a hand-made urn, of black clay, without any ornamentation, 6 inches high, and about the same width, was dug up here. It contained a few burnt bones, and what the labourers called the blade of an old razor. This urn is now in the possession of Mr. Minton, of Weston Park Farm, together with "a bronze ring fibula or brooch, of rather more than an inch in diameter, the pin being gone," which was found on the jaw of one of the skeletons, which it had stained green. The pattern is a very simple one. "A ring was also found of the same size as the fibula, and seven beads of glass. Three of these beads were about the size of peas, and of a blue colour. Another, about the same size, is flat and of a red colour; the other three are of opaque white glass, with a very faint tinge of green, and of the size of ordinary marbles. One has four little projecting spots of red upon it; the other two are ornamented with rudely cut diagonal crossing grooves." Some flattish pieces of brass, probably the common dish-shaped fibulæ, were also dug up. Roman coins are occasionally found, and skeletons are frequently dug up on the Oxfordshire side of the road towards the Five Knights.

In the collection of Mr. M. H. Bloxam, of Rugby, is a white sacrificial flint, found in the neighbouring parish of Barton-on-the-Heath by the Rev. F. C. Colville. An engraving of it appears in the *Warwickshire Antiquarian Magazine*, p. 82.

Whatever may have been the original uses of the sacred circle, it marked a political or ecclesiastical centre of some importance to the people who erected it. The roadway which passes by it extends from the Ermine way, in the neighbourhood of Gloucester, to Northampton, and continues along the southern bank of the Nene until lost in the fens. Its sides are studded with tumuli, and along its course are the remains of numerous camps of undoubted British origin. At a short distance on the northern side of the road are a series of strong entrenchments, or fortified posts, evidently the frontier defence of a tribe or tribes against a possible foe on the north. Many of these fortified positions are within the shire of Warwick. The people who are recorded by Ptolemy and Dio Cassius as inhabiting the southern portion of Warwickshire, part of Oxfordshire, and Gloucestershire, were the Dobuni, the inhabitants of the country by the river. To these people we must assign the erection of the stones at Rollright. Their dead were buried there; their footprints may be traced within our historic shire of Warwick.

St. Augustine and the Tythes.

THE elder Disraeli tells us in his charming and ever fresh "Curiosities of Literature," that "Before colleges were established, in the monasteries where the schools were held, the professors of rhetoric frequently gave their pupils the life of some saint for a trial of their talent at amplification. The students being constantly at a loss to furnish out their pages, invented most of these wonderful adventures." Joslin observes that "The Christians used to collect out of Ovid, Livy, and other pagan poets and historians, the miracles and portents to be found there, and accommodate them to their own monks and saints," never dreaming that some day they might become articles of faith. It is to this we may ascribe many of the wonderful stories which have come down to us from monkish chroniclers respecting the county of Warwick and other counties. We may discern within these marvellous stories some truth, and they probably are mere amplifications of historic fact, which have been altered to suit the purpose of the monks and ecclesiastics—to inculcate some lesson under the guise of a miracle.

The story of the Rollright Stones and the many barrows and remains which have been found in the neighbourhood point to it as an old ecclesiastical centre, around which old faiths and superstitions would linger longer than in other and less striking localities.

The story of St. Augustine is as well known as that of Gregory the Great, who, seeing some young English slaves publicly exposed for sale in the market place at Rome, was struck by the beauty of their form, their bright complexions, and long fair hair. He inquired to what country they belonged, and was told that they were Angles. He answered, with a sigh, "They would not be Angles, but angels, if they were but Christians." He continued his inquiries, and playing on the names of their country and their king, he showed great anxiety that the people so highly endowed by nature should not be left in ignorance of Christian truth. At first he wished to visit England himself to disseminate the Gospel, but being prevented, he, when Pope, sent Augustine, prior of the convent of St. Andrew at Rome, and forty monks on a mission to England in the year 597. Augustine, who found Ethelbert, the Bretwalda, married to a Christian princess, Bertha, was kindly received, and the result of his labours was the reintroduction of Christianity into England. There is some reason to believe that Christianity had not entirely succumbed before the Saxon idols, for it is said that

Augustine met the British bishops at a place in a remote part of Mercia, known as Augustine's Oak, which Brompton places on the confines of the Britons and the West Saxons. It has been thought that Hagley was the spot; others have brought the place nearer the county of Oxford, and not far from the Rollrich itself. From what passed between the older bishops and Augustine, it would seem as if the story of the tythes in connection with Long Compton was intimately connected with the conference. Augustine died in 604, the year in which the following event, as related by Capgrave, is said to have occurred at Long Compton, in the vale immediately to the north-east of the stone circle of Rollrich:—

"About the year of our Saviour's Incarnation, D.C. iiii., St. Augustine, being arrived in England to preach the Gospel, came hither; whereupon the priest of this parish repaired to him and made a complaint that the lord of the town, not paying his tithes, though admonished, was by him excommunicated, and yet stood more obstinate. St. Augustine, therefore, conventing him for that fault, demanded the reason of such his refusal. 'Knoweth thee not,' quoth he, 'that they are not thine, but God's?' To whom the knight answered, 'Did not I plow and sow the land? I will, therefore, have the tenth sheaf as well as the nine.' Whereupon St. Augustine reply'd, 'If thou wilt not pay them I will excommunicate thee;' and so, hastening to the altar, publickly said, 'I command that no excommunicated person be present at Masse:' which words were no sooner spoke than a dead man, that lay buried at the entrance to the church, immediately arose out of his grave, went without the compass of the churchyard, and there stood still during the time of Mass; which being finished, St. Augustine went to him and said 'I command thee, in the name of God, that thou tell me who thou art!' To whom he made answer, 'I was patron of this place in the time of the Britons, and though frequently warned by the priest, yet never would pay him my tithes, and so died excommunicated and was thrust into hell.' Which answer occasioned St. Augustine to command him 'to show where the priest was buried that so excommunicated him;' who, being accordingly directed to his grave, said, to the end that all men may know that life and death are in the hands of God, to whom nothing is impossible, 'Arise in His name, for we have need of thee!' Who thereupon came out of his grave and stood before them. To whom St. Augustine said, 'Brother, dost thou know this man?' 'Yes,' quoth he; 'but I would that I had never known him, for he was always a rebel to the church, a withholder of his tithes, and even to his last a very wicked man, which occasioned me to excommunicate him.'

"Augustine replied, 'Brother, thou knowest that God is merciful, therefore we must have pity on this miserable creature, who is the image of God, and redeemed with His blood, having so long endured the pains of hell.' Whereupon, delivering to him a scourge, he kneeled down, and craving absolution with tears, had it granted; and so by St. Augustine's command, returning to his grave again, was immediately resolved to dust.

"Then said Augustine to the priest, 'How long hast thou been buried?' 'Above an hundred and fifty years,' quoth he. *Aug.* 'How hast thou fared hitherto?' 'Well,' quoth the priest, 'enjoying the delights of eternal life.' *Aug.* 'Art thou contented that I should pray unto God that thou mayst return again to us; and by thy preaching reduce many souls unto Him that are deceived by the devil?' 'Far be it from thee, O Father!' quoth the priest, 'that thou should so disturb my quiet as to bring me back to the troublesome life of this world.' *Aug.* 'Go thy way then, and rest in peace, praying for me and for the universal Church of God.' So, accordingly entering his grave, he fell also to dust. Then turned St. Augustine to the knight, and said, 'Wilt thou now pay thy tithes to God, my son?' who, trembling and weeping, fell at his feet, and confessing his offence craved pardon; and, shaving himself, became a follower of St. Augustine all the days of his life.

"'Hoc miraculum videbitur illis incredible, qui credunt aliquid Deo esse impossibile; sed nulli dubium est, quod nunquam Anglorum duras cervices Christi jugo se submisissent, nisi per magna miracula divinitus sibi ostensa.'"

This story appears to show that there were rebellious subjects against the supremacy of St. Augustine and Rome, and though Selden rejects the story as a monkish fable, Bishop Kennett, in his "Parochial Antiquities,"* seems to think that, divested of its miraculous disguise, it might be true, taking into consideration that Augustine possibly was in the neighbourhood at the time assigned. The story was first told in the twelfth century, as far as can be ascertained.

The church of Long Compton is dedicated to St. Peter, and though the present building does not show any architectural signs of antiquity, there has been a church here from a very early period. There is a recumbent effigy in the south porch, which the villagers associate with St. Augustine and the tythes.

* Article "Tythes," c. x. s. 2.

St. Ecwyn.

Alcester—the Alauna Dubonorum of the Itineraries—to which allusion is made in Alcock's Arbour, was once the seat of a flourishing industry. The smiths who toiled there were "vitious" from prosperity. They inhabited an old Roman station on a great highway, and were the Birmingham men of the early Saxon days. They toiled early and late. They cared not for Sunday, or priest, and when St. Ecwyn, the third Bishop of Worcester, came to preach to them, they sang and hammered at their anvils, as if it was as necessary to their salvation as the words of the saint himself. They were ignorant, and when St. Ecwyn called to them and they answered him not, save by plying their hammers more loud than ever, he cursed them. He cursed their trade. He even anticipated the Darwinian theory, and gave them tails. The Alcester smiths never survived this; their trade fell away. They no longer took pride in their work. They felt like beasts, for they had a tale attached to them which they could not tell. It is now a quiet, quaint old town, and its trade is represented by the making of a few needles only—a warning to those who will not listen to the preaching of saints!

Holy Edith.

AMONG the records of religious houses, there are none which occupy a higher position or have purer annals than the Nunnery of Polesworth, whose walls

"The holy Edith graced."

It is situated within a few miles of Tamworth, and the story of its foundation and refoundation is thus told :—

"King Egbert having but one son, called Arnulph, who was a leper, and hearing by a bishop which came from Ireland that the then King of Connaught had a nun to his daughter, called Modwen, that healed all diseased people repairing to her, sent his said son, at the persuasion of that bishop, into Ireland, where he was accordingly cured by the same holy woman; which great favour so pleased King Egbert, that he forthwith invited St. Modwen to come into England, promising that he would found a monastery for her and her convent, of which tender she soon after accepted, forasmuch as the religious house wherein she resided was by wars betwixt those petty kings of Ireland burnt and wasted, and brought over with her two of her fellow nuns.

"Whereupon the king, having a great opinion of her sanctity, recommended his daughter Edith unto her, to be instructed in religion after the rule of St. Benet, giving her a dwelling place in the Forest of Arden, then called Trendall, where the said Edith, together with St. Lynne and St. Ogithe, lived together in a holy manner, and soon after founded a monastery for them on the bank of the river Anker, at this place called Polesworth—the first, *poll*, importing a deepness of water, and the other, *worth*, a dwelling or habitation—constituting the said Edith abbess thereof.

"Which monastery being so founded and endowed, continued to her or her successors till the Norman Conquest. That Sir Robert Marmion, having the Castle of Tamworth and the territories thereabouts bestowed upon him by the Conqueror, expelled the Romans from hence, so that they were constrained to resort to Oldbury (a cell belonging to the house); but within the compass of a twelvemonth after this their expulsion, the said R. Marmion making a costly entertainment at Tamworth Castle for divers of his friends, amongst whom was Sir Walter de Somerville, Lord of Whichmore, his sworn brother; it happened that as he lay in bed St. Edith appeared to him in the habit of a veiled nun, with a crosier in her hand, advised him that, if he did not restore the Abbey of Polesworth unto her successors, he should have an evil death and go to hell; and to the end that he should be more sensible of this admonition, she smote him on the side with the point of her crosier, and so vanished away. By which stroke, being much wounded, he cried out, whereupon his friends in the house were soon roused, and finding him grievously tormented with the pains of his wounds, they advised him to confess himself to the priest, and make a vow to restore those nuns to their former possessions, all which being performed his pain presently ceased; wherefore, in accomplishment of his vow, accompanied with the same Sir Walter de Somerville and the rest, he forthwith rode to Oldbury, and craving pardon of the nuns for the injury done them, brought them back hither, desiring that himself and the same Sir Somerville might be their patrons and have burial for themselves and their heirs in this abbey, namely, the Marmions in the chapter house, and the Somervilles in the cloister.

"The nunnery thus founded was dissolved by Henry VIII. in the thirtieth year of his reign, notwithstanding that the commission who were employed to take the surrender of monasteries in Warwickshire stated, 'That after strict scrutiny, not only by the fame of the county, but by examination of several persons, they found these nuns virtuous and religious women, and of good conversation, Alice FitzHerbert being then abbesse (having so continued for xxvii. years, and at that time lx. years of age), and that in this town (Polesworth) there were then xliv. tenements and but one plough, the residue of the inhabitants being artificers, who had their livelihood by this house.' They implored Lord Cromwell not to suppress the house, but this appeal was of no avail; the house was suppressed, the abbess receiving a pension of £56 13s. 4d. per annum, two of the nuns £2 13s. 4d. per annum, and twelve nuns only 11s. per annum, notwithstanding the honourable report."

Part of the church, which yet remains, is evidently the foundation of the Sir Robert Marmion of the legend. In a portion of the conventual buildings which remain there are unfinished fire-places and other signs to show that the good nuns were spending their income like other religious communities, in order that their wealth might not tempt the cupidity of the commissioners or their royal master.

In the old quadrangle of the nunnery, where these religious and virtuous ladies rambled and meditated, there yet remains a tall sun dial, dating back from the period af the Tudors. From it you can can see the obelisk marking the site of the chapel of St. Leonard at Hoo, and the misty steam of the mail train north as it rushes through the cutting in the hill side. The scenery is quiet and well wooded. Around we can trace the remains of a bygone religious life, which existed here for nigh a thousand years. None of the incised crosses on the stone coffin lids date from this distant period, but some of them are five hundred years old and tell of the lady abbesses who ruled over the foundation of St. Edith when our Henries and Edwards were kings in England. The dial bears these inscriptions—

"Hoitus utramque testis nos et meditermur in horto,"

and

"Tempora mutantur nos et mutamer in illis."

The first is surmised to have been taken from some old monkish poem now forgotten. The first "hortus" is understood as hortus paradisiacus, the second "horto" as the garden of the old convent where the dial is placed. The second inscription has a more personal application—the ever passing hours reminding us that we grow older, greyer, and more infirm. "Mutantur mutant" might be inscribed on the silent mentor of the passing hours in house as well as in garden.

The neighbourhood of Polesworth is very interesting from the remains of the hermitages and chapels scattered about the estate of the good nuns. In this neighbourhood is Pooley Hall, an elegant and interesting Tudor edifice of brick, built by Sir Thomas Cokain in the reign of Henry VIII. Here dwelt the poet Cokain, who was addressed in a poem, never before published, in this high-flown hyperbolical strain—

"These are strange stories, Sir, to you who dwelt
Under the warm sun's comfortable seat,
Whose happy seat of Porley far outvies
The fabled pleasures of blest Paradise;

Whose Canaan fills your hous with wine and oyl,
Which hous, if it were plac't above the spheare,
Would be a palace fit for Jupiter.
The inner rooms, for honest, free delight,
And providence, that these miscarre loth,
Has placed the tower a centinell for both;
So that there is nothing wanting to improve
Either your peche, or peace, or love.
Without you have the pleasure of the woods,
Fair plains, sweet meadows, and transparent floods,
With all that's good and excellent beside,
The temples, apples by Euphrate's side;
But that which does above all these aspire,
Is Delphos, brought from Greece to Warwickshire.
But oh! ungodly Hodge, who valued not,
The saving juice of the ænigmaticle pot,
Whose charming virtues wodde we to forget,
I enquire of fate; else I had been there yet.
Nor had then once dared to venture on
The cutting ayr of this our Freeland gone.
But once again, dear Sir, I mean to come
And learn to thank and to be troublesome."

Lady Godiva.

THE story of Lady Godiva is, perhaps, the best and most widely known of all the legends of Warwickshire. Hundreds of thousands have at different times "waited for the train at Coventry," and, as they watched "the three tall spires," have thought of the fair and beautiful wife of the stern Earl, who overtaxed the people. They have pictured to themselves the women coming to the lady with their children, clamouring—

"If we pay this tax we starve,"

and how she went to the Earl, and besought their relief from the tax. How he told her—

"'You would not let your finger ache
For such as *these?*' 'But I would die,' said she.
He laughed, and swore by Peter and by Paul;
He filliped at the diamond in her ear;
'O! ay, ay, ay, you talk.' 'Alas,' she said,
'But prove me what it is I would not do.'
And from a heart as rough as Esau's hand
He answered, 'Ride you naked thro' the town,
And I'll repeal it.'"

The heralds went forth, and in the hot breath of noon, with her rippled ringlets flowing, they knew how the fair Godiva flitted from pillar to pillar "like a sunbeam," and then rode through the silent streets "clothed on with chastity," and thus

> "Took the tax away,
> And gave herself an everlasting name."

It is a beautiful legend, beautifully told by the Poet Laureate, but, unfortunately, it is not true. But, unlike the story of Guy, there was a Lady Godiva—a lady historically renowned for her piety, her beauty, and her charity. She was the daughter of Thorold, Sheriff of Lincolnshire, the founder of the Abbey of Spalding. Her husband, Leofric, Earl of Mercia, had a seat at Coventry, at Cheylesmore it is surmised, as that manor was claimed by his descendants. He and his wife were liberal benefactors to the ecclesiastical foundations of Worcester, Coventry, Evesham, Chester, Leominster, Wenlock, and Stow-in-Lindsey. Coventry was the more magnificently endowed, and was wealthier than all the others. The site of the minster may now be seen to the north of Trinity Churchyard, and there are indications of the situation of the monastic buildings; but no trace of any work that can be attributed to the days of Godiva can now be found in the city of Coventry. Leofric died on August 31, 1057, but Godiva, his countess, whose name is spelt by the Saxons Godgifu, lived for many years afterwards. Her son Algarus only survived his father two years. The fate of her children is somewhat obscure, but a niece and granddaughter intermarried with the Norman Earls of Chester, from whom the present Grosvenor family claim descent.

The legend is given at length in Brompton, page 949, in Knighton, 2334, and in Roger of Wendover, i. 497. It was not heard of or mentioned by any known writer prior to the end of the fourteenth century. In the reign of Edward III. the town was fortified with gates and towers, and had embattled walls. The tax on the citizens was very heavy, notwithstanding the many benevolences in aid thereof. After the death of the Black Prince, who had a castle at Cheylesmore, we first hear of the legend which would affirm that Coventry was to be toll free.* There is no doubt that Leofric gave the city many privileges; but the ride of Godiva is purely apochryphal.

The story, as related in Dugdale, is thus given:—

"This Leofric married Godiva, a most beautiful and devout lady, sister to one Thorold, Sheriff of Lincoln, and founder of Spalding Abbey. Which Countess Godiva, bearing an extraordinary affection to this place, often and earnestly besought her husband that, for the love of God and the blessed Virgin, he would free it from that grievous servitude whereunto it was subject. But he, rebuking her for importuning him in a matter so inconsistent with his profit, commanded that she should thenceforth forbear to move therein; yet she, out of her

* It is somewhat remarkable that Warwick was made toll free by Thomas de Beauchamp. 32 Ed. III., 1358-9.

womanish pertinacity, continued to solicit him, inasmuch that he told her, if she would ride on horseback naked from one end of the town to the other, in the sight of all the people, he would. Whereupon she returned, 'Will you give me leave so to do?' and he replying, 'Yes,' the noble lady, upon an appointed day, got on horseback naked, with her hair loose, so that it covered all her body except her legs, and thus performing the journey, returned with joy to her husband; who thereupon granted to the inhabitants a charter of freedom, which immunity I rather conceive to have been a kind of manumission from such servile tenure, whereby they then held what they had under this great Earl, than only a freedom from all manner of toll except horses, as Knighton affirms. In memory whereof the picture of him and his said lady were set up in a south window of Trinity Church in this city, about King Richard the Second's time, and his right hand holding a charter, with these words written on—

'I, Leofric, for the love of thee,
Do make Coventry tol free.'"

There is a sketch of this inscription in the notebook of Dr. Stukeley, of which a fac-simile is given on the next page. It has now disappeared.

It will be seen, doubtless with surprise, that no mention is made of "Peeping Tom" in the above legend, for the inquisitive tailor is an interpolation of a later date. It was not known before the reign of Charles II.

In one account the "churl compact of thankless earth" is said to be a groom to Godiva; in another a tailor; a third says he was a Dane, a stranger to Coventry. The figure itself was placed in its present position in 1813-14, when Hertford Street was formed; previous to this it was in Grey Friar's Lane, at the house of Alderman Abraham Owen. The figure, which is of wood, is in armour; the sollerets are broad toed. The armour is

somewhat curious, and the bassinet is of the date of Henry VI. It is probably a figure of St. George, who, in Johnson's "Seven Champions of Christendom," is stated to have been born in Coventry, and was taken from one of the religious houses at the Reformation. The back of the figure is chipped away by curious sightseers, anxious to secure a relic of the inquisitive tailor.

Guy, Earl of Warwick.

"Tradition leads the stranger's step to thee,
  Home of the mighty Guy! Nor this alone,
For Nature bids us bend the willing knee
  Before the glories of her matchless throne.
In sooth, the mind could revel here at will,
  In all the dalliance of fancy dreams.
So fair the landscape, and so sweetly still,
  As if kind heaven shed there its gentlest beams."

THE earliest topographical writers on Warwickshire have gone into ecstacy over the beauties of Guy's Cliff. Leland notices its quietude and beauty, and Camden speaks of it in poetic terms, unusual in the old herald. "There," he says, "have yee a shady little wood, cleere and cristal springs, mossie bottoms and caves, medowes alwaies fresh and greene, the river rumbling heere and there among the stones with his streame making a milde noise, and gentle whispering, and besides all this solitary and still quietness, things most grateful to the Muses." Quaint old Fuller, who knew the spot well, speaks of it as "A most delicious place, so that a man in many miles riding cannot meet so much variety as there one furlong doth afford. A steep rock, full of caves in the bowels thereof, washed at the bottom with a christall river,

GUY'S CLIFFE, IN 1722.

besides many clear springs in the sides thereof, all overshadowed by a stately grove. This pleasant spot, with its thousand pleasant memories, is the scene of the last days of the fabled Saxon hero, Guy, Earl of Warwick."

The place is the very home of romance, and there are many pilgrims thither who taste of the crystal spring still flowing from Guy's Well and gaze on the moss-grown cave in which the husband of fair Phelice dwelt. They gaze on the mutilated statue cut out of the solid rock, which yet remains in the chapel, and wonder that any one could doubt the story of which there are so many material evidences. Yet, when viewed through by light of historical research, we find but little evidence of the truth of the legend. Its romance fades away, and we are brought face to face with a few dry facts only.

The roll of the Earls of Warwick, composed by John Rous, a chantry priest of Guy's Cliff, in the fifteenth century, gives us the name of Rohand, Earl of Warwick, in the time of Alfred the Great. He had a daughter, Phelice, who married Guy, son to Siward of Wallingford, the hero in question. As far as we know, Rous had little or no authority for the statements contained in the roll. It is obvious, however, that he knew the legend, for Phelice is represented as receiving from the herdsman the ring sent to her by the dying Guy. The legend, however, varies in many particulars.

Guy is stated to have been born in Warwick, and at

eight years old gave indications of the vast strength and agility which at sixteen attracted the attention of Earl Rohand, who was pleased with his skill in all manual exercises. Here he met the fair Phelice, who was as beautiful as Venus herself, and with her he fell in love. Her changeable moods pierced his heart. He thought that she was ambitious; he had no earldom to offer her—nothing but a true heart and a brave soul.

In this mood he went to the castle and received a warm welcome, and an invitation to a hunting match; but Guy pretended to be ill, and sat in a window alone bemoaning his unhappy fate. Hope, however, grew in his heart, and he avowed the love that was consuming him. To his vows and protestations Phelice turned an answer soft but clear, "With her should virginity live and die. Her youth and beauty were not in bloom, and these must not be thrown away on inferiors."

Guy was distracted, and Phelice was admonished by a vision to be more kind to him and his love. She loves him and tells him to "make his valour more glorious than the sun, to let it shine throughout the world, and she will then crown him with her heart, and soul, and life." Phelice, says he,

> "Phelice, this kiss is all that now I crave,
> And till I have purchased fame no more I'll have."

To Normandy then went Guy. Here he became the champion of an injured lady condemned to be burned.

The wrongs of the beautiful Dorinda fired his chivalrous soul, and he overthrew her false and perjured accusers. Refusing all rewards for this homage to virtue and to honour, Guy went to his ship, weighed anchor, and sailed out to sea. But the discomfited enemy followed. Philbertus, the betrayer, hired a stout ship and followed the venturesome and gallant Guy. The captain wished to flee, but no coward's heart animated Guy. "Like Englishmen," said he, "let us meet the foe; for the crown of France I would not have it reported that Guy had ever fled." The ship was put in a posture of defence, for Guy wished to bear the brunt of war himself alone. The Frenchmen, confident of victory, crowded on deck. But every blow Guy struck had more than human force, and the deck was soon a scene of blood and slaughter. Philbertus the betrayer, was amazed. He wished to flee, but Guy leaped on the Frenchman's ship, and his heroism made the soldiers cry for quarter. Like all heroes he was merciful. He gave Philbertus his life, took him on board his ship as prisoner, and sailed into that part of Normandy nigh unto Germany, and there, discharging his ship, gave the prisoners to the captain and went to the grand tournament for Blanche, the Emperor's daughter, of Almaine; for the victor by courage and might should have the damsel mounted on a milk white steed, with greyhounds by her side and a falcon on her wrist. Hundreds of knights and nobles were there, with golden glittering armour, prancing chargers, and the clanging sound of many trumpets.

Princes and dukes fell before the gallant Guy. "Devil, magician, enchanter!" said they; but Guy had no charm but good steel, a stout arm, and brave heart. Envy surrounded him, success attended him, love rewarded him; but he was modest as well as brave. He was a poor Englishman, too lowly to be more than the servant of such a princess. She was as beautiful as Phelice, and as modest. His constancy won all hearts. He came to Warwick again, when Phelice wished to receive him and praise the doughty deeds he had done.

He told her that his sword had won an emperor's daughter, but Phelice's better face made him leave her. She assured him of her love and constancy, and urged him to greater and more worthy deeds than winning a lady and her steed. Abroad again gallant Guy must go. The wind was not fair, and for six days together Guy lay idle in port. During this time fame made known in every corner of the land that a dun cow, of enormous size, was ravaging Dunsmore Heath and putting the keepers to flight. The king was at York when he heard of the havoc and slaughter which this monstrous animal had made. He offered knighthood to anyone who would destroy her, and many lamented the absence of Guy, who, hearing of the beast, went privately to give it battle. With bow, and sword, and axe, he came and found every village desolate, every cottage home empty. Men and beasts lay dead around. His heart filled with compassion, and he waited for the encounter. The furious beast glared at him with her eyes of fire. His arrows flew from her side as from adamant itself. Like the wind from the mountain side the beast came on. Her horns pierced his armour of proof, though his mighty battle axe struck her in the forehead. He wheeled his gallant steed about and struck her again. He wounded her behind the ear. The monster roared and snorted as she felt the anguish of the wound. At last she fell, and Guy, alighting, hewed at her until she expired deluged with her blood. He then rode to the next town and made known the monster's death, and then went to his ship, hoping to sail before the king could know of the deed. Fame was swifter than Guy. The king sent for him, gave him the honour of knighthood, and caused one of the ribs of the cow to be hung up in Warwick Castle, where it remains until this day.

Then Guy went abroad with three gentle knights, including Heraud of Arden, and they were beset by sixteen villains in the forest. Ten of these did Guy encounter and slay, but two of his knights were killed and Heraud wounded. In rage he turned and revenged their deaths. The would-be murderers were left a prey to the birds of the air and the raging beasts of the forest. At tournament and siege Guy distinguished himself, but lamented the loss of his companions; but at last he met Heraud in a pilgrim's garb, which much cheered his heart. He relieved Duke Seqwin, and made him and the Emperor friends. He sailed with 2,000 men to Byzantium, but storms scattered his ships, and Guy had to defend himself against three Turkish vessels, which he disabled; one got clear away; another was burnt, but the third he sent as a prize to the duke, his friend. Byzantium was besieged by 50,000 Turks and Saracens. These he defeated, and entered the city. The next day the battle was renewed, and here he defeated the proud and insolent Colbrond the pagan, the champion of the Saracen host. Here too, Heraud defeated Elendant; and the Soldan himself challenged Guy, and likewise was slain.

From hence he went to a forest near the harbour, where his ships were becalmed, in search of venison, and here he found a lion and dragon fighting, and resolved to engage the conqueror. The dragon won, and then Guy fought the dragon and conquered, and the lion lay fawning at his feet. He slew also a monstrous boar, and freed Northumberland of a dragon when he returned to England. Then we know that fair Phelice rewarded his love, and their marriage took place at Warwick amidst great festivities.

But Guy was unhappy. The presumptive pride of his youth was made clear to him. He resolved on a pilgrimage of expiation to the Holy Land. He went thither, and during the time he was absent the ferocious Danes ravaged the land, and the king and the people were desolate.

This happened in the third year of Athelstan's reign, the year of our Lord 926. There was scarcely a tower or a castle that the Danes had not destroyed as far as Winchester; and, hearing that the king with his nobles were in that city consulting about some timely means to prevent the utter loss of all, they sent messengers to him, proposing that either he would forthwith resign his crown to the Danish generals, viz., Olaf and Golanus, or submit to hold the realm of them, doing homage and fealty, and paying tribute according to their appointment; or, lastly, that the whole dispute for the kingdom should be determined in a single combat by two champions for both sides. This being added by Olaf, that if in that duel King Athelstan's champion had the victory, he would presently depart the land with his army; but otherwise, without any more ado, it should wholly belong to the Danes. Of which proposals King Athelstan accepted the last, and, calling together his nobles, offered that province (viz., Hants) for a reward to him that should conquer the Danish champion, called Colbrand; and to the end that God would direct him in the choice of one to undertake this combat he enjoined a fast for three days, in which, with earnest prayer and abundant tears, he besought His favour. But in this choice the English were exceedingly astonished, forasmuch as one Heraud, a most valiant and hardy knight of this nation, was then beyond the sea, seeking after Reynburn, the son of his lord and master, Earl Guy, that had been stolen away by merchants of a foreign country in his infancy; as also that Earl Rohand, the most valiant of a thousand, was dead; and that the same Guy, a man of extraordinary courage and skill in martial feats, shortly after his marriage with Lady Phelice before mentioned, being gone into the Holy Land on pilgrimage, was not yet returned. But it so fell out that God, being moved with the sorrowful tears and intercessions of the English, sent a good angel to comfort the king as he lay upon his bed the very night of the nativity of St. John the Baptist, directing that he should arise early on the morrow, taking two bishops with him, and get up to the top of the north gate of that city, staying there till the hour of prime, and then should he see divers poor people and pilgrims enter thereat, amongst which there would be a personable man in a pilgrim's habit, barefooted, with his head uncovered, and upon it a chaplet of white roses; and that he should entreat him, for the love of Jesus Christ, the devotion of his pilgrimage, and the preservation of England, to undertake the combat, for he should conquer the mighty Collbrand and deliver his realm from the Danish servitude. Whereupon King Athelstan, with fervent zeal, hastened betimes in the morning to mass, and sent for the Archbishop of Canterbury, with the Bishop of Chichester, to whom he related his vision, taking them along to the gate assigned.

About this time it happened that the famous Guy, before specified, returning from his pilgrimage in foreign parts, landed at Portsmouth, and, being there advertised of Sir Heraud's absence, with the occasion thereof, as also Earl Rohand's death, together with the great distress that the king and his nobles were then in, hastened towards Winchester immediately, and coming at night into an hospital but little distant from the north gate of that city (in which place afterwards the hospital in honour of the holy cross was founded), where he rested himself; on the next morning he went with other poor people to the city gate. To which place the king, being come for the purpose before specified, and espying one neatly clad in a white short-sleeved gown reaching to his mid-leg, with a garland of roses on his head and a large staff in his hand, but looking wan and much macerated by reason of his travelling barefoot, and his beard grown to a very great length, he concluded that the same was the man described to him by the angel, and, being full of joy, told those that were with him as much.

The palmer (for so was he at that time called), taking notice of the king and bishops, put off his chaplet, and reverently saluting them, entered the gate. Whereupon the king hastened down, and laying hold of his coat tendered him entertainment, with desire to hear some news; but the palmer, returning humble thanks, answered "That the hour to take up his lodging had not yet come, for that he intended first to visit the churches of that city and there offer up his prayers to God, but afterwards seek some food to refresh himself withal, which being done, he purposed to depart thence and perform such penance as he was to do for his sins." Whereunto the king replied, "The reason why we have here stayed hath been only to wait for your coming, for it is the will of God that you must encounter with that wicked Colbrand, the Saracen, for the safe guard of us all and all the English nation, and freedom thereof from the yoke of slavery. For Olaf, King of Denmark, and Golanus, of Norway, have besieged us here almost a twelvemonth, and now we have concluded a truce upon condition that we find a man to undergo the combat with Colbrand, their champion, and in case our champion shall overcome him, they are forthwith to quit the land without doing injury to any and not disturb this realm any more; therefore we do desire you, for the love of Christ our Saviour, and for the pardon of your own sins, that you will heartily undertake this duel against that cursed pagan, for the cause of God's Church and the Christian religion."

To whom the palmer answered, "Oh, my lord the

king, you may easily see that I am not in condition to take upon me this fight, being feebled and weakened by daily travel. Alas! where are your stout hearty soldiers who had wont to be in great esteem with you?"

"Ah!" quoth the king, "some of them are dead, and some of them are gone to the Holy Land and have not yet returned; I had one valiant knight, which was Earl of Warwick, called Guy, and he had a courageous servant, named Sir Heraud de Ardenne; would to God I had him here, for then should this duel be soon undertaken and the war finished," and as he spake these words tears fell from his eyes. Whereat the palmer, being very sorrowful, "besought him to forbear further grieving, assuring him that, for the love of Christ Jesus and the blessed Virgin, as also for the honour of God's holy Church, and for the soul of Guy, and Heraud his companion, he would, in the fear of God, undergo that combat." Then did they bring him into the city and to the church with ringing of bells; the *Te Deum* was begun with cheerful voices, and they entertained him with meat and drink, as also with bathing, putting apparel on him, and for the space of three weeks cheered him up with the best refreshments. After which, when the day appointed for that duel was come, the palmer rose early and heard three massses: the first of the Holy Ghost, the second of the blessed Trinity, and the third of the holy Cross. Which being ended, he forthwith armed himself with the king's best harness, and girt the sword of Constantine the Great about him, and taking St. Maurice's lance in his hand, got up on the king's best courser, being accounted of all that then beheld him the most proper and well appointed knight that they ever saw. From thence rode he through the midst of the city towards the place assigned for the combat, which was in a valley called Chiltecumbe, where he waited for Colbrand, who shortly after came, so heavily harnessed that his horse could scarce carry him, and before him a cart loaded with Danish axes, great clubs with knobs of iron, square bars of steel, lances, and iron hooks to pull his adversary to him; and so soon as he saw the palmer make towards him, calling loudly, he bade him get off his horse and cast himself down with submission; but the palmer, arming himself with the sign of the cross, and commending himself to God, put spurs to his horse to meet the giant, and in the first encounter pierced his shield so far that his own lance broke into shivers, which so enraged the giant that he bore up fiercely towards the palmer, and smote his horse with such strength that he cut off his head. The palmer, therefore, being dismounted, nimbly and with great courage directed his blow at the giant's helmet, but by reason of his height could reach no further than his shoulder. Then Colbrand smote at the palmer with a square bar of steel; but he, seeing his danger, interposed his shield, which bore off the blow, and on a sudden did so vigorously lay at the corner of the giant's target, that his club, bossed with iron, fell to the ground; which, whilst he stretched out his arm to take up, the palmer with his sword cut off his hand. Whereupon the Danes grew much dismayed; and on the other side was there as great rejoicing by King Athelstan and the English, and yet notwithstanding did Colbrand hold out the combat till the evening of that day, that by losing so much blood he fainted, so that Guy, with all his strength, fetched a blow and cut off his head.

The victory, therefore, thus happily attained, occasioned the Danes with great confusion to hurry away, and the valiant Guy to give tnanks to God, repairing forthwith to the cathedral, where he was honourably received with solemn procession by the clergy and others, and offered his weapon to God and the patron of that church before the high altar, which Knighton saith, even to his time, was kept in the vestry there, and called by the name of Colbraud's axe. But this being done, he reassumed his pilgrim's habit. Whereupon the king became most importunate with him to discover his name; but he utterly refused so to do, except to himself, and that upon his oath not to reveal it; unto which condition the king assenting, they walked out alone to a certain cross at some distance from the city; and as soon as they came thither, humbly bowing himself to the king, and saying he was Guy, Earl of Warwick, the king embraced him in his arms, kissed him, and promised him large rewards if he would live in his court; but he with much thankfulness refused to receive any, and besought the king that he would not disclose what he had said, in regard to his resolution.

"The pilgrim departed from the hall,
Out of the town he took his way,
And hastily went towards Arderne
To a hermit whom he knew there.
He dwelt in a remote part of the forest,
Where he led a holy life,
Beside Warwick, the city,
It is called the Kybbe Cliff;
On the Avon this hermitage,
As is written in the history.
But the hermit was dead;
No living man dwelt there.
Then Guy resolved
That he will never go from thence,
But he will always remain there,
And will there serve God."

The Earl Guy then bent his footsteps towards Warwick, and coming thither not known of any, for three days together took alms at the hands of his own lady, as one of those thirteen poor people unto which she daily gave relief herself, for the safety of him and her, and the health of both their souls; and having rendered thanks to her, he repaired to a hermit that resided amongst the shady woods hard by, desiring by conference with him to receive some spiritual comfort; where he abode with that holy man till his death, and upon departure out of this world, which happened within a short time, succeeded him in that cell, and continued the same course of life for the space of two years after; but then discerning death to approach, he sent to his lady their wedding ring by a trusty servant, wishing her to take care of his burial; adding also that when she came she should find him lying dead in the chapel before the altar: and, moreover, that within fifteen days after she herself should depart this life; whereupon she came accordingly, and brought with her the bishop of the diocese, as also many of the clergy and other people, and finding his body there did honourably inter it in that hermitage; and was herself afterwards buried by him, leaving her paternal inheritance to Reynburn, her only son. Which departure of our famous Guy happened in the year of our Lord D.CCCC.XXIX., and of his own age the 70th.

The legend has been told in song,* as well as in story, differing slightly in detail, but preserving all the main features of the Christian English hero—

"The proud Sir Guy, a baron bold
 In deeds of arms, the doughty knight,
That every day in England was
 With sword and spear, in field to fight.

* The anchoretic MSS. of the metrical version of Sir Guy of Warwick is one of the earliest of these. Henry of Knighton, Canon of Leicester, circa 1395, gives a prose version of Colbrand's duel in Latin.

An Englishman I was by birth.
  In faith of Christ a Christian true;
The wicked laws of infidels
  I sought by power to subdue.

Nine hundred twenty years and odd
  After our Saviour Christ, his birth—
When King Athelstan wore the crown—
  I lived here upon the earth.

Sometimes I was of Warwick Earl,
  And, as I said of very truth,
A lady's love did me constrain
  To seek strange ventnres in my youth:

To try my fame by feats of arms,
  In strange and sundry heathen lands,
Where I achieved, for her sake,
  Right dangerous conquests with my hands.

For first I sail'd to Normandy,
  And there I stoutly won in fight
The Emperor's daughter, of Almain,
  From many a valiant worthy knight.

Then passed I the seas of Greece,
  To help the Emperor to his right
Against the mighty Soldan's host
  Of puissant persons for to fight;

Where I did slay of Saracens
  And heathen pagans many a man,
And slew the Soldan's cousin dear,
  Who had to name doughty Colbron.

Ethelred, that famous knight,
  To death likewise I did pursue,
And Almain, King of Tyre, also,
  Most terrible in fight to view.

I went unto the Soldan's host,
  Being thither on embassage sent,
And brought away his head with me,
  Having slain him in his tent.

There was a dragon in the land,
  Which I also myself did slay
As he a lion did pursue—
  Most fiercely met me by the way.

From hence I pass'd the seas of Greece,
  And came to Pavy Land aright,
Where I the Duke of Pavy kill'd,
  His heinous treason to requite;

And after came into this land
  Towards fair Phelice, lady bright,
For love of whom I travelled far
  To buy my manhood and my might.

But when I had espoused her—
  I staid with her but forty days
Ere that I left this lady fair,
  And then I went beyond the seas—

All clad in grey, in pilgrim sort,
  My voyage from her I did take
Unto the blessed Holy Land,
  For Jesus Christ my Saviour's sake.

Where I Earl Jonas did redeem,
  And all his sons, which were fifteen,
Who, with the cruel Saracens,
  In prison for long time had been.

I slew the giant Amarat
  In battle fiercely hand-to-hand,
And doughty Barknard killed I,
  The mighty duke of that same land.

Then I to England came again,
  And here with Colbrand fell I fought,
An ugly giant which the Danes
  Had for their champion hither brought.

I overcame him in the field,
  And slew him dead right valiantly,
Where I the land did then redeem
  From Danish tribute utterly.

And afterwards I offered up
  The use of weapon solemnly
At Winchester; whereas I fought
  In sight of many far and nigh.

In Windsor Forest I did slay
  A boar of passing might and strength—
The like in England never was
  For hugeness, both in breadth and length!

On Dunsmore Heath I also slew
  A monstrous wild and cruel beast,
Call'd the dun cow of Dunsmore Heath,
  Which many people had oppress'd.

Some of her bones in Warwick yet
  Still for a monument do lie,
Which unto every looker's view
  As wond'rous strange they may espy.

And then to Warwick came again,
  Like pilgrim poor, and was not known;
And then I lived a hermit's life,
  A mile or more out of the town;

Where with my hands I hewed a house
  Out of a craggy rock of stone;
And lived like a palmer poor
  Within that cave myself alone:

And daily came to beg my bread—
  Phelice at my castle gate—
Not known unto my loving wife,
  Who daily mourned for her mate.

Till at the last I fell sore sick,
  Yea, sick so sore that I must die:
I sent to her a ring of gold,
  By which she knew me presently.

Then she repairing to the cave
  Before that I gave up the ghost;
Herself closed up my dying eyes,
  My Phelice fair, whom I loved most.

Then dreadful Death did me arrest,
  To bring my corpse unto the grave;
And like a palmer dyed I,
  Whereby I fought my life to save.

My body that endured this toil,
  Though now it be consumed to mould;
My statue fair, engraven in stone,
  In Warwick still you may behold."

Such is the legend of Guy. We find first that the ancient name of Guy Cliff, at least as far back as Edward III., was Gibbeclyve. It is Gibcliff in other instances. Like Bevis, of Hampton, the story has a strange likeness to the French romances of the 12th and 13th centuries. In the 14th century Guy was represented as a real personage, and in 1339 his sword and coat of mail formed the subject of a bequest, for the manuscripts of the 15th century, in Magdalen College, Oxford, treated of the combat between Guy and Colbrand as an historical incident, whereas Copeland, in 1550, took no notice whatever of the legend of the Warwickshire dun cow. It was first mentioned by Dr. Caius, who wrote the "De Bonasi Cowibus," wherein he said that at Warwick Castle, in 1552, in the place where the arms were kept, was hung up the head of a bonassus; that the bladebone of the same animal was hung up in chains from the North Gate, Coventry, and the rib was hung up in the chapel at Guy's Cliff. In 1636, the body armour of Guy was exposed at Kenilworth, and his horse armour at Warwick Castle, with his sword and dagger, and the rib of the dun cow. Evelyn visited Warwick Castle in 1654, and saw the supposed sword, staff, and the other relics of Guy. The armour exhibited at the porter's lodge of Warwick Castle as that of Guy's consists of a bassinet of the time of Edward III.; his breastplates are two shields, one of the 15th century, and the other of the time of James I.; his sword is of the time of Henry VIII.; his staff is a curious and ancient tilting lance; fair Phelice's slippers is a pair of stumped irons of the 15th century; Guy's horse armour is also of the same date. The celebrated Guy's porridge pot is, no doubt, an ancient garrison cooking utensil. Mr. Matthew Bloxam has the bladebone of the dun cow, and another rib is in St. Mary's Redcliffe Church, Bristol. The statue in the chapel at Guy's Cliff is recorded to have been cut and the chapel rebuilt by the directions of

Richard Beauchamp, Earl of Warwick, in the 15th century, when the chantry there was founded. The well was arched in at this time also. So that in reality there is nothing, except the cave, which can be assigned to an earlier date than 1450, more than 500 years after Guy had departed this life, and the place was then known as Gibcliff.

On the other hand, it is known that Rous had access to many sources of information which are not now available. Many of the deeds of Guy are supposed to be symbolized. We know that the sheriffs of the shires had great power, and that the sheriff or ældermen of the marches of Mercia had a difficult task. The Danes, who settled on the east side of the Watling Street, made frequent invasions into Warwickshire. We can trace their settlements on many points of land. Dunsmore, like the plain near Edgcote, is supposed to have been Danesmore, and the dun cow has been created out of the similar sound of Daengow, a Danish tribe who fought there. We know that a bloody battle was fought near Marton, from the arms and armour found there. There is a curious similarity in the name of both the Saracen and the Danish champion Colbrand. Whoever was the hermit at Guy's Cliff in the time of Athelstan we may never know, but we do know the names of several who resided there.

In 1870 attention was directed to some supposed

Anglo-Saxon writing in the cave reputed to be Guy's. Early in the century Mr. Daniel Lysons reported that such was the case; and in February, 1870, Mr. Ralph Carr Ellison carefully examined the panel in which the words occurred, and found the sentence, whatever it was, written twice over—once in Saxon Runic characters, as well as in partly Roman capitals.

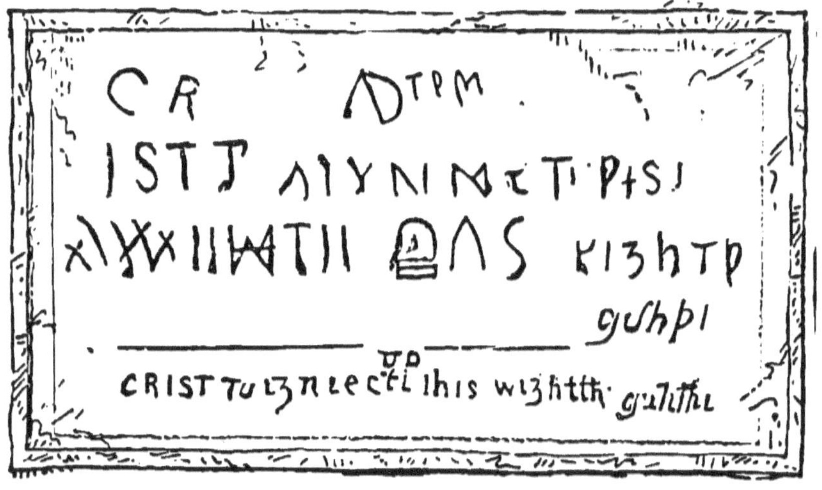

This has been referred to the 10th century, and indeed, to the lifetime of the illustrious Guy himself. The inscription has been read thus—

"Yᴅ
CRIST-TU ICNIECTI
THIS I-WIHTTH.
Guhthi"

in the Mercian dialect of Anglo-Saxon. In West Saxon it would have been—

"YT
CRIST-TU CNIHTE
THIS GEWIHT.
Goda."

This has been inferred to mean—

"Cast out, thou Christ, (thy) servant,
Or knight, this weight or burden."

Each term is repeated in Anglo-Saxon gloss. There are other letters, about which there has been much vague but ingenious conjecture. The inscription is now carefully preserved, and Lady Bertie Percy has had it carefully copied.*

* In an old quarry not far from the cave is a roughly hewn figure on a square pedestal. It is surrounded by trees and foliage. It was put up to the memory of a quarryman killed there, and bears the following inscription by the late Mr. Bertie Greathead.—

"Here lie I, Dick Ward, yeon aout i the rock
To which I ha een full monny a nock,
And this'n shall stond ill wayager a paound
Where ye loggeryeds all be six feet i the graound;
For my back's summut humpy,
And my legs ower stumpy.
Ye may loffe, and ye wooll, but never a sole
Among yeou grinners coold meack sich a hole:
Will Russel cut eers, eyes, and nosy,
The squire his sel found aout the posy.
1821."

St. Wolstan.

THE ancient town of Long Itchington, now but an unimportant village, but once one of the principal towns in the country, had the honour of being the birthplace of the great Saxon Bishop, Wolstan of Worcester.

In the library of Sir Watkin Williams Wynn, of Wynnstay, there is a manuscript life of St. Wolstan in Latin hexameters. Notices of his life and career are common in all English histories. He was the son of Æthelstan, a theyn of Long Itchington, by Wulfigu, his wife, who after his birth took monastic vows. Wolstan was at first only a secular student at Peterborough, under one Ervenius, apparently a foreigner. As a student he was distinguished for his chastity, his pious demeanour, his skill in illumination, and bodily exercises. At the age of 26, Brighteah, Bishop of Worcester, ordained him, and on becoming a priest he entered the priory of Worcester, of which, under Ealdred, a subsequent bishop, he became prior. He went about to baptize the poor, and devoted himself to religious exercises. In 1062 the bishopric of Worcester became vacant through the translation of Ealdred to the Archbishopric of York. The legates of

Pope Alexander II. were at this time in England, and they went to Worcester to persuade Wolstan to accept the vacant see. Ethling, the Abbot of Evesham, was also a candidate, but the Witan joined with the legates in urging the acceptance of the high office on Wolstan, who at this time was about 50 years of age. At last Wolstan yielded to the entreaties of his friends and was consecrated by Ealdred. He was a friend of Harold's, and appears to have ruled the diocese with considerable wisdom. He was one of those bishops who did not oppose the coronation of the Norman Conqueror, and indeed, from some reason or other, the Conqueror was well received at first by Warwickshiremen. In 1076 Wolstan was summoned by Lanfranc and William to surrender his bishopric to a more learned ecclesiastic, who would be more subservient to the new rulers of England. The conduct of Wolstan on the occasion is known to every reader of English history. The chief motive of Wolstan's life seems to have been a reverent love for the memory of Edward the Confessor, and to this his recognition of William must be in a great measure ascribed. The story is well told by the author of the following ballad,* which tells the rest of the story :—

* The ballad, of which these verses are an extract, was written by a lady, who signed herself Annabel C———. They appeared, I believe, originally in "Gems from Modern Poets." London, 1849.

"The Saxon, with bowed spirit,
Weepeth and cannot rest,
For other lords inherit
The land he loveth best.

The Norman lord hath made him
In his own home a slave;
But nothing can degrade him,
For his heart is true and brave.

And Norman William reigneth
Where Harold reigned of yore,
Save that no heart remaineth
In men's service as before.

He hath smote the English people
With his gleaming sword of steel;
He hath trod the English people
Beneath his armed heel.

Their old domains are given
To his greedy stranger band:
Like hunted harts they're driven
Throughout their own dear land.

Oh, Harold, where's thy power?
Oh, Harold, where's thy peer?
So fair an English flower
No more shall we see here.

One English bishop only
Is left his flock to feed:
His children, few and lonely,
Have him alone in need.

Where the Saxon dead are lying
The Norman king doth stand;
And each in splendour vying
Press round the alien band.

Now to that king unholy,
  With his Normans gathered round,
The Saxon bishop lowly
  Must bow him to the ground.

And does he lowly enter
  Or bow him to the ground?
Within that glittering centre
  No firmer step is found.

His mind is fixed on heaven;
  He hath no lord on earth;
He who the staff had given
  He trusts hath there his birth.

With head erect, unshaken,
  Before the king he stands,
Who bids the staff be taken
  From his true pastoral hands.

He yields it not so lightly,
  But grasps it strong and bold;
He grasps it firm and tightly;
  He will not loose his hold.

And with it from them turning,
  He strode where through the gloom
A silver lamp was burning
  Before a royal tomb.

The hues of evening, streaming
  Through windows o'er his head,
The clear, pure lamplight gleaming,
  A glory round him shed.

His robe he round him gathers;
  He stays his hasty tread;
In the old tongue of his fathers
  He speaks unto the dead:

'Oh king, our Edward, hearken!
  I had this staff from thee,
There are tempest-clouds that darken,
  Thou its defender be.'

Again he turned him proudly
  To the strange king's alien band,
And, with voice unshaken, loudly
  He spake with outstretch'd hand:

''Twas a better man who gave it
  Than ye boast of in your race,
And he alone shall have it,
  This be its resting place!'

He raised his hand to heaven,
  He smote the Saxon's tomb;
No mandate then is given—
  They dare not speak his doom.

Deep in the flint imbedded,
  As if in yielding clay,
The staff to stone is wedded
  Not to be rent away.

He laid his jewelled mitre,
  Ring, pall, and cope away,
And with calmer looks and brighter
  Went with the monks to pray.

They who ne'er feared in battle,
  But gave it hearty cheer,
Who loved their armour's rattle,
  Now held their breath for fear.

The king looked to those around him;
  They looked unto the king;
But never a word they found him
  That any help could bring.

Then spake the king in anger,
'Make ye the staff to yield!'
They had liefer heard the clangour
Of the fight in battle-field!

'Now hold it firm, De Tracy!
Doth it yield unto thy hand?
Doth strong Sir Humphry Lacy
Find it an osier wand?

Vere, Vernon, Mowbray, shake it!
Ye all are mighty men;
Now good Lord Montfort take it,
And show thy strength again!'

Now Lanfranc's self is trying,
To make it shake and fall;
But the hand beneath him lying
Is stronger than them all.

The king cries out in wonder,
The archbishop can but weep,
And all hearts that roof under
To heaven in praises leap;

For He who reigns in heaven
Hath stayed their hands from sin,
So may they be forgiven
The wicked thoughts within!

'My brother, we have erred,'
The grieved archbishop said,
'Thou wisely hast referred
To the Judge of quick and dead.

He ever judgeth truly;
He sees not as we see;
He know'st thou serv'st Him truly,
In just simplicity.

Better a little learning,
With love and faith always,
Than earthly knowledge, yearning
For empty human praise.

We have erred, have erred, my brother,
Take back the staff to thee!
The hand strong 'gainst all other
An infant's then will be.'

Then rose that prelate holy,
As a simple priest might rise,
And came to the altar slowly—
No triumph in his eyes.

A moment his lips are praying,
On the staff he lays his hand,
Ah! see! it is obeying!
The stone is but as sand.

Then Lanfranc craves his blessing,
And kneels down at his feet,
Thus Wolfstan sore distressing
By honour more than meet.

So he falleth down and striveth
That he be blessed instead;
Then to Him who blessing giveth,
Each kneels in solemn dread.

A Legend of Arden.

WHO, loving Shakespeare as a Warwickshire man should, and as an Englishman ought, does not know the story of Mariana and the Moated Grange? The echoes of the song where she is first discovered, in "Measure for Measure" (Act iv. Scene 1)—

> "Take, oh take, those lips away,
> That so sweetly were forsworn,"—

linger lovingly on the ear; and even if Shakespeare's description is not known, Tennyson's song of intense weariness, the lay of the deserted yet loving heart of Mariana, is known. Never, perhaps, shall we truly know which of the many moated areas of the county of Warwick suggested to Shakespeare his idea of the moated grange. But we have still existing an old moated house, preserving the same substantial front as it did in the time of Shakespeare, when it was inhabited by the painstaking and persevering county antiquary, Henry Ferrers, of Baddésley Clinton. There are many amongst Warwickshire men who fondly regard this old house at Baddesley as *the* Moated Grange. They remember that in the neighbouring village of Snitterfield Shakespeare's father was, in all probability, born. They know that many of his relations resided at Rowington for a long period; amongst the "haunts" of Shakespeare's youth we must include the precincts of the Grey House at Baddesley, and the shady haunts of Hey Wood, a portion of the primeval forest of Arden, and around which at the present time many of the giants of the old forest yet stand in gaunt majesty. Beneath their shade we might hope to behold the melancholy Jacques, and anon Rosalind and Touchstone. The neighbourhood is even more identified with "Measure for Measure," a play believed to have been written with special reference to Lord Grey, whose life was then in danger from the machinations of his enemies. In this neighbourhood we may trace the monastery to which the duke retreated, the nunnery of the votarists of St. Clare, as well as the moated grange. Strangely, too, there had been an Isabel Shakespeare in the adjacent nunnery, "*quondam priorissa de Wraxall*," as she is termed in the register of the Guild of St. Ann, at Knoll, in the nineteenth year of the reign of Henry VII. The foundation of Wroxall is the subject of the last of the monkish legends we have gathered together. The story runs thus:—

"That one Richard, shortly after the Conquest, holding the lordship of Hatton and likewise this place of Wroxall of Henry then Earl of Warwick, had issue a son, called Hugh, who was a person of great stature, and bore the same arms as the Montforts of Beaudesert (near Henley), in this county, did, being a branch of the same family as was thought; which Hugh going to warfare in the Holy Land was there taken prisoner, and so continued in great hardship there for the space of seven years. But at length he, considering that St. Leonard was the saint to whom his parish church had been dedicated, and the many miracles :hat God had often wrought by the merits of that His glorious confessor, made his addresses by earnest prayers :o him for deliverance; whereupon St. Leonard appeared ·o him in his sleep, in the habit of a black monk, bidding iim arise and go home and found at his church a house ·f nuns of St. Benet's order; but the knight awaking ook this for no other than a dream, till that the same aint appeared to him a second time in like manner. Iowbeit then, with much spiritual gladness and rejoicing, e made a vow to God and St. Leonard that he would per- ›rm his command, which vow was no sooner made than iat he became miraculously carried thence with his tters and set in Wroxall Woods, not far distant from s own house; yet knew not where he was till a shepherd ' his own passing through those thickets accidentally und him, and after some communication (though he was first not a little affrighted in respect he saw a person so ·ergrown with hair), discovered all unto him. Where- ›on his lady and children, having advertisement, came :thwith to him, but believed not he was her husband till he showed her a piece of a ring that had been broken betwixt them, which so soon as she applied the other part, in her own custody, closed therewith. And shortly after, having given solemn thanks to God, our Lady, and St. Leonard, and praying for some divine revelation where he should erect that monastery so promised by his said vow, he had special direction where to build it, by certain stones pitched in the ground in the very place where the altar was afterwards set. After the structure whereof, two of his daughters were made nuns thereof, a lady from the nuns of Wilton being fetched to direct them in the rule of St. Benedict."

The church and the site of the monastic buildings are now visible, in consequence of the old hall being pulled down which was built over the site. The place can now be traced, but the present structure is later than Hugh Hatton. The origin of the legend is obviously the result of a vow, if Hugh did not avail himself of the aid which Lord Bateman of the ballad is said to have done. The site is, however, memorable as having been the seat of Sir Christopher Wren. The present proprietor, Mr. James Dugdale, built the present mansion in 1867. It contains a fine collection of oil and water colour paintings by the best modern masters. The house was designed by Mr. Walter Scott, of Liverpool.

Robin Hood.

)F the many popular traditions that have come down o us, that of Robin Hood and his merry men has been he most popular for the longest period. We have an ntimate acquaintance with Little John, Will Scarlett, Allan-a-Dale, and Friar Tuck. We loll with them under he merry greenwood, and every glade of Barnsdale nd Sherwood seems known to us. We know the tricks layed on the Sheriff of Nottingham. We know the allad of the Tinker of Banbury, and how he made the ishop of Hereford dance in his boots. Robin Hood has l the attributes of a popular hero. He was of noble rth, deprived of his inheritance. He chose the merry e of an outlaw, and with a rough and steady sense of stice took from the rich and gave to the poor. The or blessed the man who felt for their wrongs and ·ir sufferings. They did not care for any abstruse law ethics. There was the noble hero, who defied the law l gave them out of the plentitude of his heart something .t had been extorted from proud, avaricious, or grasp- ecclesiastics. Yet the whole story is involved in ıbt, and we are indebted to Dr. Stukeley for the hint that it is possible that he may have been a native of Warwickshire.

That Robin Hood was born at Loxley no one, who does not deny his existence altogether, would presume to doubt. There are but two, or at the most three, Loxley's in England, and which of these may claim the honour of being the birthplace of the bold outlaw, the hero of song, of ballads, and the greenwood, is a question open for discussion. Robin Hood is claimed by Yorkshire and Nottinghamshire as their special hero. Sherwood and Barnsdale re-echo with his name. A Lockslcy has been found near Sheffield to claim him as a son. The Loxley in Staffordshire has neither claim nor probability of being connected with Robin Hood. If he was not a native of Sherwood, he might have been born on the fringe of the forest of Arden.

In the MS. collection of the late Robert Wheler, of Stratford, relating to Warwickshire antiquities, it is recorded that "At the north side of Coughton Church there is a window, almost at the lower end, towards the belfry, wherein at the bottom is this written on the glass under the pictures of divers men :—

"'This window was made, and these men following with the money that Robin Hood and his men got.'"

Coughton Church is almost within sight of Loxley near Stratford, and we are led to consider the evidence which can be brought to bear on the history of the popular forester.

Robin Hood, according to the majority of his biographers, was born at Loxley, or Lockesley, about the year 1160. He is said to have been of noble parentage —an earl, in fact, whose real name was Robert Fizooth or Fitzodo, and Dr. Stukeley deduces him from Ralph Fitzooth, a Norman, who came to England with William Rufus, and married Maud de Gaunt, daughter of Gilbert, Earl of Kyme and Lindsey. This statement may or may not be worthy of credence, but there was a Robert Fitzodo living at Loxley, then spelt Lockesley, at this time, which is a very curious coincidence. It is thus mentioned in Dugdale, "Whether Robertus, fil. Odonis, who lived in Henry the Second's time, was the first that had it, by the Earl of Warwick's grant, or whether it was his father, I am not sure; but that the said Robert possessed it, and made it his place of residence, there is no doubt, for in his grant to the Canons of Kenilworth of XCC. acres of his demesne lands here, with a messuage, loft and croft, and Xs. rent, which for XI. marks of silver he sold them, he writes himself Robertus, fil. Odonis de Lockesleia; and, besides this so sold by him, he gave unto them, for the health of his father's soul, whose body lay buried in that monastery, and for the good state of himself and his posterity, pasturage for X. oxen and sheep in his demesne lands there. Which Robert left issue only three daughters, his heirs, whose matches and descendants I have here recorded." One of these married a Bagot, and another a scion of the ancient family of the Trussells, of Billesley. There is a farther pedigree of these Fitzodos in Dugdale's account of Harbury, from which it appears that this Robert had a son called Odo, who had issue a son known as Robert FitzOdo, of Herberbury, who by his deed recorded to Edward I. in the rolls of Chancery bestowed upon the monks of Combe his manor house, &c., for the health of his soul, and that of his wife Elizabeth.

One of the earliest notices of Robin Hood which is undisputed is in "The Vision of Piers Plowman," generally ascribed to one Robert Langland, and written within a century after the date of the supposed death of the outlaw. Sloth, in this early poem, says :—

> "I cannot perfectlie my paternoster as Prest it singeth;
> But I can rymes of Robin Hood and Randulf Earl of Chester."

The connection of the name of Robin Hood with Randulf Earl of Chester is most singular, for in the year 1152-3 Henry FitzEmpress, then Duke of Normandy, upon making peace with King Stephen, rewarded Randulf Earl of Chester, surnamed Gernons, for the services he had rendered to him, with many large estates, of which he had dispossessed some of his enemies. Amongst them was the whole fee of Radulphus, filius Odonis, wherever it could be found.* Here is the outlawry of a FitzOdo by Henry II. in the 12th century, and the gift of his lands to Ranulf Earl of Chester, in nearly the same terms as mentioned by the author of "Piers Plowman," who, it must be recollected, did not live far from the Warwickshire borders.

In the curious pedigree of Robin Hood published by Dr. Stukeley, the outlaw's descent from Gilbert de Gaunt in the female line is made out; and as he is called the Earl of Huntington in the oldest ballads and on his supposed tombstone at Kirklees, it is still more curious, as Mr. Planché has pointed out, that in 1184 the earldom of Huntington lapsed to the Crown on the death of Simon de St. Liz; and again, in 1237, on the death of John Le Scot without issue. It is probable, if Robin Hood had such a pedigree, he may have preferred a claim to the earldom when 24 years of age and again when 77 for the outlaw did not die, according to the tombstone, till 1247.

The tradition of Robin Hood must not be lightly cast aside. The surmise of his Warwickshire origin is amongst the many literary romances of the county, and time may throw some further light upon it.

* Cottoman MS.—Thornton, Hist. Notts.—Planché's "Rambles with Robin Hood."

Amy Robsart.

THE name of Amy Robsart is indelibly mixed up with the glories and the decay of the princely Castle of Kenilworth, through the novel of Sir Walter Scott. When "the tall gentleman who leaned heavily on his stick" visited the remains of Kenilworth Castle more than sixty years ago, probably he himself never dreamed that his pen would give so great a popularity and almost immortality to the tragedy which he associated with the pageantry of Elizabeth's visit in 1575. Wherever English books are read, the ruins of Kenilworth Castle have received a new charm from the magic wand of the "Ariosto of the North." Year after year pilgrims have strolled among the crumbling ruins of Kenilworth, more deeply interested in the Pleasaunce, in Mervyn's Tower, in the site of the old lake, in the probable scene of the meeting between Elizabeth and Amy Robsart, and in the endeavour to trace the exact sites indicated by Scott's romance, than in the great siege, its early feudal history, or even the magnificent pageantry with which Leicester welcomed his royal mistress, the virgin Queen.

It seems a sacrilege to tear away this veil of fiction, so attractively woven by the great Wizard of the North, and to dissect this romance of history and class it with the legends and traditions of the past. Not one in a hundred ever dreams of questioning the accuracy of Scott's great romance. Not one in fifty would be willing to have a glorious dream of love, and loyalty, and devotion dispelled.

Every reader knows Amy Robsart's story. How she was inveigled from her father, Sir Hugh Robsart's home in Devonshire, and privately married to Robert Dudley Earl of Leicester, who placed her at Cumnor Place, the residence of his servant, Anthony Forster, a gloomy misanthropic man, whilst the Earl attended the Court as a bachelor beloved by the Queen, who would have married him but for this secret; and how Amy followed him to Kenilworth and was present during those brilliant festivities in July, 1575. How she was taken from thence and hurried back to Cumnor to meet a horrible and ghastly death at the very moment of her reconciliation with her husband and recognition as his wife. It is no new story. It may be found in Leicester's "Commonwealth," and in the introduction to the novel itself. We have the story in another form in Mickle's ballad, with the exception of the visit to Kenilworth. The sense of secrecy and mystery has done much to hide the true facts of this romantic story.

There are documents extant which give us a full account of Amy Robsart, her life, marriage, and melancholy and somewhat mysterious death. Amy was the daughter and heiress of Sir John Robsart, of Siderstern, in the county of Norfolk, and was born at Stanfield Hall, which has since acquired an unhappy notoriety, in 1532. On the 4th of June, 1550, she was married to Sir Robert Dudley, in presence of Edward VI., with great pomp, and the youthful king's diary records many of the facts. The marriage, therefore, was not secret. Amy was never Countess of Leicester, for she died three years before her husband was created earl. She was not at the princely pageants at Kenilworth, for she had been dead fifteen years when they took place. Kenilworth was not in Dudley's possession until he was created earl. His brother Ambrose was created Earl of Warwick in 1557, and it is possible that she may have visited her brother-in-law at the castle, and have stayed at Moreton Morrell, which tradition says was the case. Sir Richard Varney was a relative of the Verneys of Compton Murdac, now known as Compton Verney, and the present Lord Willoughby de Broke claims kindred with him. His character, like that of Anthony Forster, was needlessly blackened by Scott, who seems to have perverted, through ignorance or design, the marriage of Dudley with Douglas Howard, Lady Sheffield, in 1573, which was a secret marriage, for the purpose of his story, and made Amy Robsart the heroine, although she had been in her grave fifteen years.

The death of Amy Robsart was, however, a mystery, which will probably never be made clear. She did die suddenly—nominally from the effects of a fall down "a pair of stairs," at Cumnor, when all the servants of the house were at Abingdon fair. The curious and minute facts preserved show how anxious Dudley was that no blame or suspicion should fall upon him; how he sent his "good cousin" Blount to inquire into the facts; how the said cousin tarried at the inn at Abingdon, and "pumped" the host as to the news of the place, without declaring his business or his motives; how he found that Anthony Forster was in good repute; how Amy herself had insisted on the servants going to Abingdon fair, although it was Sunday, and was left in the house almost alone; how a coroner's inquest was held, but no satisfactory result ensued, and no definite details were given of the cause of death; how the foreman of the jury had written to Dudley, who had reiterated his desire for a full inquiry; how the general belief was that Amy, wearied with her husband's long absence and apparent neglect, had apparently tired of life, and had probably ended her own life by a fall down stairs—possibly accidental, or possibly designed. Ultimately the jury, after sitting from the 10th to the 13th of September—the accident happened on the 8th—returned a verdict of "Mischance," which was tantamount to "Accidental death." Forster and the other attendants were acquitted of any acts of violence. There was no unseemly haste over the inquiry or funeral; the proceedings were conducted in due legal form, and the only doubt is as to the exact means by which Amy Robsart died. The implications on the character of Varney and Forster are shaken by the contemporary facts; the absence of the servants was fully explained as occurring at Amy's own special wish; her letter to Mr. Flowerdew shows her desponding spirit, and thence it is highly probable that her death was accidental from the fall, or possibly from her own design. In any case, no charge of complicity against Dudley is proved by the existing facts, and he is at least entitled to the benefit of very serious doubts as to his alleged guilt.

The old hall was of considerable extent, and was built round a court or quadrangle, of about seventy-two feet in length and fifty in breadth. The principal entrance was on the north side, under an archway, with rooms on either side of it; above these "the long gallery" extended the whole length of that side of the building. At the west end of this apartment the flight of stone stairs, at the bottom of which the body of the unfortunate Lady Leicester was said to have been found, led down to the quadrangle and great hall of the edifice, which was at right angles to the long gallery. Over a room beyond the hall was the apartment celebrated by the name of

"Lady Dudley's Chamber," and indeed so great an interest had the fate of that hapless lady excited, that the whole place was generally called at Cumnor "Dudley Castle." On the south side were some apartments, which bore traces of superior magnificence, but which were in a state of dilapidation. The old inn, called the Bear and Ragged Staff, is an object of interest even now. She was buried at the Church of our Lady, in Oxford, on Sunday, the 22nd of September, 1560. The full account of the funeral ceremony is given in a very illegible manuscript among the Dugdale MSS. in the Bodleian Library, but it is unfortunately far too long to quote here. It contains numerous interesting passages, showing the great pomp and ceremony with which the body was brought from "Glocester College, a lytell without the towne of Oxford," to St. Mary's Church, where, "in the mydell eyle in the upper ende, was made a hearse" with all due appurtenances. The procession to the church must have been a very imposing sight on that Sunday morning, now over 300 years ago, for "after the pore men and women in gownes" came the "universities, 2 and 2 together, accordinge to the degres of the colleges, and before every house the officers with ther staves," then "the quere in surplesses singenge, and after them the minestar." After them followed the officials from the Herald's College, all in their mourning habits, and "the corpes borne by 8 talle yeoman, for the way was farre," then the chief mourners and others, and lastly "the mayor of Oxford and his brethren." They entered in at the west door of the church, and the body was placed on the hearse, and on "eche syde of the hersse stod 2 gentlemen holding the bannerroles, and at the feet stood he that held the great banner," and the service began, first "sarteyne prayers, then the 10 commandments, the quire answering

CUMNOR CHURCH.

in peyke-songe, then the pystle and the gospell began, and after the gospell the offeringe," and when this was finished "the sermon began, made by Doctor Babyngton, whose antheme was *Beati mortui qui in Domino moriuntur.*" Dudley was not present at the funeral.

On the north side of the chancel of Cumnor Church

is the tomb of Anthony Forster, a monument of grey marble, surrounded by a canopy of the same, supported by two pillars. On the back of the tomb, on brass plates, are engraved a man in armour and his wife in the habit of the times, both kneeling before a faldstool, together with the figures of three children kneeling behind their mother. A long epitaph assigns to him a large share of the virtues which most adorn the human character.

After the death of Forster, Cumnor Place was long uninhabited, and stories are still prevalent among the inhabitants of Cumnor of the spirit which frequented the deserted mansion.

"And in that manor now no more
Is cheerful feast and sprightly ball,
For ever since that dreary hour
Have spirits haunted Cumnor Hall.

The village maids, with fearful glance,
Avoid the ancient moss-grown wall,
Nor ever lead the merry dance
Among the groves of Cumnor Hall.

Full many a traveller oft hath sigh'd,
And pensive wept the Countess' fall,
As wandering onward they've espied
The haunted tow'rs of Cumnor Hall."

The apparition was said to appear in the form of a young and beautiful woman, superbly attired, and was mostly seen on the steps, the immediate scene of the barbarous act. The tradition of the place relates that the ghost was at last removed from the house, and laid to rest in a pond at a short distance from it.

The Dream of Thomas Oken.

On the border land of fiction is the story of the dream of Thomas Oken, the last master of the old guild at Warwick, and the great benefactor to the town. The following sketch embodies the generel idea that Oken was prompted to give so largely and liberally to Warwick by a dream. The names introduced and the persons are those of Warwick burgesses then living :—

I.—HALLOWED WORDS.

The moon was shining brightly in the black-blue heavens, the air was cold—bitterly cold—the Winter King had locked this old realm up in iron bonds. He reigned supreme o'er hill and fell, and his breath cut through our Warwickshire uplands and gentle undulating dales with a severity that few had remembered in this broad kingdom of ours, even in the days of the good old-fashioned Christmases. For it was Christmas time, when the moon shone as brightly as a burnished silver buckler on the steel-cold icy heavens. The tall tower of St. Mary's stood out sharply cut against the northern heavens as the glorious old bells pealed forth

WARWICK CASTLE.

the welcome to glad time when human hearts are supposed to be peculiarly under the influence of Divine love, and Christ reigns in verity upon the earth, and our hard souls melt in the genial rays of charity and love.

It was on such a Christmas-eve when the lights shone joyously forth from window and tower of the old Castle of Warwick. There had been glorious doings in the hall, for Lord Dudley had commanded the yule log to be burnt amidst rejoicings and mirth, and the wassail bowl had been quaffed, and the King of Misrule, with his numerous and attendant jesters, had for the time been lords of the hour; cold and hunger had been forgotten, for it was indeed

"Merry in the hall."

Beards had wagged, all and every one had loyally and truly wished that they might speedily "see the like again." The merry party passed out of the castle gates, as the bells pealed out to announce that Christmas had indeed come. Then some turned over the narrow stone bridge and passed into Bridge End, while the larger number came through Castle Street into the old town. There were lights glistening in the windows, and the prickly holly was stuck into the diamond panes of many a window in the houses of the well-to-do burghers of Warwick. The gilt vane of the High Street Cross seemed to dance and sparkle in the moonlight in the eyes of the merry roysterers, whose wits had been sharpened by the spiced ale and wassail of my Lord of Warwick.

"I'll take a gold rial that old Thomas Oken is fast asleep at this hour," said Miles Hirons. "The old curmudgeon, since he got rich, can never enjoy himself as he used to do in the old Guildhall, and keep merry Christmas with his townsfolk."

"He is always fashed with his silks and velvets," muttered bold Will Arden. "He has lost his soul in the pursuit of wealth; and as for Joan, she seems like an old witch from Wolvey Heath, so shrewd and cunning she looks as she measures out the bright sarsnet, as if she grudged to part with the silk for the bright angels from the satchel of our dames."

"Aye," said an old rosy-nosed, blink-eyed individual, "they take on now, but we recollect them poor enough; yet whether king or queen reigned he flourished in that scrimpy old house of his."

"Yes," said Miles Hirons, "he is bewitched by that old foreigner, Nicholas Iffler, who, I take it, is a descendant or an imp of old Nick's himself. The Lord preserve us!"

Yet so it was. The success of honest industry gave rise to envious tongues and detracting words. Perhaps, too, there was some reason for the free remarks of the joyous fellows who spoke full of Christmas fun. Mistress Oken was a careful helpmate for the prosperous mercer, who had held his own during the changes of the previous half century, until he was one of the most prosperous, if not the richest, burgesses in the old borough. He was the mainstay of the fussy little Recorder, who a year or two afterwards met with the special notice of the good Queen Bess; and even as the bells chimed out, the newly-elected bailiff of the town under the new charter was sitting by Thomas Oken's fireside with some four or five of the other burgesses and well-to-do burghers —Richard Ellyn, Thomas Burges, Richard Bothe, Nicholas Iffler, and others, amongst whom was a priestly-looking personage, to whom the party paid great deference.

The room was plainly but comfortably furnished, and the old oak table and shining buffets were loaded with good cheer, amongst which were some curious glasses and robust-looking bottles, which were evidently of foreign manufacture.

As the voices of the street roysterers went by, singing the old refrain of "Jolly good ale and old," Nicholas Iffler was busily engaged in drawing the cork of a bottle. "Mien Got," said the old man, "ale is good, but a flask of Rhine is better. Do you not think so Mistress Oken?" and he handed the beaded sparkling wine to the lady of the house, in one of the slender crystal glasses which were then but rarely seen in the houses of commoners in England.

"It is heart cheering," said the old dame. "May our gracious Queen be happy and reign long."

There was a long-drawn "Amen" from the corner in which the priestly-looking individual sat. "Amen," said Master Thomas Cartwright, for it was he. "Well said, dame; may she live long, and maintain our faith in unsullied purity. Let that be our Christian wish."

"But over the good wine which is the juice of the grape from the sunny hill-sides of my own land," said Iffler, "for I live here amongst you in peace, and in the enjoyment of my faith, Master Cartwright, through the indulgence of our Queen and the munificence of my Lord Dudley."

"Aye," chimed in the burghers, "since my Lord of Leicester has held the Castle of Kenilworth, and his worshipful brother has lived at the castle, there has been good trade for you and all of us."

"To our gracious Queen," said they all, and they quaffed the fine Rhenish which Old Iffler had brought as a gift to Dame Oken from his Westphalian home.

"Christmas," said Master Cartwright, "is but a relic of the old pagan and Popish times, but it has a truer and higher celebration in the human heart. There charity should reign; there the love of the poor should dwell, even as it did in the heart of our Lord and Master."

"Truly so," said Thomas Oken. "I have known the hard frowns of poverty, and how blessed it is to know that those who are richer than we are care for us, but they seldom think of it."

"My Lord of Leicester has had his heart so influenced by this Christian spirit," said Cartwright, "that he has determined to endow the old guild at Honyngate for twelve poor soldiers, who have been maimed or disabled in her Majesty's wars, for ever. May the grace of heaven bless the gift."

A simultaneous "Amen" burst forth, for Thomas Cartwright was known to be a godly man—a man who prayed from the heart as the spirit moved him, before his sermon and homilies. He was the first preacher in the Church of England that had done such a thing, and he was high in favour with the Earl of Leicester, who was about to advance him to the mastership of the newly-formed hospital.

The evening passed gaily on with sound conversation and merry thoughts, until the bells of the old church struck upon the ear.

"Christmas is at hand," said the preacher. "In the midst of our mirth let us not forget the Giver of all good—the merciful Father. May He bless this Christmas-day to us all; may He soften our hearts, so that we may soothe the sorrows of the poor, and enable us to help them forward in the cause of righteousness and truth!"

The loving cup was then passed round, and the old

burghers went out into the cold air to their several homes. When all had departed save the preacher, Thomas Oken said to him, "Can I do aught to bless and sanctify this Christmas? Can I replace on the earth any of the good men who have hallowed it?"

"Look to your own heart for an answer," said Cartwright as, amid the blessings of the hour, they parted for the night.

II.—THE DREAM.

Good old Thomas Oken retired to his rest troubled in mind on that Christmas morn. The moon shone brightly he could see, and the chill air pervaded even the snug bedchamber. The air seemed laden with the sound of merry Christmas bells; they rung and tingled in the good old mercer's ears until he could scarcely believe but what he heard them. As his eyes sank in slumber and his head fell heavy on the pillow, his last thoughts were, "Can I do aught to bless and sanctify this Christmas?" He had not been asleep long ere he was conscious of something unusual in the bedchamber. It was no longer the dark, sombre apartment, with the moonlight peeping in through the lattice panes; the old oak rafters became endowed with somewhat of their old life—fresh branches sprang out from each gnarled trunk, and were speedily covered with hanging verdure; glad flowers blossomed from the floor;

a clear bright light flooded the room; and he saw before him an angelic figure, pensively leaning and watching the country beyond. Thomas Oken looked, and he saw estates at Baddesley, Harbury, and Beausale, studded with the fleecy sheep, and the sunlight seemed to fructify the herbage—so glorious did it appear. He saw that the shepherd was in his own likeness, and he felt that joyousness of heart which he had felt when a boy, and had played on the old common, and had gone to roam among the rocks at Guy's Cliff. He then thought of the words of the preacher, and he looked within his heart, and he found it dry and withered. Each palpitating membrane was stamped with gold rials and silver pennies, and there was only one spot yet untouched and real, and there he found stamped the words, "I was poor and was never deserted. I was poor, and He always fed me. He has guided my footseps, and how have I rewarded Him? He has blessed my labours, but who will reap the fruits?" He could see around these words the picture of his life—his early struggles; his poverty; his peddling career. His pleading with his dear Joan in their courting days. How their lives had been blessed, and how the first sorrow came on them when their dear child died. Then came the dark days of struggle again in troublous times which followed, until he first met Nicholas Iffler, who could not only tell him of the best mart to buy his goods, but who found him two noble customers in the Lords Dudley to purchase them. Even the virgin Queen had inquired where the handsome silks with which my Lord of Leicester had slashed his doublet had been purchased, and had commanded a brocaded robe from the stores and warehouses of the mercer of Castle Street. All this he saw depicted on his heart, but there was a part on which nothing was written. His charity had been merely formal. He had given his offering to the church, and had not been unmindful of the poor, like his neighbours, but his seed had not been blessed. "God alone blesses the cheerful giver," and Thomas Oken had not given cheerfully. He saw that he was the shepherd of his flock in charge simply for another. Then the words of Thomas Cartwright had power, "Look to your own heart for an answer," and there you will see how this Christmas may be sanctified and blessed. He saw that whilst he was tending his sheep there were poor and ignorant lookers on; envious hearts were backbiting him. Some were toiling up noisome steeps, and others were groaning in dirty sloughs and complaining of the exaction of the tax gatherers. Thomas Oken groaned in spirit. A film passed over his eyes, and then he saw that the scene had changed. The old town which he had known throughout his life was before him. It was altered it is true, yet strangely familiar. The golden autumn was over the land. The air was fragrant with the glorious flowers, and the ripe corn nodded its heavy head in bounteous plenty. Merry parties passed along, and he could hear the silver notes of the bells of St. Mary floating along the Avon. He apparently passed along the Honyngate, but how changed. It was cleanly paved, and the High Street looked bright and sunny. The lowing kine were passing to and from the large area of common land, and the brethren of the hospital were still in the old gowns. But how changed the street. The High Cross was no longer there. The old church was altered, but he could see his old house in evergreen freshness of youth. Crowds were flocking to the church, and he followed them. There he heard the word of God expounded and the duty of Christian charity inculcated to large crowds of grateful hearers. But near the Chapter House door a poor widow knelt, and by her side were two orphan children. He could hear their prayer for the good, the holy, and the charitable, who had alike blessed them and had been blessed. On looking up he saw that all eyes were fixed upon a small brass plate, on which a man and woman were pourtrayed, and underneath were these words:—

"Of your charite give thanks for the soules of Thomas Oken and Joane his wyff, on whose soules Jesus hath mercy, Jesus hath mercy. Amen. Remember the charyte for the pore for ever. Anno Domini M.CCCCC.LXXIII."

What was this he heard—accents of love and tenderness around him, yet all was so strange and unwonted.

The preacher spoke of the good which one man can do if so disposed, and how his good deeds will live and blossom and bear fruit abundantly.

All this seemed so clear and bright to Thomas Oken, that he wondered that he had not always thought so. He felt and knew that the spirit of Christmas was over this and had blessed the work. He thought of how the dry and dusty leaves had blossomed and the flowers sprang out of the same beneficent influence. He had searched his own heart, and he felt that he could bless and sanctify this Christmas in the thirteenth year of her Grace, and in the year of our Lord, 1570.

III.—THE DEED OF FEOFFMENT.

The sun shone brilliantly on that Christmas morning. The hoar frost had figured each diamond pane and had flung its rayed crystals over the light tracery of the branches of the trees and shrubs when Thomas Oken came down to breakfast. Mistress Oken observed that he looked sad and thoughtful as he returned the Christmas greeting of the household. Master Cartwright also came to that sumptuous breakfast, where the "jolly good ale and old" took the place of more effeminate beverages, and as he gazed on Oken's face he said "that He who searcheth all hearts had been at work in his friend's." He knew that the day would be sanctified and be made memorable, and that Warwick's foremost burgher would emulate the example of England's most famous noble, and that the coming year would be memorable as the year of charity in the old town of Warwick.

The answer had been truly sought for and found. The symbolical heart had but little left to be filled up, and it was speedily done. Ere the 1st day of January a deed of feoffment had been drawn up, and Thomas Oken gave his estates at Beausale, Harbury, Baddesley, and Warwick to the bailiff, Thomas Burgess, and the Corporation for ever, so that out of the profits arising the poor men's children might be taught and the townsmen's children receive a better education in the King's School. To this one-fourth of the whole was directed to be applied. One-third of the sum was directed to be applied to the relief of the poor. One-sixth to those sermons in St. Mary's which he had heard in his dream. The market place and the town gateways were to be kept clean and in repair. The merry roysterers were not forgotten, for they were to have ale when they cut down the Whitsuntide ivy at the High Cross, and bonfires on Midsummer-eve and the even of St. Peter. A good dinner was to be given to certain members of the Corporation and burghers, and, when all was paid, the residue was to be devoted to the payment of stallages and to the repair of the town bridge.

Nor was this all. His race was nearly run; but at his death he left further monies for the enlargement of the common; for plate to be used by the Corporation; for dowers to ten poor maidens; by further donations to the poor. He directed that the brass plate should be inserted in the walls of the Chapter House in St. Mary's Church. Neither did he forget the neighbouring towns of Stratford and Banbury. This example was followed by his friend Nicholas Iffler, whose grateful heart and liberal mind endowed almshouses for the poor, and the land he gave provided a local habitation also for the recipients of Thomas Oken's bounty. These things did Thomas Oken to bless and sanctify Christmas, for his heart was opened, and his soul returned to his God who gave it on the 30th of July, 1573, in the fifteenth year of the reign of her Grace Elizabeth Regina; and the poor of Warwick yet bless the name of Thomas Oken, for his good deeds have blossomed and increased. Many a poor man's heart has been comforted and his path made easy by the dream and fulfilment of the old Warwick mercer on that famous Christmas-eve.

THE

Romantic Episodes

OF

WARWICKSHIRE.

Prince Fremund.

THERE are but few visitors to Leamington who do not know the soft and sylvan scenery of Offchurch. The village church, though restored, has many signs of antiquity. A recently found carved cap of a circular-headed window, on which is figured a serpent, seems to belong to the original church, founded here, according to the Saxon chronicle, by Offa, King of Mercia, whom Charlemagne called the greatest of the western kings (circa A.D. 690), in memory of his son, Prince Fremund, who was treacherously slain between Long Itchington and Harbury. Between these villages a few years ago some Anglo-Saxon spear-heads and bosses were found.* Unfortunately there is no confirmatory evidence of the burial of Fremund here; but that Offa had a residence near the site of the present seat of the Dowager Countess of Aylesford, called Offchurch Bury, is certain. On the side of the parish nearest the Fosse way numerous relics of a battle-field have been found, and are preserved at the Bury. The death of Fremund is recorded by Camden, who quotes an old chronicler as his authority. He says, "Not far from Offchurch is

* They were in the possession of the late Mrs. Buffery, of Emscotte, who promised them to the Warwick Museum.

Urtundon, now Long Itchingdon, and Harbury. Neither verily are these two places memorable for any other cause, but for that Fremund, sonne to King Offa, was betwixt them villianously, in times past, slaine by those that forelayed him, a man of great renowne and singular piety to Godward, unto whom nothing else procured envie and evill will, but because in an unhappy time hee had by happy conduct quelled the audacious courage of his enemies. Which death of his, notwithstanding, turned to his greater glorie, for, beeing buried at his father's palace, now called Off.Church, hee liveth yet unto posterity as who, beeing ranuged in the catalogue of our saints, hath among the multitude received Divine honors; and whose life is by an ancient writer set out in a good poeme, out of which let it bee no offence to put downe these few verses following touching the murderer who, upon an ambitious desire of the kingdom, slew him :—

"'Non sperans visio Fremundo, regis honor optato se posse sui, melitur in ejus
Immeritan tacito mortem, gladioque profanus
Servio exerto servus, dominique jacentis
Tale nihil veritum sano caput amput ab ictio
Tatis apud Wydford Fremundum palma coronat,
Dum simul et sontes occidit, et occidit, informis.

"'Past hope, whiles Fremund lived to speed of wished regalty.
All secret and unworthy means he plots to make him dye,
With naked sword, prophane, slane he, assaileth cowardly
His lord unwares, and as he lay beheads him cruelly.
At Wydford thus Prince Fremund did his glorious crown attaine,
Whiles slaying guilty folke, at once himself is guiltlesse slaine.'"

The Siege of Kenilworth.

The Great Siege of Kenilworth.

THE story of the first commoner who married a princess of England is one of the most romantic episodes in the history of our land. The hoary walls of Kenilworth have no better story to tell. The desolate halls do not speak of this, but the tall keep frowned on the scene, and the boundary walls then, as now, marked the extent of the wards of this great midland fortress. The castle was but little more than a century old when it came into the hands of Simon de Montfort, as part of his wife's dower. It owed its existence to Geoffry de Clinton, the chamberlain of Henry I., and we know it was erected between the years 1123 and 1125. To this period the great keep, now known as Cæsar's Tower, must be ascribed. The castle was garrisoned for the King in the reign of Henry II., during the struggle between him and his sons, and the soldiers remained within the walls for seventy-seven days. In 1184, the walls were repaired at a cost of £26 6s. 9d. The history of the purely Norman castle now closes. In the reign of John, the castle was still in the hands of the Crown, and was held for the King by the Sheriff, and between the fourteenth and seventeenth years of the reign of John the castle was greatly re-edified and repaired, at a cost of £937 9s. These works are now to be traced in Lunn's Tower, Water Tower, in the outworks on the east, and in a portion of the western walls. In the reign of his son, Henry III., the greater portion of the outer walls were rebuilt and repaired. The castle was one of the largest and most perfect and complete fortresses in the kingdom, when Simon de Montfort, in 1238, came to England and claimed the Earldom of Leicester in right of his mother Amicia. By the royal favour and authority he married Eleanor, the Countess Dowager of Pembroke, the King's sister, notwithstanding the opposition of the Earl of Cornwall, the King's brother, and many of the powerful English barons, who viewed with jealousy this promotion of a foreign subject and his alliance with the royal family. Simon de Montfort was soon the popular idol, the trusted friend of nobles and commoners, a master of the arts of war and of peace, a benefactor of the clergy, and a defender of the realm against foreign encroachments. During the next fourteen years Simon de Montfort ruled in Guienne with ability and honour. He was the popular idol of England, though in disgrace with the King.

The history of the English Parliament dates from this era. At Oxford, on the 11th of June, 1258, the Mad Parliament, as it was termed, met and chose a council of twenty-four to rule the kingdom and to give advice to the King. Amongst the representatives of the barons in this council was Peter de Montfort, Lord of Beaudesert, near Henley in Arden, who adhered to the fortunes of his great namesake, and who subsequently had the honour of presiding over the first assemblage of the knights of the shire who represented the Commons in Parliament. There were many changes and shifting scenes in the next five years; a perpetual struggle between the barons and the King for power. In April, 1263, the great Earl of Leicester placed himself at the head of the forces of the barons, and forced the King to comply with their demands. A hollow truce followed. In May, 1264, hostilities again broke out, and on the 14th of the month the famous battle of Lewes was fought, and the King, together with Prince Edward, became prisoners to the Earl. With Simon de Montfort fought many of the Warwickshire knights and barons. The end was at hand.

In 1265, Simon de Montfort summoned what was in reality the first English Parliament, and over this assembly of knights of the shire and representatives of the cities and boroughs of England William Trussell, of Billesley, a Warwickshire knight of considerable ability, presided as speaker. In the meantime treachery was rampant among the forces of the barons. Prince Edward found himself at the head of a large force, whilst Simon de Montfort, still in charge of the King, guarded at Hereford the Severn and the marches of Wales. The energy of Prince Edward destroyed the boats and bridges, but could not prevent the stout Earl from fording the river and marching to Evesham, where he encamped early in August, in the hope of being joined by his son Simon, who was in charge of Kenilworth, ere he gave battle to the Prince; but young Simon was surprised at night in a ravine near Kenilworth, the exact site of which is not known, and Prince Edward seized his stores, treasure, and many of his knights, and forced the rest to take shelter within the walls of Kenilworth. On the morning of the 4th of August, the Earl's barber discerned from the towers of the abbey that the standards of young Simon were in sight; but the shrewd Earl saw that they were in the hands of enemies. On the front and rear the columns of Prince Edward advanced, and in a masterly manner surrounded the Earl's forces. "They have learned from me the art of war," he exclaimed. "The Lord have mercy on our souls, for I see that our bodies are Prince Edward's." After partaking of the sacrament, the Earl first attempted to force his way to Kenilworth, but, failing in this, he marshalled his forces on the summit of a hill to the north of the town, which is still pointed out, and here met the attack of the royal forces. In one of these charges the King, who was a prisoner, was unhorsed, and was rescued by the Prince. Leicester's horse was killed. His friends fell around him, and, at last, the great Earl died, sword in hand, and the battle of Evesham was a royal victory. The treatment of the Earl's body and that of his son was barbarous even in a barbarous age; but ultimately their remains were interred in front of the high altar of Evesham's princely abbey. What few of his followers escaped made their way to Kenilworth, to the Isle of Axholm, or to the Cinque Ports to join young Simon, whilst the people mourned the death of "Sir Simon the Righteous." Liberty seemed dead. The laws which had been bought so dearly were set at naught. Rapine ruled the land. Young Simon released Richard, King of the Romans, from Kenilworth, notwithstanding the wild cry of vengeance from the knights, who heard with horror the treatment of the Earl's body on Evesham's corn fields. The men of the Cinque Ports ravaged the coasts, and in the midst of all these disturbances came Ottobone, the Pope's legate, to preach clemency and forgiveness. It is pleasing to know that Prince Edward gave his voice to the cause of moderation. Young Simon received, at Northampton, promises of pardon if he surrendered the castle; but the wild spirits who garrisoned it scorned the idea, unless the order was given by the Countess of Leicester, who was then abroad, and Earl Simon escaped to France.

A year elapsed ere the King found himself strong enough to attack the insurgents who held the Castle of

Kenilworth. They were bold and valorous knights. Under the command of John Gifford, the governor, they surprised Warwick Castle, took Earl Manders and his countess prisoners, and obliged them to pay 1,900 marks for their ransom. They demolished the walls of Warwick Castle between the towers, and thus prevented the county town from protecting a hostile force. They ravaged the country round, and boasted that they had enough provisions for several years' consumption. In the meantime, the dispersed bands of insurgents were defeated near Chesterfield, and many of them, including Sir Henry of Hastings, found their way to Kenilworth, and awaited the return of Sir Simon and his foreign auxiliaries. Sir Henry of Hastings was warmly welcomed as their leader. Sir William de la Cowe and Sir John de la Warre, the warders of the castle, surrendered to him their authority, and they awaited with complacency the threatened siege.

They listened to William, Archbishop of Edessa, treated him courteously, but refused the terms of surrender. They saw the meadows around the castle filled with the tents and pavilions of the King's adherents, but they blanched not. They threw open their gates, whilst they manned their hoards, and made ready their mangonels and petaries. Simon de Montfort was the famous military engineer of his time. His castle was fitted with all the warlike engines then known, and the garrison heeded not the efforts of the Royal Engineers to supplant and overpower them. Edward had been a pupil of De Montfort's, but the attackers were outmatched by the defenders. A wooden tower, of wondrous height and breadth, was constructed by Edward, at an enormous cost, from whose floor more than two hundred balistarii poured arrows and other missiles on the garrison, but the stones accurately aimed from a mangonel within destroyed it. A machine called "a bear," which sheltered a number of archers, met the same fate, and was levelled by one of the petaries of the besieged. The garrison made daily sallies, threatening even the King's supply of provisions. The Brays were then but newly formed, and seem to have sustained equally with the castle the fortunes of the siege. Seeing how little the castle was vulnerable to his attacks, the King caused a number of barges to be brought from Chester in order to attack the castle from the lake, but this attempt was foiled also. The legate of the Pope was unceasing in his efforts as a mediator. On St. Bartholomew's, August 24th, the siege had lasted two months, and the Parliament then assembled desired peace. They granted the King money, but they asked that the disinherited should be offered terms. They propounded what is termed the Dictum or Ban of Kenilworth, which recognised the right of those in arms to release their estates and compound for their misdemeanours by a pecuniary fine, equivalent to five years' ransom of their estates, and with this a complete indemnity. Still the garrison were obdurable. The terms were rejected, and the forty days of grace elapsed without the terms being accepted. Then the Pope's legate, dressed in his red cape, surrounded by the bishops, mounted a tall tower within sight of the garrison, and formally excommunicated them. He was met with jeers and scorn. The walls were gay with pennons and standards, and a mock legate in a white cape uttered a jesting excommunication against the besiegers. They knew that their friends were in arms in the Isle of Ely, and they laughed at the King, his Parliament, and the legate from behind those massive walls. Six weary months had the siege continued, and on the 11th of December the King ordered all the carpenters in the kingdom to assemble at Nottingham. The Sheriff of Oxford was ordered to attend, with the whole *posse comitatus*, in order to overwhelm the contumaceous garrison by sheer force. The King, however, had powerful allies in disease and famine, and ultimately the garrison marched out in warlike array, their ranks thinned by death, when only two days' provisions remained in the castle.

During the tumult of the siege there occurred one of those solemn and romantic episodes which sanctify even war. Suddenly the clang of arms ceased. The drawbridge was lowered, the postern gate was opened, and there issued from the castle a funeral cortege carrying the body of some knight who had been captured and who had died in captivity. The warriors paused as choristers and priest went by, with lighted tapers, chanting the De Profundis, and restored the remains of the deceased knight to his companions in arms.

The castle was again in the hands of the King, and he granted it to Edward, his second son, who held it till 1295, when he bequeathed it to his son Thomas. To him we owe much that is beautiful in the castle ruins; but the thousand visitors do not think of the rude defenders of the freedom of the people. They people the desolate halls with the gorgeous finery of the Tudors. Visitors sigh over the imaginary sorrow of Amy Robsart, and gaze out of the windows of Mervyn's Bower, and dream of her beauty, her wrongs, and her sorrows, whilst the stout Earl and his comrades, who did so much for the freedom of the nation, are remembered only by the huge stones which remain of his petaries and mangonels.

The Royal Favourite.

EDWARD LONGSHANKS was dead, and Edward II., first Prince of Wales, reigned in his stead. Guy Beauchamp lived in the Castle of Warwick, which had been in some measure restored since the raid of John Gifford, and Thomas, Earl of Lancaster, had beautified Kenilworth. There had been jousts and tournaments at Kenilworth. Guy had distinguished himself in the Scotch wars, but, like many of the barons, was disgusted with the wanton lasciviousness of the King and his foolish fondness for foreign favourites. In his father's days Edward had shown this weakness, and now he was King he insulted both nobles and people by his conduct.

Foremost amongst the Court favourites was Piers Gaveston, a Gascon. He had been banished the realm by Edward I., and the first act of Edward II. (1307) was to recall his favourite and harass Walter Langton, Bishop of Litchfield and Coventry, through whose complaints Gaveston had been banished. The bishop was imprisoned, his goods seized, and his movables given to Piers, who had married the daughter of Gilbert de Clare, the King's Consul. We have a vivid description of the handsome Gascon in the chronicles of the time. His features were cast in the finest classic mould. His eyes were dark, soft, and lustrous, so was his hair, which clustered in thick waxing masses over his broad intellectual forehead. But the great charm of this God-like countenance after all was in his sweet expression, especially when his smile was brightened by the display of an even set of teeth (as the chronicles tell us), "as white as egg-shells." Witty, brave, and highly accomplished, with the most irresistibly pleasing manners, he had likewise a colossal figure, as graceful as an Antinous, towering high even over the noble forms of tall companions. To these physical advantages were superadded mental endowments of the highest order. Thus gifted with a sparkling and brilliant intellect, Gaveston's mind had been early imbued with all the fascinating charms of the soft and chivalrous literature of the troubadours or minstrels of his native Gascony. But although so endowed by nature, and by high cultivation, with such singular advantages of a majestic and commanding presence, grace of form, and bewitching manners, and so capable of creating the most passionate love and affection for him, he was utterly destitute of those higher qualities which serve to procure lasting esteem and regard. A life of sensual enjoyment and luxurious magnificence was, unhappily, too well suited to the impulsive passions of the young Plantagenet, for he and his friend "Perot," as he used to call him by a pet name, ran together in couples through every scene of loose intrigue and coarse debauchery. In vain was remonstrance made to the weak King. He created his favourite Earl of Cornwall, and loaded him with favours and presents. So great had become the scandal, that the barons and earls combined together to banish the favourite out of the kingdom. In this compact, Guy, Earl of Warwick, bore a part. The Earls of Arundel, Lincoln, Pembroke, Gloucester, and Hereford lent their influence, and Piers Gaveston was banished by the authority of Parliament; but Gaveston went first to Bristol, and from thence to Ireland, where the King made him Lord-Deputy, and sent him presents. In 1309, the earls, finding that the King wasted his money on his favourite, permitted his return. He was met by the King joyfully at Chester, and the treasures of the realm were left to him. He took a table and a pair of tressels of gold, which he gave to a merchant, Armeric de Friscobald, and sent them to Gascony. This table was one of England's heirlooms, and was reputed to have belonged to King Arthur himself. Again he was banished to Flanders, but at Candlemas, 1311, he was home again. His arrogance was felt past endurance. The Earl of Gloucester was dubbed "a Bastard," the Earl of Lincoln, "Bursten Bellie," the Earl of Warwick "the

Black Hound of Arden," and Thomas, Earl of Lancaster, was "a Churl." These hard words did not alleviate the wrath of the nobles, and they resolved on revenge.

The spring of 1312 had not melted into summer ere the earls were in arms. The King left Gaveston in Scarborough Castle and came himself towards Warwick. The lords besieged Scarborough, and finally compelled Gaveston to surrender. They promised him his ife and to take him to the King. The Earl of Pembroke ındertook to escort Gaveston as far as Wallingford, but ıt Deddington they rested, whilst Pembroke went to visit his wife, who was in the neighbourhood, and Gaveston vas left under a weak guard. In the night the Earl of Warwick, Gaveston's relentless enemy, seized the opporunity and obtained admission into the castle and made Gaveston his prisoner. Gaveston, who was then in bed, overcome with the profound sleep of fatigue and long vatchfulness, was roughly startled from his slumbers, nd compelled to dress with all possible speed, and come own the court yard. Here, to his utter surprise and larm, he found himself face to face with his most etested foe. Warwick strode up to him, and with a erocious grin of exultation, told him that "'the Black Dog of Arden' is come to keep his oath which he has worn, that you should one day feel his teeth. That ay is come at last, and with the blessing of God I hall not perjure myself." Gaveston could not be induced to walk as fast as his escort, so they compelled him to mount upon a mule so as to enable them to reach Warwick before nightfall. In this way he was conducted in a sort of rude triumph. As the procession approached the drawbridge, and before it passed through the strong gates of the frowning towers which guarded the entrance to the old castle, of which now not one stone can be traced, it was received with menacing shouts of exultation and ferocious yells, accompanied by a loud crash of discordant military music. Gaveston was immediately conducted to the great hall, where he found those proud barons whom he had so often derided and insulted assembled in dread array. It appears that he was detained in prison in a detached tower of the castle for a few days after his arrival, in order that the barons should make arrangements for some sort of trial; for during this delay Pembroke, either affecting surprise and indignation, or really afraid of the consequences to himself, formally called upon Warwick to release him. But he was answered by the Earl of Gloucester, and told that Warwick acted with the full concurrence of the barons. He then started off to Oxford, and asked the clergy and the Corporation to rescue Gaveston; but they all resolutely declined to interfere for his safety. A sort of council of war was then assembled in Warwick Castle which was attended by the Earl of Lancaster, then residing in the Royal Palace of Kenilworth, the Earl f Gloucester, Arundel, Hereford, Warwick, and others whose names have been preserved in the chronicles of he time. Gaveston's colossal strength and agility, his urpassing beauty of countenance and grace of form, his laring, almost reckless courage in the battle field, his oyal title of Earl of Cornwall, even his marriage with . princess of the blood royal of England, but above all iis paramount influence over the King, were all now itterly useless to him in presence of this awful tribunal. During this mock deliberation, some one, fearing the consequences of a fatal verdict, suggested the advisability of delay; but a deep voice from an ancient, grave man from the back of the hall called out, "You have caught the fox; if you let him go now, you will have to hunt him again." The fate of Gaveston was decided. Then he proud favourite, seeing the inevitable approach of death, came down from his old haughty insolence of demeanour, and threw himself upon his knees before the Earl of Lancaster, "the Old Hog," as he used to call him, imploring him abjectly to spare his life. However, uch appeal was in vain, for the Earl is said to have xclaimed, in reply, "Take him away! take him away!" Ie was then conducted from that dread fortress to the lace of execution, on Blacklow Hill, on Gaucrslie Heath, ear Guy's Cliff, and there his head was struck off, on he 20th of June, 1312, and in the twenty-ninth year of is age.

The place for execution was well chosen. It was a secluded spot outside the jurisdiction of the Earl of Warwick, just within that of the Earl of Lancaster, the King's cousin. It overlooks a fair scene, but no one on that same day took heed of that. We are told that when Gaveston's head was cut off it rolled into a thicket underneath the rock, from which it was taken by a friar preacher (the priest who was probably ordered to give him the last rites of the Church) and secretly carried off by him concealed in his hood. He carried it to the monastery of the Grey Friars at Oxford. Some of the brethren came over shortly after, brought away the body also, and then buried the remains in their own church. In two years afterwards they were removed by the King's orders, and re-interred in the King's own church, at King's Langley, with great pomp. Edward himself deposited two palls of cloth of gold on the coffin with his own hands.

There are but few now allowed to visit the scene of this wild revenge. On a piece of rock is inserted, "P. Gaveston, 1st July, 1312," and above this the late Mr. Bertie Greathead erected a simple cross, with the following inscription:—

> "In the hollow of this rock
> was beheaded,
> On the 1st day of July, 1312,
> by Barons lawless as himself,
> PIERS GAVESTON, Earl of Cornwall,
> In life and death
> a memorable instance of misrule."

This date, however, is wrong. Hollingshead says that it took place on Tuesday, the 20th of June. Dr. P. O'Callaghan * points that the execution took place on the fast day of Saints Protatius and Gervasius, two of our earliest Christian martyrs, and supposed to have been twin brothers, who were beheaded by the Emperor Diocletian, at Milan, in the fourth century. Their feast lay is the 19th of June, so that the old and the new in-scription appear to have had eleven days added, instead of deducted, to make it agree with the present style.

It is a curious circumstance that all the actors in this bloody tragedy met with a violent death. Thomas Plantagenet, Earl of Lancaster, the King's first cousin, o whom Gaveston appealed in vain for mercy, was put o death in a brutal manner near Pontefract Castle, in orkshire, in 1321, and in the thirty-sixth year of is age. Humphrey de Bohun, Earl of Hereford and onstable of England, was run through the body by a ike thrust through a crevice in the wooden flooring of ie bridge, in the famous battle of Boroughbridge, so in 1321, and in the forty-third year of his age. dmond Fitzallen, Earl of Arundel, was beheaded at ereford, in 1326, in the forty-fifth year of his age. ylmer de Valence, Earl of Pembroke, who played such treacherous part in the betrayal of Gaveston, was stabbed

* To Dr. O'Callaghan's courtesy and researches I have been indebted · some of the particulars of this sketch.

to the heart by an assassin in France, while attending Queen Isabella, in 1323, at the age of forty-seven. Guy de Beauchamp, Earl of Warwick, "the Black Dog of Arden" (as he was nicknamed by Gaveston), was the only one who died in his bed, at Warwick Castle. But then it was by poison, which was supposed to have been administered to him by some adherent of Gaveston, in revenge for the active part which he took in his murder. His death took place only three years after Gaveston's, and in the thirty-sixth year of his age. His infant son was entrusted to the Despencers, the successors to Gaveston, in the favour of the King. The Castle of Warwick was razed to the ground, so that one stone did not rest upon another, and the princely mansion was only worth 6s. 8d. for the herbage that grew in the ditches.

Within sight of that rock on the heath, the King directly met retributive justice. His favourite, Despencer was beheaded, his wife and son deserted him, and it was at Kenilworth Castle that he was compelled to sign his abdication, and to relinquish for ever the throne of England, which he had so long and so un worthily occupied. Henry Plantagenet, son of Thomas who was murdered at Pontefract, succeeded his father who was then residing in the Royal Palace of Keni worth, and as he was naturally disposed to treat th captive King, his relative, with lenity and kindnes Edward was transferred to Berkeley Castle; here he wa subjected to the greatest cruelties and indignities. At length, by private orders of Mortimer, the queen's paramour, two murderers were secretly introduced into his sleeping chamber at night. These hired assassins pressed the wretched King down on his bed with a heavy oak table, and when by this contrivance they had secured their victim in an immovable and unresisting position, they thrust a red hot piece of iron through a horn up into his bowels, and so his death was effected after the most frightful pains and torments. The guards and servants were horrified by the awful screams with which the dying King filled the whole castle in his agonies. Thus the degenerate, selfish, and perjured King terminated his inglorious career on the 21st day of September, 1327, at the premature age of forty-three.

The Forget-me-Not.

> "And oh! be sure ye bring me this—
> The love link 'tis of pure and precious thought,
> Moments blest of love-engendered bliss,
> Balm of the soul!
> Yes; bring the blue, gold-eyed Forget-me-Not."

AT the time when John-o'-Gaunt had just finished that portion of Kenilworth Castle which is now known as Lancaster's Buildings, his son, Henry Bolingbroke, Duke of Hereford, was a widower. On a day variously named, but which, from an ancient MS. which gives a detailed account of the occurrence, was on the 16th of September, 1397, there was a list royal prepared at Gosford Green, in the neighbourhood of Coventry, with a sumptuous theatre, to witness a wager of battle between Henry Bolingbroke and Thomas Mowbray, Duke of Norfolk.

The night before Henry found a home at Baginton—then the home of the Bagots. The site of the castle where they dwelt can still be discerned. Mowbray lodged at the embattled mansion at Culudon, where a battered ruin alone attests the former strength of the old crenelated dwelling of the Segraves and subsequently of the Berkleys. This duel gave rise to the historical legend attached to the Forget-me-Not. The combat is thus and best told in an ancient MSS. :—

"*A Combate to be foughte betwixte ye Duke of Herefordc and Thomas Mowbraye, fyrst Duke of Northefolke and Marshall of England.*

"Henry, Earl of Derbeye (soune of John of Gaunte, Duke of Lancaster, and fowrthe begotten soune of Edwarde ye Thirde), being but a little before created Duke of Hereforde, a prudente and politique p'soune, beganne to consider howe that Kinge Richarde, his cousine germayne, did little regarde the counseile of his uncles or other grave p'sounes, but did set his wille and appetite instead of Law and Reasonne; on a daye being in ye compaignye of Thomas Mowbraye, firste Duke of Northefolke, beganne to break his mynde unto him (rather lamentinge on the behalfe of his cousine germayne the Kinge, than for any malice that he bare unto him) tellinge him that the Kinge little esteemed or regarded the nobles and princes of his Realme, but that he soughte occasions (as much as in him did lye), to destroye the greater p'te of them, nothinge esteeminge the blotte of honor, the damage of the weale publique, the murmuringe of the nobility, the grudge of the Com'ons, nor the wonderinge of all men, at his unprincely doinge, desired the Duke of Northefolke (w'ch was one of the Kinge's Privey Counsaile, and well harde [heard] with him) to advertise ye Kinge to tourne the leafe, and to take a better lesson.

"When the Duke of Northefolke had harde his device at fulle, he toke it not in good parte, but reckened that he had got a praye [prey], by w'ch he shoulde obtaine greater favoure of the Kinge than ever he had, so that at that time dissembled the matter (as in deede he was a deep dissembler) and having fytte opportunitye, opened the whole matter unto the Kinge, and aggravatinge the same to make yt appear unto him more haynous [heinous] broughte the Kinge in great dislikinge with the Duke of Hereforde. Neverthelesse, his furye beinge somewhat appeased, he determined to hear bothe p'tyes [parties] indifferently, and called unto him the Duke of Lancaster and his Counsaile, and also the Dukes of Hereforde and Northefolke, and caused the accuser to reporte openly to him the worde to him declar'd, w'ch rehersed them againe, as he had before related them to the Kinge. When Duke Henry harde the tale otherwise reported than he either thought or sayde (somwhat disquieted w'th ye untrewthe of ye matter) besoughte ye Kinge that he would not conceave any evil opinion of him until he understoode more of ye matter; and towrninge [turning] him to his accuser, declared woorde [word] and woorde what he had saide, and showed the cause whereupon he spake them, affirminge that if the

Kinge wolde p'mitte [permit] and suffer him he wolde p'vc [prove] his accuser a false forger of seditious tales by the stroke of a speare, and dynte [dint] of a worde. The Duke of Northefolke affirmed constantly his sayinge to be trewe, and refused not the combate. The Kinge demannded of them bothe if they wolde agree betweene themselves, w'ch they bothe refused; and then he granted them the battell, and assigned them ye place to be at *Coventree* [*Coventry*] citye, in ye monthe of Auguste next ensueinge, where he caused a sumpteous theatre and list Roiall [Royal] to be prepared.

"At the day appoynted, the 2 valiaunte Dukes came to Coventree, accompaignied with ye nobles and gentiles [gentry] of their linages, w'ch encouraged them to ye uttermoste. At ye daye of compate and fyghte, the Duke of Aumarle, that daye high marshall, entred into the list with a great compaignie of men, apparailed in silk sendale, embroudered with silver both richly and curiouslye, every man having a tipped staffe to keep ye field in order. About the time of prime, came to the barriers of the list the Duke of Hereford, mounted upon a whyte courser, barbed with blewe and green velute [velvet] embroudered sompteouslye w'th swannes and anteloppes of goldesmithes woorke, armed at all points. The constable and marshall came to ye barriers demandinge of him what he was? who answered, 'I am Henrye, Duke of Herforde, w'ch am come hether to do my devoyre againste Thomas

Mowbraye, Duke of Northefolke, as a traitor untewe to God, the Kinge, his realme, and me.' Then incontinente he sware upon the Holy Evangeliste that his quarrel was just and trewe, and thereupon he desired that he myghte enter the liste. Then he put his sworde (w'ch before he held naked in his hande), and put down his visor, and made a crosse in his forehead, and w'th speare in his hand entred into ye list and descended from his horse, and set him downe in a chair of green velute, which was set in a traves of greene and blewe velute at thone [the one] end of the list, and there reposed himselfe, expectinge the cominge of his adversarye. Soon after him entered into the field with great pompe King Richarde, acco'mpanied w'th all ye pieres [peers] of his realme; and there came w'th him also the Erle of St. Paule, who came in poste out of Fraunce, to see this challenge p'formed. The Kinge had aboute ten thousand men in harnesse, lest some fraye or tumult myghte rise amongst his nobles by parte takinge, or quarrelling. When the Kinge was set on his stage, w'ch was richly hanged, and pleasauntly adourned [adorned] a Kinge of Armes made open p'clamation, p'hibitinge [prohibiting] all men, in ye Kynge's name and ye high constable and marshall's names, upon paine of deathe, not to enterprise, to approache any parte of ye listes except suche as were appointed to order and marshall ye fielde. Which p'clamation ended, another heraulde cried,

'Behold here Henrye Lancaster, Duke of Hereforde, appealante [appellant] w'ch is entered into ye lists Royall, to do his devoyre against Thomas Moybraye, Duke of Northefolke, defendant, upon payne to be proved false and recreante.' The Duke of Northefolke hovered on horseback at the entrye of the list, his horse beinge barbed with crimson velute embroudered with Lyons of sylver and mulberry trees. And when he had made his othe before the constable and marshall, that his quarrell was just and trewe, he entred ye field manfully, sayinge aloude, 'God ayde [aid] him that hath ye righte,' and then he dismounted from his horse, and sate downe in the chayre, which was crimson velute, curtened aboute with whyte and red damask.

"The L. Marshall vewed theyre speares to see that they were at once equall lengthe, and delivered th' one speare himselfe to the Duke of Hereforde, and sent the other speare to the Duke of Northefolke by a knighte. Then the heraulde p'claimed that the travesses and chargres of ye champions should be removed, commandinge them on ye Kinge's behalf to mount on horsebacke and to address themselves to the battayle and combate. The Duke of Hereforde was quicklye horsed, and closed his barrier, and caste his speare into ye reste, and (when ye trumpet sounded), sette forwardes courageouslye towarde his enemy 6 or 7 paces. The Duke of Northefolke was not fully sette forwarde when ye Kinge cast down his warder, and the herald's cried, 'Ho, Ho!' The Kinge then caused their speares to be taken from them, and commanded them to repair unto their chayres, where they remained 2 long houres while ye Kinge and his counsaile deliberately consulted what way was best to be taken in so weighty a cause.

"Then the heraulde [herald] cried, 'Silence!' and Sir John Borcye, Secretary to the Kinge, reade ye sentence and determination of the Kinge and his counsaile, in the long rolle, pronouncing it in this manner: 'My lords and masters, I intimate and notifie unto you by ye Kinge's Ma'tie [majesty], and his honourable counsayle, that Henry of Lancaster, appealante, and Thomas, Duke of Northefolke, defendante, have honourably and valiantly appeared here within the list Royale this daye, and have been ready to darraine to battaile like 2 valiant knightes, and hardye champions, but because ye matters is greate and waighty between those 2 great princes, the Kinge and his counsayle have taken this order:—Firste, that Henrye, Duke of Herefordc, for divers considerations, and because he hath displeased the Kinge, shall, within XV. dayes next followinge, dep'te [depart], oute of the realme for terme of X. years, w'thoute retourninge, except he be by the Kinge repealed againe, upon ye paine of deathe.' The heraulde then again cried 'O yes!' and then ye ecretary pronounced :—'Thomas Mowbraye, Duke of Northefolke, by th' ordinance of the Kinge and his ounsayle, because he had sowen [sown] sedition in this ealme, by his woordes, whereof he could make no profe proof] shall avoyde the realm of Englande, and dwell n Hungrye, Bochame, Pruce, or where he like, and never etourn again into Englande, nor approache ye borders r confines of ye same, upon paine of deathe, and that e Kinge wolde staye ye p'ftes [profits] and revenewes f hys landes in his own hande until he have receaved uche sommes [sums] of money as the Duke have taken p of the Kinge's Treasurer for the wages of ye garrison f Callyce w'ch weare still unpaied.'

"When these judgments were thus develged, the inge called before him those two exiles, and made hem sweare that th' one should never come w'th in ace where th' other was (willingly), or keep compaignye [company] to go there in any forrayne [foreign] gione, w'ch othe [oath] they humbly receaved, and ep'td [departed] from the Lystes [lists]. It was supposed that the Kinge mistrusted, that if they two oulde joyne in one againe, and conspire to revenge ainste him, that they mighte worke him much trouble, d for that cause to have designed this othe. Then e Duke of Northefolke (w'ch supposed he should have en borne out by ye Kinge), repented sore of his terpryze, and dep'ted sorrowfully out of the realme into Almayne, and at the last came to Hungrye, where (through thought and melancholie) he diseased [died]. The Duke of Hereforde took his leave of ye King at Elsham, which there released 4 yeares of his banishment; and so he tooke his journeye to Callice, and so into France, where, having gotten estimation with Charles, the French Kinge, had like (by ye helpe of ye

KENILWORTH FROM THE MEADOWS.

said Kinge) to have married th' only daughter of John, Duke of Bery, uncle to the French Kinge, if Kinge Richarde (for fear of ye mischiefe that thereby might ensue unto his p'soune [person], if the Duke were so strongly alyed [allied], because ye Com'ons of England loved him dearly, and greatly desired his retourne) had not cast a stop in his waye."

Yet, notwithstanding this, the banished Duke found favour with the Duke and Duchess of Bretagne. Like Richard II., he had for his badge the humble *myosotis*, and during his exile he is said to have twined in his collar of S.S. As a remembrance when leaving the Duchess, he is said to have given her this badge as a token of remembrance, and his *mot* or watchword *Souveigne vous de moy.* On becoming King he found Joan of Navarre a widow. He remembered his kind hostess, and redeemed his badge by showing he forgot her not, and made her his queen. Those who remember this as they gaze on Kenilworth, or the pasture of Gosford Green, will perhaps picture to themselves Henry and Joan, side by side in their tomb in Canterbury Cathedral, whilst on the other side lies the stiff form of the Black Prince, whose son Henry deposed, if he did not put him to a violent and ignominious death. At Kenilworth, at least, Richard II. was a prisoner.

The Last of the Beauchamps.

THE history of the Beauchamp family belongs to the history of the kingdom. During the thirteenth and fourteenth centuries they were the heroes of romance and chivalry. The bear and ragged staff were seen in the front of every battle where an Englishman fought. The greatest treasures of England were entrusted to their keeping, for to them again and again was entrusted the governorship of Dover and of Calais. The early life of the first of the great Beauchamps, and the closing scenes of the life of the last heroes of the name, were marked by romantic episodes and vicissitudes of fortune, which show on what a slender thread the glory of a great family rested in the fourteenth and fifteenth centuries of our era.

When Guy de Beauchamp, the rude judge and captor of Piers Gaveston, died, he left two youthful sons as the heirs of his name and his family honours. He had tried to secure their well-being by obtaining a grant from Edward II. that his executors should have charge of his lands, during the minority of his heir, by duly accounting to the King's Exchequer for the same. But when

Guy was dead, his lands were seized, and by one of those strange pieces of retribution which sometimes happen, the custody of the lands of the captor of one favourite of Edward II. was granted to another. The heir of the Beauchamps was very young when his lands and castles passed to the hands of Hugh le Despencer on the death of "the Black Hound of Arden" in 1315.

It seemed as if the sun of the Beauchamps had set, for their castle was levelled to the ground, and the youthful Earl was in the hands of the enemies of his house. But the Despencers were not to live. The chivalrous Edward III. had a sympathetic feeling for the bereaved and youthful Earl of Warwick. He gave him his estates and a command in his army. He led the van at Crecy on that glorious Saturday when the Black Prince won his spurs and his crest from the chivalry of France. He fought and conquered at Poictiers, and with the spoils and ransom that fell to his lot began to fortify and rebuild the Castle of Warwick and the churches of the old borough. When he died, in 1370, and was buried in the choir of St. Mary's Church, which he built, and where his effigy can still be seen, his second son, Thomas, succeeded him. He was for some time governor to the young King Richard II.; but subsequently he fell into disgrace, and though he employed himself in completing the works his father had begun at Warwick, he was arrested and banished, and afterwards thrown into the

Tower of London, where the Beauchamp Tower marks the site of his incarceration. It was not till Henry of Lancaster became King that he recovered his liberty and his rights. He died in 1401, and the brass effigies of himself and his Countess are placed near the entrance of the Beauchamp Chapel, which owes its existence to the will of their only son, Richard, who succeeded his father. It was this Earl Richard who visited the Holy Land. He negotiated the famous treaty of marriage between Henry V. and Catherine, daughter of Charles VI. of France, after the "crowning mercy of St. Crispin's-day," on the field of Agincourt. He succeeded the Duke of Bedford as Regent of France, and died in Rouen in 1439. His tomb stands in the chapel which bears his name, on the south side of St. Mary's Church. His son was created Duke of Warwick, with certain rights of precedency, but died at the early age of twenty-two years, leaving an infant daughter, who speedily followed him to the grave. His estates came to his sister Ann, the last heiress of the Beauchamps, then the wife of Richard Neville, who is known in history as the "Stout Earl of Warwick," the "King Maker." Her history is the most remarkable and romantic of all her race.

Ann Beauchamp was born at Caversham, in Oxfordshire, on the 3rd of July, 1429. Her mother, Isabel Despencer, was the second wife of Richard Beauchamp, and widow of Richard Beauchamp, Earl of Worcester, cousin to her second husband. In consequence of this relationship, a dispensation from the Pope was necessary to legalize the marriage. Her brother Henry, when only ten years of age (1433-4), had married Cicely Neville, the daughter of Richard Neville, Earl of Salisbury, and on the same day Anne Beauchamp was espoused by Richard Neville, brother to Cicely. When the infant daughter to the Duke of Warwick died, Richard Neville was created Earl of Warwick, and he and his Countess, Anne, then entailed the Castle of Warwick, with numerous lordships in sixteen counties, upon their joint issue, or the issue of Anne, and, in default, upon the heirs of Margaret, the eldest daughter of Richard Beauchamp by his first wife, Elizabeth, daughter and heiress of Thomas, Lord Berkeley. Margaret was married to John Talbot, Earl of Shrewsbury, and from their eldest son, John, the Dudleys and the De Lisles derived their descent from the Beauchamps, and made their claim on the estates.

Notwithstanding the fame and the power of Richard Neville, there is but little in the county of Warwick hat is associated with his name. There are a few ncised and carved wall markings in one of the rooms n Guy's Tower which may belong to his time, and on he side of the steep hill which rises in front of Tysoe Church, to the left of the road, there is the figure of a horse cut, which is known to the country people, from the colour of the soil exposed, as the Red Horse.* It is traditionally asserted that this figure was cut to celebrate the victory which Richard Neville gained at the battle of Towton, on Palm Sunday, 1461. On that day the Yorkists were placed in circumstances of extreme peril. They had followed the Lancastrian army as far as York, and when the Earl of Warwick saw the superior forces of Queen Margaret, his stout heart appears almost to have failed him. He ordered his charger to be brought forth, and in face of the whole army stabbed it to the heart, at the same time solemnly swearing, by the cross on his sword hilt, that on that day the hazards of the common soldier should be his also, and that, though the Yorkist soldiers might run away, he would alone oppose the hosts of the Lancastrians. "*Let him fly that fly will,*" said he, "*I will tarry with him that will tarry with me.*" The battle was the most hotly contested of the many battles of the Roses. It is said that those who buried the dead counted no less than 38,000 corpses on the field.

The somewhat hasty love match of Edward IV. with Elizabeth Woodville, the widow of Sir John Grey,

* Fifty years ago the horse was a conspicuous feature in the landscape, but now it is hidden from view by the plantations, and is much smaller than the old figure, which Dugdale states was annually scoured by a freeholder of the parish, who held his lands under that tenure. The figure measured 34 feet from croup to chest; from ear to nose, 7 feet 6 inches; from the shoulder to the ears, 14 feet; to the ground 16 feet, or 57 hands high.

whom the amorous King had met on theforest lands of the neighbouring county of Northants, appears to have been the primary cause of the estrangement which subsequently took place between Edward IV. and Richard Neville, the latter aggravating the Yorkist by demanding what the former was sometimes unwilling to give; but throughout the terrific and bloody struggle which we know as the "War of the Roses," though "the King Maker" occupies a foremost place, we have but occasional glimpses of his wife, Anne, the heiress of the Beauchamps.

In the vicissitudes of that time, kings and queens were victors and fugitives in their turn. We see the heroic Margaret of Anjou through the din of the battles, now a queen, now a supplicant for a freebooter's protection; now taking the lives of the greatest of the land, and again fleeing to save her own. It was a time when dukes and earls might one day be victorious and powerful, and the next day be begging bread to satisfy their hunger.

It was in 1469 that the Earl of Warwick turned against his kinsman and friend, Edward of York, and embroiled the country again in civil war. The Duke of Clarence, Edward's eldest brother, followed the fortunes of the Earl, and on the 12th of July, 1469, espoused his daughter Isabel in the church of Notre Dame, at Calais, and received as her dower half the lands of the Beauchamps—the inheritance of her mother. Anne Beauchamp and her youngest daughter, the Lady Anne Neville, were present at the ceremony, which was performed by George Neville, Archbishop of York.

Whilst the ceremony was proceeding there was a large and tumultuous gathering in the north; an army, if such it may be called, assembled and marched towards London. They were opposed by Herbert, the new created Earl of Pembroke, and a number of Welsh levies. The hostile forces met on the very borderland of Warwickshire, at Edgecote, in Oxfordshire, on July 26th, when the Welsh were utterly defeated. Lord Rivers, the father of Elizabeth Woodville, and Sir John, her brother, were captured and beheaded at Northampton. Urgent messages were sent to Warwick and to Clarence to come to the King's assistance. They found the King at Olney almost defenceless. The insurgents departed on Warwick addressing a few words to them. A few days subsequently, Edward was captured in his camp at Wolvey Heath by the Earl of Warwick, and taken prisoner to the Earl's great northern stronghold at Middleham, in Yorkshire. Up to this time Warwick appears to have been solicitous only to show his power and secure his old supremacy in the State, for he marched against some insurgent Lancastrians, who had entered England from Scotland, defeated them, and then released

Edward at York. Quarrels, bickerings, and jealousy were now common, and early in 1470 Warwick and Clarence, with their wives and other ladies, fled the kingdom to Calais, where they found the guns of the fortress turned against them by Warwick's own lieutenant. Whilst waiting before Calais, Warwick became a grandfather, for the Lady Isabel was confined of a son, the unfortunate Edward Plantagenet, who lived to be the last of his race and name. The wily Louis XI. of France gave England's great military commander a warm welcome. It was now that Warwick conceived the idea of betrothing his daughter, the Lady Anne, to the Prince of Wales, the son of Henry VI. and Margaret of Anjou. To this project Louis lent a willing ear. It was twelve months after the marriage of the Duke of Clarence and the slaughter at Edgecote that Warwick met the unfortunate Margaret of Anjou at the old palatial fortress of Angers. There Prince Edward first saw Anne Neville. There the stout Earl knelt at the feet of the still young Queen, the enemy of whose fortunes he had been. Margaret was bitter; and a quarter of an hour elapsed ere she would grant the Earl's pardon. There was witness to the scene many of those destined to play a part in the tragedy of the next fourteen years. We know also that at this meeting Anne Beauchamp was present, and she survived them all.

Margaret could not at first consent that the Lady

Anne Neville should be the wife of her darling son. She, however, obtained a clause in the agreement, by which Anne Neville was to remain in the hands and keeping of the Queen, and that the marriage should not be perfected until the Earl had recovered the kingdom of England, or the greater part thereof, for the House of Lancaster.* It would appear, therefore, as the Earl of Warwick fell a few months afterwards, that the consummation of this marriage contract never took place. When the ceremony, whatever it was, took place at Amboise, at the end of July, 1470, Edward was but seventeen years of age, and the Lady Anne a young girl of fourteen summers, for Anne was born at Warwick Castle in 1456. In pursuance of this contract, the King Maker took the first opportunity of embarking for England, and on the 4th of August left Angers, and on the 13th of September disembarked what forces he had at Plymouth and Dartmouth, and in an incredibly short space of time, so great was his popularity, he found himself at the head of 60,000 men. Edward IV. had delayed too long his preparations. In a few days he was a fugitive and an exile, and his Queen an inmate of the sanctuary at Westminster, instead of occupying a royal palace. Richard, Duke of Gloucester, accompanied his brother, but the false and fickle Clarence was made the

* "Manner and Guiding of the Earl of Warwick at Angers." Harl. MSS. 513, fol. 169 b.

Protector of the realm during the minority of Edward, Prince of Wales.

The crown was entailed on Clarence in the event of Prince Edward dying without issue. But the voluptuous Edward IV. was as bold and as courageous as ever. He landed, six months after his flight, from Lynn at Ravenspur, in Yorkshire, with 2,000 men. He marched unopposed to Leicester and Warwick, where the Duke of Clarence deserted to him with 4,000 men. Edward was anxious to fight, but for some reason Warwick, who was at Coventry with a superior force, declined the combat, and in twenty-eight days from his landing at Ravenspur, Edward entered London with acclamation. On the 14th of April the Battle of Barnet was fought, and was the death scene of the stout Earl and his brother, the Marquis of Montagu. The Duke of Gloucester distinguished himself in this fight. Queen Margaret landed at Weymouth on the day of the battle of Barnet, and found sanctuary at the Abbey of Beaulieu, where Anne Beauchamp and her young daughter had also found shelter. Here the Earl of Pembroke and other Lancastrian barons found these ladies, for there yet remained another chance for victory, but that chance disappeared in the bloody field of Tewkesbury, when Edward, Prince of Wales, met with his early death, too probably by the hands of the King's relatives. Queen Margaret was arrested in a church near Tewkesbury, by Sir William Stanley, and taken to Coventry, where she first heard that she was no longer a mother. She figured in the triumphal procession of Edward IV. into London, after which she was committed to the Tower, and in a few hours was a widow. With her for a time the Lady Anne found shelter; but she was speedily removed by the Duke of Clarence and placed with her sister Isabel. Anne Beauchamp remained in the sanctuary at Beaulieu for some time, and then escaped privily to the north, where she had still many friends, for her noble husband was not yet forgotten.

Clarence was even now but a young man, yet he claimed at once in right of his wife all the possessions of the King Maker. He appears to have placed the Lady Anne in some obscure street in London as a kitchen maid, in order that the Duke of Gloucester, his brother, should not marry her. In this wretched yard Richard found the heiress of the Nevilles and the Beauchamps. Contrary to Shakespeare's version, Anne appears to have had no aversion to Richard, whom she had known in her father's halls at Middleham, and went gladly with him to the sanctuary of St. Martin-le-Grand, from whence she was placed under the guardianship of her uncle, George Neville, Archbishop of York. Richard then appealed to the King and Council, and was allowed to marry Lady Anne, but the date and place of his marriage is uncertain. She, however, bore him a son in 1473. Now commenced a fierce quarrel between the brothers over the estates, for the Duke of Gloucester naturally claimed a moiety of the inheritance of the King Maker, but Clarence insisted on his exclusive right to the whole of the inheritance. "He may well have my lady sister-in-law," said he; "but we will part no livelihood." Subsequently both brothers appealed to the King, and supported their cause by divers subtle and acute arguments. In 1474 an Act of Parliament was passed, which divided the inheritance of the two sisters between the brothers; but no mention was made of the unfortunate and wretched mother, who was left in want and almost beggary. Richard left the Court of his brother shortly after his marriage, and went to reside in the north, where he was governor and chief seneschal of the Duchy of Lancaster.

On the 2nd December, 1476, Isabel, the wife of the Duke of Clarence, died in Warwick Castle, it is alleged by poison. Early in 1478, Clarence fell a victim to his own folly and wild tongue, and was drowned, so it is popularly said, in a butt of Malmsey wine in the Tower of London. The tragedy of the White Buck of Arrow had taken place the previous year. One of the Hugfords of Emscote was made governor of Warwick Castle during the minority of Edward Plantagenet, Earl of Warwick, the son of the Duke of Clarence.

On July 6, 1483, Richard, Duke of Gloucester, and his consort, Anne Neville, were crowned at Westminster Abbey. In August, Richard proceeded in state to visit the northern portion of his dominions. At Warwick he was joined by "his gentle Queen, and in the old hall of the castle he received the ambassador of Elizabeth of Castile, as well as the envoys of the King of France and the Duke of Burgundy, who came to congratulate him on his accession." On the 15th of August we find him at Coventry, on the 17th at Leicester, and on the 22nd at Nottingham. At York, on September 8th, he was crowned again, and in the procession walked Edward, his son, then a child ten years of age. The Queen, his mother, the Lady Anne, walked by his side, holding him by her left hand. It was a proud day for Richard, for he that day created his son Prince of Wales and Earl of Chester; but in seven months the child was dead. He died in Middleham Castle, the scene of his birth and his parents' happy childhood, on the 9th of April, 1484. On the 16th of March, 1485, Anne Neville died at the early age of twenty-eight. The battle of Bosworth was fought on August 22nd of the same year, and none remained of the Nevilles or the Beauchamps, save the children of Clarence, but Anne Beauchamp, who survived fathers, husbands, daughters, and fortune. Born to a high destiny, she was now but a beggar and an outcast, a prey to misfortune.

The latter days of this unfortunate lady are involved in obscurity. In the third year of Henry VII. (1488) she re-appears on the scene, but only to give legal force to the seizure of her lands by the King. A new Act of Parliament was passed annulling the Act which gave the estates of the King Maker and his wife to the Dukes of Clarence and Gloucester "as against all reason, conscience, and course of nature, and contrary to the laws of God and man." In consideration of the true and faithful service and allegiance by her borne to King Henry VII., as also that she never gave cause for such disherison, he restored to her possession of the premises, with power to alienate the same or any part thereof. The cause of this Act was soon apparent, for on the 13th of December the same year she executed a deed of feoffment and a fine thereon. She conveyed the whole on the King, and entailed it upon the male issue of his body, with remainder to herself and her heirs. Thirteen manors in Warwickshire were included in this deed, with a hundred and five others, and two years afterwards she received an assignment of the manor of Sutton for her maintenance. Where she died, when she died, or how she lived during the remaining years of her life, is involved in obscurity.

Her two grandchildren, the son and daughter of the Duke of Clarence, survived her. Edward, who was knighted by Richard III. at York, was sent for security to Sheriff Hutton, in Yorkshire. After the death of Richard on the field of Bosworth, he was imprisoned by Henry VII. in the Tower, and in the year 1499 he plotted with Perkin Warbeck to escape. On the 21st of November he was brought to trial before the Earl of Oxford as High Steward of England. He was urged to confess, and throw himself on the King's mercy, and he did so. He was condemned to death, and was beheaded on Tower Hill on the 28th of the same month. He was the last male Plantagenet, the last heir of the Beauchamps, and the hope of the house of York; the last Earl of Warwick of the old line. He was killed in order that no obstacle should remain in the way of the marriage of Catherine of Arragon with the heir of Henry VII.

His sister, Margaret, lived longer, but met her death on the same spot forty-four years afterwards. She had married Sir Richard Pole, and was the mother of the famous Cardinal Pole. In 1513, Henry VIII. being then on the throne, Margaret petitioned Parliament, being then a widow, as the sister and heir of her brother, that she might inherit his estate and dignity, and so be styled the Countess of Salisbury, which was granted. What estates she received were taken away by attainder in 1539-40 for alleged privity to the conspiracy of Henry Marquis of Exeter. On the 27th of May, 1541, Elizabeth Plantagenet was dragged to the block on Tower

Hill by the hair of her head, and died in the sixty-eighth year of her age, and thus perished the last scion of the Beauchamps in the direct line of descent.

The Castle of Warwick, the monument of their greatness and their power, yet remains to us. The towers built by Clarence and Gloucester have not been finished. Since the death of the heiress of the Beauchamps, the castle has been alternately a gaol and a palace. The sad fire on Advent Sunday, 1871, though it did not destroy any portion of the castle erected by the Beauchamps, revealed the old walls and arched doorways through which the armed retainers had marched into the great hall, and the passages leading to the ladies' chamber, from whence Anne Beauchamp witnessed the revelry in the hall below. Something of this has been preserved by the restorers of the castle. The hall may be seen now in all its fair and stately proportions, but more beautiful than when the home of the last of the Beauchamps.

The White Buck of Arrow.

It was but natural that throughout the Wars of the Roses, Warwickshire and Warwickshire men should play an important part. Though Warwick Castle was one of the seats of Richard Neville, Earl of Warwick, which he had acquired by right of his wife, Anne Beauchamp, Kenilworth was held by the Lancastrians, and Henry VI. was loved at Coventry, and the city of Godiva remained true to the Red Rose throughout the long and bloody struggle for the English crown. The famous Parliament which attained Richard, Duke of York, his wife, the fair "Rose of Raby," his sons, the Nevilles and their friends, sat at Coventry on the 20th of November, 1459. From that moment reconciliation between the rival parties was impossible. The respective claims of the Houses of York and Lancaster could only be decided by the sword. The noblemen and gentry of Warwickshire took different sides. Those on the west and south followed the fortunes of the great Earl, but others cast their lot with the Lancastrians among the latter was Sir John Grey, of Astley. Among the former were William Lucy, of Charlecote, and Thomas Burdett, of Arrow. At this time many of the Warwickshire families were represented by minors or heiresses, for the wars with France had shorn the midland shire of the pride and flower of its chivalry. The undulatory country of mid-England had many charms for Edward IV., for it was on the boundary of the county that Elizabeth Woodville had cast herself at his feet on behalf of her infant children. Her husband, Sir John Grey, had been slain at the second battle of St. Albans, and his estates had been forfeited as a traitor. Edward's susceptible heart was touched by the pleadings of the beautiful widow in the forest glades of Whittlebury, and Elizabeth did not plead in vain. Joquetta, the wife of the Duke of Bedford, had planned the meeting, and did not misjudge the result. The meeting took place almost within view of the castellated seat of the De Lyons, of Warkworth, from whom the Woodvilles claimed descent, and in this fair and sylvan scene royal sunshine gladdened the fortunes of the Lords of Astley and Fillingley, as well as of the Woodvilles. In the calm woodlands Edward found a queen and Elizabeth a throne and a husband. It mattered little in these times that the Greys had hitherto been Lancastrians and had suffered for the cause. They now assumed the badge of the White Rose in honour of their relative, and little recked that with royal favours and honours they were accepting troublous days, which led to the headsman's block.

Whilst Clarence ruled at Warwick and Sir Edmund Neville, the friend of the King, was owner of the joint estates of Hastings and Bergavenny, in right of his wife, the heiress of Beauchamp, Earl of Worcester, Edward found friends and sport in Warwickshire. He had forgiven apparently the treachery of "false and perjured Clarence," and lived only in the smiles of his wife's relatives, whom he had ennobled and raised to positions of honour.

The character of George, Duke of Clarence, is stamped in history and immortalized by Shakespeare. That he was weak and treacherous, we know. That he was avaricious and ambitious, we have abundant evidence. He deserted his kingly brother as well as his powerful father-in-law; yet he found many friends, but none more faithful or unfortunate than Thomas Burdett, Lord of Arrow.

The Burdetts were an old Warwickshire family, long settled on the eastern side of the county. As far back as 1151 (fifth Henry II.), William Burdett obtained from the Earl of Leicester a grant of a piece of land between Seckington and Shuttington, and thereon founded a small monastery, known as Aucote Priory, in expiation of the murder of his wife, whom he slew on his return from the Holy Land. It appears that, like Othello, his jealousy was excited by the foul tongue of his steward, who met him on his return to England, and to hide his own attempts to dishonour his master, slandered the lady, and thus caused her death. In the reign of Edward I., Robert Burdett married Elizabeth Camvill, a descendant of the noble family who founded the Abbey of Combe. By this marriage the Burdetts became possessed of Arrow, and for many years held important positions in the county. On the 4th February, 1333 (seventh Edward III.), Robert Burdett received a licence to impark his woods at Arrow. The family furnished sheriffs and knights of the shire in successive reigns. They fought in the wars of Henry V. and VI. Nicholas Burdett was Chief Butler of Normandy, and Governor of Eureux in that duchy, and was slain at the battle of Pontoise in 1439-40. His son Thomas was one of the gentlemen of the household of George, Duke of Clarence.

In 1476, Isabella Neville, the wife of Clarence, died, it was alleged, by poison, though both she and her sister, Lady Anne, appear to have been consumptive. Shortly afterwards, Charles the Rash, Duke of Burgundy, was killed at Nancy, leaving his daughter, Mary, heiress to his immense estates. Clarence's sister, Margaret, was stepmother to this lady, and he proposed to marry the young heiress with his sister's connivance and consent. The weak but ambitious Duke was already rich and had many friends. He was known to be unscrupulous and untrustworthy, and this proposition raised the jealousy of Edward and the family of the Grey's and Woodvilles; indeed, one of the latter was also a suitor for the lady's hand. Edward opposed the marriage with all his power, and Clarence retired full of disdain, vowing vengeance in no measured terms. Spies were set to watch him, and his incautious words soon reached the Court. While he was absent, the King was hunting in Warwickshire in the latter part of the year 1477, and in the course of his sport killed in the park of Arrow a white buck belonging to Thomas Burdett.* This gentleman was so enraged at the killing of his favourite buck, that in his anger he passionately wished the horns in the King's belly. Watching eyes and greedy ears carried with ready tongue and willing lips this expression to the King, and Burdett was arraigned, tried, and executed for high treason in consequence. About the same time one Stacey, a priest in Clarence's household, was arrested and tried for having recourse to damnable magic, by burning certain images to hasten the death of the Lord Beauchamp. Whilst under the agony of the rack, he implicated Thomas Burdett as his accomplice. He, too, was executed, but both died protesting their innocence.

The Duke of Clarence was absent when the trial and

* The spot where the buck was killed is traditionally said to be in the immediate neighbourhood of the church.

execution of his servants took place. On hearing of it, he presented himself at the council, and denounced the proceeding in violent language. He was unsparing in his epithets, and at last the King interfered, and Clarence was committed to the Tower. He was publicly tried by his Peers on a variety of charges some formidable enough, but others absurd. Witnesses were found to depose to the truth of them, and Clarence was condemned to death. His conduct must have been outrageous, for the Commons and their Speaker prayed for his execution. He was executed in private—drowned, it is said, by his own desire, in a butt of Malmsey wine. His estates, or at least a large portion of them, fell to the lot of the Queen's relatives, Warwick Castle falling by Act of Parliament to his son, but ultimately came into the possession of Richard III.

Thomas Burdett appears to have been unfortunate in his attachments. By his first wife, Agnes Waldeif, he had one son, Richard Burdett; but he was divorced from her by reason of their nearness of kindred, and in 1464-5, having married another wife, he obtained the King's license to alienate his lands to his younger son, John, and thus disinherit Richard. Whilst being drawn from the Tower to the place of execution, he saw in Westchepe, near St. Thomas à Becket's Hospital, now Mercer's Chapel, his eldest son. The thought of the wrong that he had done his boy appears to have struck the doomed man with remorse. He requested the cavalcade to stop for a moment, in order that he might ask his son's forgiveness for the wrong he had done him, for he thought that this deed was the cause of God's vengeance against him.

Richard Burdett, his eldest son, had married Jocosa (Joyce), the daughter of Sir Simon Montford, of Coleshill, and by her had two sons and a daughter. The sons died without issue in his lifetime, but before their death Richard had instituted a suit against his half-brother, John, for the recovery of his estates. The cause was decided against him. Subsequently his father's second wife, Margaret, who had married Thomas Woodhill, and her son, John, agreed to levy a fine on the manor of Arrow and other lands, whereby Richard became possessed of them, with remainder to his heirs. On Richard's death, without male heirs, John, to prevent these entailed estates passing into the hands of strangers —for Richard's widow had married Hugh Conway, Treasurer of Ireland, and her daughter Anne had married Edward Conway (the younger brother of Hugh)—claimed that the fine should be annulled, and in support thereof alleged that he had been in arms on behalf of the Earl of Richmond, with Henry, Duke of Buckingham, and had been a faithful servant to Henry VII. He was in the retinue of Sir Edmund Howard when he presented this claim in 1512 (fourth Henry VIII.), and in high favour at Court, but the suit dragged its weary length along for many years. It was not until after Sir John Burdett's death that it was agreed that Edward Conway and his heirs should have the manor of Arrow, with other lordships, and that Bramcote, Seckington, Compton Scorfin, and Wilmcote should be the portion of Thomas Burdett, the son of Sir John. From Thomas the Burdetts now living trace an unbroken descent. Many of them have been distinguished, but none more so than Angela Georgina, daughter of the famous Sir Francis Burdett, whom we know as Baroness Burdett-Coutts.

The Conways long continued lords of Arrow. They served their country as statesmen, as soldiers, and as sailors. In 1683, Popham Seymour inherited the estates of his cousin, the Earl of Conway, and, on the 17th March, 1702, his brother Francis, who succeeded him, became Lord Conway, and Baron Conway of Ragley, county of Warwick. Ragley, the present seat of the lords of Arrow, was acquired by purchase in the reign of Elizabeth. The present Lord of Arrow is the Most Honourable Francis Hugh George Seymour, Marquis of Hertford.

The Foundling's Gratitude.

On a promontory overlooking the Feldon stands the beacon tower of Burton Dasset. It is one of the three old beacons which in time past cast their lurid glare from cresset and tower over the undulating face of Warwickshire. The others were at Bickenhill and High Cross. The tower at Burton is singular in construction, and was erected in the fourteenth century, for the Belknaps, lords of Dasset, held their lands under the condition of providing a beacon on this oolitic ridge, which forms a spur of the Edge hills. The large, interesting church shows the ancient importance of this old town, now represented by four or five farm houses. On the south side of the church is a large well, which has been long the conduit from which the neighbours have derived their water supply. From hence the eye travels over the level plain of Kineton towards the wooded heights of Brailes. From hence can be seen the fringe of trees which marks the boundary of Northants. In the east the heights of Shuckburgh may be discerned, and on the north the rolling, billowy land of the liassic sea to the bounds of Arden. A spectator on this hill could have discerned the march of the troops of Royalist and Roundhead prior to that fatal October Sunday, in 1644, when King and Parliament first met in hostile array on the fair plain beneath. From the adjacent church tower Cromwell is said to have viewed the battle, and was so shocked that he slid down the bell ropes and ran away. Whether this story, published in the lifetime of the Protector, is true or false, it is certain that the fire on the old beacon

BEACON AT BURTON DASSET.

tower first told the Parliament and the citizens of London that blood had been shed, and that the result was not adverse to the popular side.

The parish of Burton Dasset includes the hamlets of Northend, pronounced "Norend," and Knightcote, and there are some interesting remains of old ecclesiastical buildings at Northend, which is the most populous portion of the parish. These hamlets are the recipients of a charity which may be appropriately termed "A Foundling's Gratitude." The story is interesting, as it shows that the ancient inhabitants discovered that they might entertain angels unawares.

The story is variously told; but it appears that towards the close of the reign of Henry VI., or early in the reign of Edward IV., when the Wars of the Roses were desolating the land, and the "Red Horse" was freshly cut, a poor foundling besought help from the inhabitants of the then populous and flourishing village of Burton Dasset. He was repulsed from their doors, but found a home and a welcome at Northend, beneath the shadow of the hill on which the beacon tower is now built. At what age the foundling was when he sought food and shelter on these bleak hills no one knows; whether he was, or afterwards became a sweep, a shoemaker, or a sailor, the accounts which have come down to us do not say with certainty; but the welcome he received appears to have touched the heart of John Kimbell, for in that troublous time of war and desolation, when the King Maker was dead and his widow penniless, he gave what he had to the people who had befriended him, and their descendants even now enjoy the benefits of this far-off charity. The historic facts connected with the gift are these, which are taken from the "Report on the Charities of Warwickshire":—

"John Kimbell, by deed fourteenth of Edward IV., conveyed a messuage and two yard lands in Mollington to Ralph Wallis and his heirs, in trust that the rents should be employed as follows:—7s. towards the use and repairs of the parish church of Burton Dasset, and 2d. in bread to be given to all the poor householders in Knightcote and Northend, in the name of dole, and all the residue to be employed in such manner as the trustees and inhabitants should direct. The estate was, 7th March, 1815, conveyed to Thomas Ledbrook and seven others on trust, reciting that the open fields in Mollington had been enclosed, and that certain exchanges had been made. The premises now consist of the old house and barn, &c., and four parcels of arable land, containing 47a. 2r. 37p., let (1825) at the yearly rent of £70; it is now (1872) let at the yearly rent of £120. In addition, the trustees are possessed of a house in Knightcote, with a small garden, and about a quarter of an acre of land besides, which they purchased in 1815, for the use of the schoolmaster, which he occupies at the rent of 1s. per week. Out of the rents, 7s. is paid to the churchwardens, and a dole of bread, now a fourpenny loaf, to every house in the two hamlets, which, in 1825, cost £3 10s. The sum of £30 a year is paid to William Ledbrook (formerly a baker), who acts as schoolmaster to the poor children of Knightcote, to teach them reading, writing, and arithmetic free. The rest was applied to the repair of the highways in the two hamlets, and a dinner at the annual meeting of the feoffees till 1871, when a resolution was passed to supply the hamlet of Knightcote with water from Burton hills, for which purpose the sum of £300 was borrowed to defray the expenses, to be paid back by instalments out of Kimbell's charity; consequently, a small moiety only will now be given for the roads till this debt is paid off."

"William Ledbrook, gentleman, of Burton Hill, in the parish of Burton Dasset, by deed of conveyance, bearing date September 16, 1864, to five trustees, viz., William Fairbrother, Edmund Griffin, William Bishop, Thomas A. Bawcutt, and John Bloxham (all of this parish), farmers, conveyed to the said trustees, their heirs, and assigns, a messuage, cottage, or tenement, with the buildings, gardens, and appurtenances thereto belonging, and also a close of land, containing six acres, in Knightcote, in the parish of Burton Dasset, upon trust, to let the same, and receive the rents, and pay and apply the same for ever in aid and support of the salary of the schoolmaster and schoolmistress of the parochial school of and for the parish of Burton Dasset, and also in aid of and for the support of a choir in the parish church of Burton Dasset, and the Episcopal Chapel at Northend in the same parish, in such proportions and manner, or wholly in any one to the exclusion of the other or others of the said objects, the vicar and churchwardens for the time being each to have two votes at any meeting of the trustees. The land is now let at £18 per annum, and the cottage is leased unto the original owner for thirty years, at a rent of sixpence per annum, if she should so long live, after whose death the cottage may probably let for about £5 per annum, making altogether £23 per annum."

An Old Love Story.

ON a steep eminence overhanging the river Thame, n
far from the ford which gives the hundred of Hemling
ford its name, is the fortified mansion of the Bracebridg
and the church of Kingsbury. In the time of t
Heptarchy, some of the Mercian kings held their Co
on this fair spot. In later times it was the ea
home of the Bracebridges, the descendants of t
Lincolnshire squire, Peter de Bracebridge, who,
the Norman times, left his home in the fens and ca
wooing to Warwickshire, where he wedded the f
Amicia, granddaughter to the oft-quoted Turchill,
Sheriff of Warwickshire during the time of the C
fessor. During the troublous Plantagenet days,
Bracebridges fought bravely and held their heads amo
the proudest knights and squires of the land. The
fortified their home at Kingsbury, and the existing fort
fications show an interesting example of the crenel
house of the fourteenth and fifteenth centuries. With
these romantic walls, during the time when the feuds o
Yorkist and Lancastrian disturbed the land, and t
bear and ragged staff was the universal cognizance of th

nidlands, fair Alice Bracebridge dwelt and loved. She hought that she was loved also, and that John Arden. he heir of Peddimore, dreamed of her fair face as he vandered round Park Hall and thought of his Saxon ncestry and the misfortunes of his house. His mother elonged to another race, for his father, Walter Arden. ad wedded Eleanor, the daughter of John Hampden, the ncestor of the famous Buckinghamshire squire. They id not look with favour upon the alliance of their son rith the poor and proud Bracebridges, who owed to the rdens their estates and position in Warwickshire.

Richard Bracebridge, of Kingsbury, was not made of at yielding stuff to brook in silence or in disdain the ejected alliance of his family by his kinsmen, the Ardens Peddimore. The lover was pining by the side of the hame, and Alice was watching the flowers brought own by the slow stream from her absent lover. Her ghs and tears melted the old squire's heart, and early e morning he called his retainers to boot and saddle d rode to the hall of the Ardens and brought away e unreluctant heir to his moated house at Kingsbury. e raid was unexpected, and the disconsolate parents on eir return home were loud in their demands for redress. steal a man's daughter was a venial offence, but to duct a son was unpardonable. The Ardens appealed law—they represented the matter to King Edward ., to the lords of the land, and demanded justice and the restitution of their son and heir, but in the meantime, John Arden remained within the strong walls of Kingsbury and comforted himself with the company of Alice Bracebridge. It was a soft imprisonment, and it mattered but little to them what kings, lords, and lawyers might say or do. They little cared when Sir Simon Montford, of Coleshill, and Sir Richard Bingham, the judge, then living at Middleton, took the matter into their grave deliberation and decreed that the pair should be married in February, 1474, and that the lady should have a portion of 200 marks as a jointure settled upon her. Richard Bracebridge, in expiation of the trespass he had committed, was ordered to give Walter Arden the best horse that could be chosen in Kingsbury Park. When Walter died he made John Bracebridge one of his executors. For many years—for more than two centuries—the descendants of John Arden and Alice Bracebridge lived lords of Peddimore at Park Hall, and then founded the Staffordshire family of that name.

The double moat yet remains at Peddimore, and the home of the Bracebridges is silently going to decay, like the family. Within the fortified walls there remains the dwelling house erected in the time of Elizabeth, when the last Bracebridge, of Kingsbury, sold his paternal estate, and the death of the last of the Bracebridges was recorded when Charles Holte Bracebridge, of Atherston Hall, was laid in his grave.

The Church of Expiation.

N a gentle elevation in the very midst of the old forest nd of Arden, near to many of the monarchs of the old oodland, stands the solitary church of Baddesley linton. Its grey tower is scarcely seen amid the trees y which it is surrounded, even by visitors to the flower-rewn glades of Haywood. On the south side, a vene-able yew tree stretches its sombre arms over the moss-rown graves of the old inhabitants. Stately elms and eeches fringe the lonely graveyard, and a quiet walk ads to the moated house of Baddesley Clinton. In this tensely quiet spot it needs no effort of the imagination conjure up Mariana and her dreary days of longing r the coming of the false lover, to whom Shakespeare is given an undying notoriety, and Tennyson has em-edded in one of his sweetest lyrics. Though there are ore than a hundred moated areas in Warwickshire, ddesley Clinton is in some respects an unique example a fortified manor house of the fifteenth century. Its ll over the porch, its long passages and internal arrange-ents, give it an interest not possessed even by the ger and statelier fortified mansion of Maxstoke. The history and descent of the house has been poetically rendered by Henry Ferrers, the painstaking antiquary, who once lived here, and whose descendants yet occupy their ancestral home. This Henry Ferrers occupied the house in Vinegar Yard, Westminster, which acquired such an unenviable notoriety in the Gunpowder Plot.

> "This seate and soyle from Saxon Bade, a man of honest fame,
> Who held it in the Saxon time, of Baddesley tooke th e name.
> When Edward King the Confessour did weare the English crowne,
> The same was then possest by ———* a man of som renowne;
> And England being conquer'd, in lot it did alyghte
> To Giffry Wirce, of noble birth, an Andegavian knighte:
> A member hamlet all this while, of Hampton here at hand,
> With Hampton so to Moulbray went, as all the Wirce's land.
> Now Moulbray, lord of all, doth parte these twoo, and grants this one
> To Bisege; in that name it runs awhyle, and then is gone
> To Clinton as his heyre, who leaves it to a younger son;
> And in that time the name of Baddesley Clinton was begun.
> From them agayne, by wedding of their heyre, at first came
> To Conisby, and after him to Foukes, who weds the same.
> From Foukes to Dudley by a sale, and so to Burdet past;
> To Mitley, next by Mitley's will it came to Brome at last.
> Brome honors much the place, and after some descents of Brome
> To Ferrers, for a daughter's part of theyr's in match it comes.
> In this last name it lasteth still, and so long—longer shall;
> As God shall please, who is the Lord, and King, and God of all."

The Bromes mentioned in this bit of antiquarian rhyme occupied a somewhat prominent position in this neighbourhood and at Warwick in the fifteenth and sixteenth centuries. The family appear to have derived their name from Brome's Place, or Brome Hall, a moated mansion, of which some remains exist in the neighbouring

* A blank in the original.

parish of Lapworth. For several generations in the fifteenth century they were tanners in Bridge End, Warwick, where their ancient residence, known as Brome's Place, yet remains.

In the eighth Henry VI., John Brome was one of the burgesses for the town of Warwick, and his son married Beatrice Shirley, the granddaughter of Sir Hugh Shirley, who fell at Shrewsbury fight, and he

BROME'S PLACE, BRIDGE END, WARWICK.

was Lord of Baddesley Clinton, and stood high in favour with Henry VI. and the Lancastrian party. On the accession of Edward IV. he ceased to be employed in the public service. He devoted himself apparently to the improvement of his estate, and the advancement of his children. His eldest daughter, Jocosa, became prioress of the neighbouring nunnery of Wroxall, and his son Thomas proprietor of the

Woodloes, a substantial moated house not far from the priory at Warwick, which from time immemorial had been held by the cooks of the earls of Warwick. John Herthill, steward to Neville, the great Earl of Warwick, had mortgaged the manor of Woodloes to John Brome, and wished to redeem it, but the latter refused to part with the land. Herthill then stabbed him in the porch of the White Friars, London, and it is said that Thomas Brome smiled when he saw his father stabbed, for his father forgave him doing so in his will. His eldest son, Nicholas, succeeded his father at Baddesley Clinton, and resenting his murder, he some three years afterwards waylaid Herthill in Longbridge fields, on his way to Barford to keep the Earl of Warwick's Court, and after a short encounter slew him. For this he had to pay for certain masses in the church of St. Mary, Warwick, and in his church of Baddesley Clinton. Nicholas was a man of many wives as well as violent passions, for coming into his parlour at Baddesley Clinton he found the parish priest "chucking his wife under the chin," which so enraged him that he killed the priest. He procured the pardon of the King and the Pope for this, but was enjoined to do certain acts in expiation thereof. He "built the steeple of Packwood church," and raised the tower of Baddesley church from the ground, and bought three bells for it. He raised the body of the church ten feet higher, and there are many evidences of his work in the manor house adjoining. He lived until the reign of Henry VIII., August 29, 1517, and the church of his expiation has recently been restored, and the monuments of the Bromes and Ferrers cleaned and repaired. From the intermarriage of his daughter Constance with Sir Edward Ferrers, the manor and mansion descended to the family who now inhabit it.

The Bromes continued to reside at the Woodloes, which they modified in the reign of Elizabeth, for some time, and they had a town house on or near the spot where the present gateway stands leading to Warwick Castle. The present house of the Woodloes has the same chimneys and some of the windows intact, but the house was rebuilt on a site considerably to the north of the old house during the present century.

There is a strange anecdote told of one of the family of the Bromes at Chilton Cantelow, Somersetshire,* where one Theophilus Brome was buried on the 18th of August, 1670. He requested that his head might be taken off and preserved in the farm-house, where a head is still shown. The tenants have not been able to bury it, through the noises which ensue. The sexton, in trying to do so, broke his spade.

* Collinson's "History," ii. 339.

Willoughby the Explorer.

THE spirit of adventure is not confined to any age or to any shire. The love of a maritime life and a roving career has seduced many a boy from his home and friends. In the midland shires the families are numerous who have sons at sea. It seems as if the spirit of the old Vikings could not sleep in the midland vales which were assigned to the followers of Guthrin by Alfred the Great. Every now and then a yearning for the wild freedom of the océan comes over the home-nurtured youth, and he goes to seek his fortune abroad.

The Edwardian wars, and the cruel battles which marked the civil strife of the Roses, gave a natural outlet to these adventurous spirits; but when Richard III. fell on the field of Bosworth, and Henry of Richmond had been *fêted* at Coventry, and had seized the rich heritage of the Beauchamps, peace reigned on the troubled land, new thoughts and new aims found willing hands and hearts to seek other fields for action. In 1497, eighteen months before Columbus saw the mainland of tropical America, Sebastian Cabot, then in the service of Henry VII., had landed on the coast of Labrador. It was then that this distinguished navigator thought of a north-west passage to India. In 1517, he was sent by Henry VIII. to Labrador again, and entered Hudson's Bay. After a short service in Spain, he came again to England, when the youthful Edward VI. allowed him a pension, and sought his counsel on all naval matters. About this time Cabot revived his idea of finding a northern route to India, and the first Arctic expedition by the north-east route was planned.

There was living at this time one Sir Hugh Willoughby, of Middleton Hall, near Sutton Coldfield. He was a man of high lineage and military renown. His family had long settled at Willoughby-on-the-Wold, in the county of Nottingham. His ancestor, Bugg, first took the surname of Willoughby, and in the thirteenth century, by marriage with the heiress of the house of Bec, the head of the family became Lord Willoughby de Eresby. In 1320, the family were in possession of the estate of Wollaton, Nottinghamshire, and by marriage with Margaret, a sister and co-heir of Sir Baldwin Freville, Hugh Willoughby became Lord of Middleton. He died in 1431-2, and his widow married Sir Richard Bingham, one of the justices of the King's Bench, who resided at Middleton till his death in 1452-3; but the last of the Frevilles lived to see her grandson, Henry Willoughby, knighted for his gallant conduct at the famous battle of Stoke. At her death, Sir Henry, the father of Sir Hugh Willoughby, became Lord of Middleton in right of his grandmother, and his descendants still hold the lordship.

Sir Hugh was the son of Sir Henry by his third wife, Ellen Egerton, of Wrinchall, Cheshire, whose mother was one of the Gresleys, and it appears that he was early destined for a military career. His father's second wife was connected with the Brandons, Lady Jane Grey, and the Dudleys, and they led the way to fame and fortune. In 1542, Hugh Willoughby went on the Scottish expedition under the Earl of Hereford, who was subsequently Earl of Warwick and Duke of Northumberland, the father of Ambrose, the "good Earl of Warwick," Robert Earl of Leicester, and Guildford Dudley, the unfortunate husband of Lady Jane Grey. In this Scotch expedition Hugh Willoughby greatly distinguished himself. He bravely defended Fort Lowder in 1549-50. His military career stopped with the disgrace of the Duke of Somerset. He married Jane Streeley, the daughter of Sir Nicholas Streeley, who resided near Wollaton, and she bore him a son, Henry. Of these we hear no more. Men's minds were full of the discovery of new lands. New sources of trade were being opened up by the Spanish and the Portuguese, but no stranger was allowed to interfere. At this period, Cabot's scheme for a north-east route to Cathay (China) became popular, and in 1527, the "Mystery Company and Fellowship of Merchant Adventurers for the Discovery of Unknown Lands" was incorporated. Of this company Cabot was governor, and, under his direction, a great expedition was planned, and Sir Hugh Willoughby appointed commander-in-chief.

The expedition consisted of three vessels; the *Bona Esperanza*, of 120 tons, was commanded by Sir Hugh in person, and William Gefferson was sailing master; the *Edward Bonaventura*, 160 tons, was under the command of Richard Chancelour, Stephen Borough being sailing master, and the *Bona Confidentia*, 90 tons, which was placed under the command of Master Cornelius Durfoorth. Each vessel was sheathed with lead, and furnished with a pinnace and a boat. The plans of operation were drawn out by Cabot, and the most quaint and minute instructions were given to the commanders to regulate their conduct and their crews. These regulations were thirty-three in number. There were regulations for morning and evening prayer, for the reading of the Scriptures, and other religious exercises. "Carding, dicing, and such other devilish games" were prohibited. When Sir Hugh came to a strange country, he was instructed to make the people drunk, in order that the secret of their hearts might ooze out, and, by the thirtieth item, he was enjoined not to be frightened if he saw any people wearing "lyons and beares skinnes, having long bowes and arrowes," "for such be worn oftentimes more to feare strangers than to any other end." The young King

Edward wrote to all the kings inhabiting the north-east parts of the world towards the mighty empire of Cathay, in English, Latin, Greek, and other languages, bidding them greeting, and, on the 11th May, 1553, these three ships weighed anchor at Deptford, and proceeded on their perilous voyage.

There is preserved an account of the voyage, written at the dictation of Richard Chancelour, pilot major of the voyage, by Clement Adams, "schoolemaster to the Queene's henshmen," and from his and other descriptions of the departure we learn how keen was the interest felt in this voyage; how readily the £6,000 was subscribed towards the outfit of the ships. At Ratcliff the crew saluted their acquaintance "one his wife, another his children, and another his kinsfolkes, and another his friend dearer than his kinsfolkes." The "great ships" then dropped down to Greenwich, where the Court was towed by the boats. "The mariners were all apparelled in watchet or sky coloured cloth. The courtiers came running out, and the people flocked together, standing very thicke upon the shore; the Privie Councel they looked out at the windows of the Court, and the rest ran up to the toppes of the towers; the shippes hereupon discharged their ordinance and shoot off their pieces after the manner of war and of the sea, insomuch that the tops of the hills resounded therewith; the valleys and the waters gave an echo, and the mariners they shouted in such sort, that the sky rang again with the noise thereof. One stood on the poop of his ship and by his gesture bade farewell to his friends in the best manner he could. Another walked upon the hatches, another climbed the shrouds, another stood on the main yard, and another on the top of the ship." But, alas! the good King Edward lay sick and ill, and ere the adventurous voyagers had reached the sea he died and left the realm a prey to enemies.

At Gravesend the veteran Cabot visited the ships, with many gentlemen, and gentlewomen, and bade them good-bye, and after tasting the best cheer the voyagers could give them, liberally rewarded the mariners. He asked them to pray for the good fortune and the success of the adventure and then departed commending them all to the governance of God. It was six weeks from the time of leaving Ratcliff ere the expedition finally got to sea. They had to tarry for wind and tide at every point in the river and along the lowlying flats of the east coast—Sir Hugh's diary gives us a few dates of these hindrances—but on the 23rd of June, 1553, they fairly got to sea. They cast many a long, lingering look on their native and, which many of them were not to see again, and others were to return with fame and glory. Willoughby had left his son behind him. Richard Chancelour was married to a sister of Robert Dudley, and he was leaving wo sons behind him in England, while he sailed over the sea of uncertainty to the unknown realms beyond the North Cape, which, up to that time, no English ship had doubled, or, at all events sailed eastward of the Wardhuys.

On the 14th of August, 1553, Sir Hugh Willoughby, in the *Bona Esperanza*, came in sight of land. This was probably that part of the coast of Nova Zembla lying between the Northern and Southern Goose Cape, Gussinii Noss. The mainland of Russia was first seen by Sir Hugh on the 23rd of August, and he landed the same day. This fact makes him the first Englishman who trod Russian territory from the sea, for the *Edward Bonaventura*, with Chancelour on board, did not cast anchor on the southern coast of the White Sea till the 24th, when she was off the settlement "Possad" of Nenocksa, not far from the Korelian mouth of the Dwina, where he waited for the other ships, but the junction was not to be.

On the 14th of September, Sir Hugh effected a fresh landing on the Lapland coast, in a bay westward of the island of Nokujeff, where pretty good anchorage was found. He sailed subsequently with both vessels in a south-easterly direction towards the White Sea, and had he continued this course, we are told by a Russian geographer, he would probably have reached the monastery of Ssolovertz or joined Chancelour at Nenocksa; but he appears to have been caught in a whirlpool at Cape Natoi Noss, and this decided them to return to the bay which they had left, and which is distinguished by the bold, rocky isles of Nokujeff. They were in this bay on the 18th of September.

In the meantime Chancelour reached Wardhuys in Norway, and after waiting for some time he sailed on his voyage, notwithstanding the dissuasions of some Scottishmen, until he reached "a land of everlasting sunshine, shining with a continual light and brightness clearly upon the huge and mighty sea." He had reached the dominions of Ivan Vassilovich, the Czar of Russia, and Master Chancelour paid him a visit at his court at Moscow, a journey that entailed a sledge drive of fifteen hundred miles. Thus he laid the foundation of that Russian friendship and esteem which secured us peace until our day. He regained his ship and reached England in the following spring.

In the summer of 1554, some Russian fishermen plying their calling on the eastern coast of Lapland had their attention attracted by some large craft lying between the black and craggy Nokujeff and the shore. They went to them and found that they were the floating tombs of Sir Hugh and seventy of his unfortunate companions. The unfortunate knight had been caught by a severe winter where there was neither men or fuel. His diary gives a fearful account of the sufferings of the crews. The chaplain was with Chancelour, and there were merchants in both ships, of the name of Alexander and Richard Gardiner. The snow-wreathed bodies of his sixty-five men frozen to death affected Sir Hugh, for we learn from his diary that he was alive at the end of January, 1554. The discovery of the bodies and ships was reported to the Governor, and by him to the Czar, who ordered everything to be sealed up, and the ships to be sent to Cholmogorn. The untimely fate of Sir Hugh excited but little attention at the time; Lady Jane Grey had been beheaded; the country was subjected to the bigoted rule of Queen Mary, and when the soiled clothes of the knight, preserved at Wollaston, were brought home, but few cared for the man who had been so unfortunate. A century afterwards there was another Willoughby at Middleton, a naturalist, and a friend of Ray the botanist. His history of birds and fishes was published, and he died in 1672, in the thirty-seventh year of his age. To him we are indebted for much relating to the natural history of Warwickshire.

The black and rocky edge of Nokujeff still rises 400 feet above the sea level. Here should be the monument of the first of our Arctic explorers, and his portrait should be preserved amongst the worthies of the county.

A Tudor Tragedy.

WHILST all that was mortal of Sir Hugh Willoughby was enshrined in an icy shroud on the desolate coast of Lapland, a tragedy was being enacted on the eastern boundaries of Warwickshire, which has furnished a theme for the historian and the romancer. The neighbourhood of Wolvey is full of romance. The story of the seizure of Edward IV. here by the King Maker, the fate of the neighbouring grange, of the hermits on the heath, of the Templars, of the Burdetts, of Bramcote, are full of interest. The scene of the tragedy at Shireford lies about a mile north of Wolvey, between that village and Burton Hastings, for here stood in the first year of the reign of Queen Mary a fair manor house, inhabited by Sir Walter Smyth and his young wife. The story is preserved in Dugdale, and has been reprinted in Burke's "Vicissitudes of Families," and in Howitt's "Visits to Remarkable Places."

Shireford had been long in the possession of the family of Purefoy, and in the reign of Henry VIII. it passed into the hands, by purchase, of a Mr. H. Smyth, a wealthy citizen of Spon Street, Coventry; the Purefoy's retiring to their ancient mansion of Fenny Drayton, some six miles further north along the Watling Street. The new possessor of Shireford had a good estate at Fletchampstead, near Coventry, and was a man of charitable disposition. His son, Walter Smyth, succeeded to his estates, was married, and had a son and heir, Richard Smyth, grown to man's estate. On the death of his first wife, Sir Walter was an aged man, and thought it time that his son was married. He mentioned the circumstance to Mr. Thomas Chetwin, of Ingestre, in Staffordshire, a gentleman of ancient family and fair estate, and with whom the Purefoys had been connected. Mr. Chetwin entertained the offer on behalf of Dorothy, one of his daughters, and was contented to give £500 portion with her. "But no sooner had the old knight seen the young lady than that he became a suitor for himself, being so captivated with her beauty, that he tendered as much for her, besides a good jointure, as he should have received in case the match had gone on for his son. Which liberal offer so wrought upon Mr. Chetwin, as that he spared not for arguments to persuade his daughter to accept of Sir Walter for her husband. Whereupon the marriage ensued accordingly, but with what a tragique issue will quickly be seen; for it was not long ere that, her affections wandering after younger men, she gave entertainment to one Mr. William Robinson (then of Drayton Basset, a young gentleman of about twenty-two years of age) son of George Robinson, a rich mercer of London, and grew so impatient at all impediments which might hinder her full enjoyment of him, that she rested not till she had contrived a way to be rid of her husband. For which purpose corrupting her waiting gentlewoman, and a groom of the stable, she resolved, by their help, and the assistance of Robinson, to strangle him in his bed, appointing the time and manner how it should be effected; and though Robinson failed in coming on the designated night (perhaps through a right apprehension of so direfull a fact), she in no whit staggered in her resolutions, for watching her husband till he was fallen asleep, she then let in those assasinates before specified, and casting a long towell about his neck, caused the groom to lye upon him to keep him from struggling, whilst herself and the maid, straining the towell, stopt his breath. It seems, the good old man little thought that his lady had acted therein, for when they first cast the towell about his neck, he cryed out, 'Help, Doll, help!' But, having thus dispatcht the work, they carryed him into another room, where a close stool was plac'd, upon which they set him; and, after an hour, that the maid and groom were silently got away, to palliate the business, she made an outcry in the house, wringing her hands, pulling her hair, and weeping extreamly, with pretence that, missing him for some time out of bed, she went to see what the matter was, and found him accidentally in that posture; which subtill and feigned shews of sorrow prevented all suspicion of his violent death; and, not long after, went to London, setting so high a value upon her beauty, that Robinson, her former darling (perhaps for not keeping touch with her, as before hath been said), became neglected. But, within two years following, it so hapned, that this woful deed of darkness was brought to light by the groom before specified, who, being entertained with Mr. Richard Smyth, son and heir to the murdered knight, and attending him to Coventre with divers other servants, became so sensible of his villany, when he was in his cups, that out of good nature he took his master to a side, and upon his knees besought forgiveness from him for acting in the murther of his father, declaring all the circumstances thereof. Whereupon Mr. Smyth discreetly gave him good words, but wisht some others that he trusted to have an eye to him, that he might not escape, when he had slept and better considered what might be the issue thereof. Notwithstanding which direction, he fled away with his master's best horse, and, hasting presently into Wales, attempted to go beyond sea; but being hindred by contrary winds, after three essays to launch out, was so happily pursued by Mr. Smyth, who spared for no cost in sending to several ports, that he was found out, and brought prisoner to Warwick; as was also the lady and her gentlewoman, all of them, with great boldness, denying the fact, and the groom most impudently charging Mr. Smyth with endeavour of corrupting him to accuse the lady (his mother-in-law) falsely, to the end that he might get her joynture. But upon his arraignment, so smitten was he at apprehension of the guilt, that he publickly acknowledged it, and stoutly justified what he had so said to be true to the face of the lady and the maid; who, at first, with much seeming confidence, pleaded their innocency, till at length, seeing the particular circumstances thus discovered, they both confessed the fact; for which, having judgement to dye, the lady was burnt at a stake, near the hermitage on Wolvey Heath (towards the side of Shirford Lordship), where the country people to this day shew the place, and the groom with the maid suffered death at Warwick. This was about the third year of Q. Mary's reign, it being May 15, 1 Mariæ, that Sir Walter's murther so happened."

Such is the story as told by Dugdale. It is asserted that a reprieve was granted to the young wife, but, in consequence of the horse of the messenger foundering near Cloudesley Bush, it did not arrive in time.

The subsequent fate of the estate of Shireford is remarkable as showing the sharp and overreaching spirit of the times. Richard Smyth by his first wife had only one daughter, Margaret by name; whilst she was yet a child he fancied that he had no probability of male issue, and therefore proposed to Sir John Littleton, of Frankley, in Worcestershire, to form an alliance between Margaret Smyth and William Littleton, Sir John's third son. He offered in consideration of such marriage to settle all his lands in remainder after his decease, without other issue, upon the said William and Margaret and their lawful children, but in default of such issue to descend to his family and heirs. This draught agreement was prepared and sent to Sir John to have engrossed, and on the day appointed Richard Smyth went to Frankley to execute the deed. Here he found a goodly company of Sir John Littleton's friends and excellent entertainment. The writings were brought forward in their presence and began to be read, when Sir John's keeper came hurriedly in and said "that there were two bucks at lair in the park which carried a glass in their tails for Mr. Smyth's dogs to look in." Now Mr. Smyth loved coursing, and he had brought his greyhounds with him, but appeared to hesitate. The keeper said that the market people passing through the park might rouse the deer. Sir John urged Mr. Smyth to seal the deeds, vowing they were according to the original draught. In a weak moment Mr. Smyth did so, and went forth into the park. The youthful pair were then married, though only nine years old, and lived in the house at Frankley with Sir John.

Some six years after this, William Littleton was killed

by a fall from his horse, when Richard Smyth demanded his daughter, as she had no children; but to this Sir John demurred, and, on the deeds being produced, it was found that, in default of William dying without issue, the Smyth estates were to devolve upon William's heir, which was his eldest brother Gilbert. In the meantime, Margaret was married to Sir John's second son, Gilbert. Great suits of law followed the discovery of this perfidy, and when, on the death of Gilbert, the estates descended to his son John, the litigation was continued until the latter was drawn into the street brawl of the Earl of Essex with Catesby and Winter, in the forty-second year of the reign of Elizabeth (1601), when he died in prison, and the estates were forfeited.

When James I. came to the crown, he restored these lands to Muriel, the widow of John Littleton, and it appears that her nephew, John, the son of George and Margaret, was staying here on the eve of the hunting match at Dunchurch, 1605, and though solicited to join his brothers there, he sullenly refused to go. Stephen Littleton, of Holbeach, the son of Margaret and George, lost his life and estate for his participation in the plot. Muriel Littleton sold Shireford, or Shelford, as it is now called, to Sergeant Hele, a great lawyer, who divided it between his five sons, amongst whom it was the subject of a family contention, when King Charles II. again reigned over England.

Reformers and Martyrs.

ALONG the Watling Street way we find the traces of our reformers and our martyrs. From Cesterover to Willey, the pinnacled tower of Lutterworth is a conspicuous object in the landscape. Here Wickliff preached, wrote, and died. It was along the little river Swift that his honoured dust was borne, when his bones were torn from his grave thirty-one years after his decease, burnt, and cast into the river. "Each separate atom," as Fuller quaintly puts it, "became a germ of truth." The rivulet carried the ashes to the Avon, the Avon to the Severn, the Severn to the ocean, and from thence all over the world. No one can forget how stoutly John of Gaunt, then Lord of Kenilworth, stood the friend of Wickliff when cited to London to answer for his opinions. Luther was equally well supported, when, 150 years afterwards, he stood before the diet of Worms. Honest John Lacey, the parish priest of Chesterton, was not afraid to harbour Sir John Oldcastle, the good Lord Cobham, when an outlaw for his religious opinions, for we find that King Henry V. granted the old priest a pardon for so doing in the third year of his reign (1415-6). In the very year of the battle of Bosworth, when Coventry was full of renewed zeal for the Lancastrians, eight men and one woman were charged with heretical doctrines, and were forced to recant and do penance, because they did not believe that Popes were successors to St. Peter, and that prayer and alms availeth not the dead. They did not believe in either purgatory or pilgrimages, but in the saving influence of faith and God's mercy. They even thought it better to give alms to the poor than to make offerings to images of saints. They thought that every man should know the Lord's prayer, and that bread should be alone the representative of the sacrament of the Lord's Supper. In the year 1488, Margery Goit was accused of denying the doctrine of transubstantiation, and was ordered to do penance.

It was not until the year 1519, when Henry VIII. had been on the throne ten years, that the faggot and stake were used at Coventry to repress heretical opinions. In that year six godly men and one woman were burned on the Little Park for Protestant heresies, and their goods seized by the Sheriff. There is preserved, in the ninth volume of the Stafford MSS., verses indicative of the puritanic spirit, and of the aspirations for a Christian life, written at Sutton Coldfield. It is dated May, 1546 (thirty-eighth Henry VIII.), the year before Edward VI. ascended the throne :—

"Aryse yerly
Remember God shortly
Blesse the surely
Serve God devoutly
And the world besely
Fear God inwardly
Love thy prynce int'ly
And praye for him humbly
Worke thy dede wysely
Gyffe thy armes secretly
Eate thy meate merely
Goo thy waye sadly
Learne virtue dayly
Answer demurely
Chyde not wilfully
Stryke not hastely
Deale not to largely
Laugh not loudly
Goo to dyn appetly
Sytt thereat manly
Eat not surfetly
Ryse therefro tempatly
Comon not to boldely
Use not thy tong libally
Loke nott sowrely
Love not thy wyfe jeleusly
But loke on her pleasauntly
Chastyce thy chyld duly
Pay thy dettes truly
Spend mesureably
Do thy s'ves hedely
Kep thy offyce redely
Be arrayed honestly
Here ye masse devoutly
Paye thy s'vant ryghtuesly
Bourde not brodely
Ask thy dettes gently
Speak for thy ryght boldly
Maynteyne trueth manly
Crafte not pryvayly
Take god sound patyetly

And thank him tend'ly
Bewar othes accustomably
Nor swere not depely
Love thy wyffe faythfully
Suffer her resonably
Loke on thy daughter dyligently
Make thy bargain discreetly
At supp eat slenderly
Ayris therefrom sob'ly
Drynke thereat but softely
And then geave thanks hertly
To God that sends all to the
And go to bed in charyte."

When the Coventry heretics were doing penance, Hugh Latimer, of Thurcaston, was fifteen years old, and full of zeal for the papacy. When he became the first Protestant Bishop of Worcester, he found many zealous friends living almost within sight of his birthplace. Amongst the numerous servants and dependents of the monasteries was John Glover, of Baxterley, formerly an official connected with the Cistercian Abbey of Merivale, and subsequently a retainer of Lord Ferrers, who took back the Abbey lands his ancestor gave the monks more than 300 years before. Baxterley is pleasantly situated on a bend of the ridge on which Hartshill and Oldbury are placed, which overlooks a large portion of the great Leicestershire vale. Here John Glover built a hall, and here received Master Hugh Latimer as his guest, with his friend and servant, Austin Bernher. There is an entry in the church books recording the fact that the venerable old divine preached there. Robert Glover, the martyr, had married a niece of Latimer, and early in the reign of Edward VI. resided occasionally with his brothers, John and William, at the Manor House, at Mancetter, which yet remains adjoining the churchyard. One of the adjacent houses was, in 1555, inhabited by Mr. Thomas Lewis (who owned a moiety of the manor) and his wife. Edward VI. was dead, and Mary reigned in England, and Dr. Banes was Bishop of Lichfield and Coventry.

Coventry, renowned for its religious pageants, for its splendid churches, for its cathedral, and ancient halls, was at once the home of popish bigotry, and staunch Protestantism. In the reign of Henry VIII. it had been noted as the home of sectaries, yet there was a strong repugnance to destroy the ecclesiastical monuments of their fathers. Miracle plays had been common, and the pageantry of the priests pleased the mass of the people. On the 8th of February, 1555, Lawrence Saunders, a minister of Bread Street Chapel, London, was burnt for heresy in Coventry. Originally designed for a merchant, he was educated at Eton School, and apprenticed to Sir William Chester. Saunders, however, preferred the ministry, and after being educated at Cambridge, became the incumbent of Church Langton, in Leicestershire, and of All Hallows, Bread Street, London. When the persecutions of Queen Mary began, Saunders went on preaching as before in defiance of the Queen's proclamation. After preaching against the errors

COVENTRY CHURCHES AND ITS PAGEANTS.

of Popery at Northampton, he was arrested and suffered imprisonment for a year and three months, notwithstanding he was offered mercy by the Bishops of Winchester and London, with whom he had frequent disputes, if he would recant and return to the Church of Rome. He refused these terms, and wrote a letter of condolence to Cranmer, Ridley, and Latimer, then in prison at Oxford. On the 4th of February, 1555, Bishop Bonner went to the Marshalsea Prison, London, degraded him, and deprived him of his official character, and on the following morning, Mordaunt, the sheriff, delivered him to the Queen's Guard, who were appointed to conduct him to the city of Coventry, there to be burned. On the 8th of February, he was conducted to the stake placed in the park, just outside the city walls. Here he was offered pardon if he would revoke his heresies; but this Saunders refused to do, and after a humble prayer he, clad in a shirt and old black gown, folded his arms around the stake to which he was about to be chained, and kissed it, saying, "Welcome the cross of Christ! Welcome everlasting life!" He was then fastened to the stake, the flames ascended round him, and he was soon in the presence of his Maker.

There are many signs that the execution of Saunders created a widespread feeling of enthusiasm. He had been the friend of the Glovers, at Mancetter, and here his memory and his fate were mourned. Mrs. Lewis appears to have gone to mass regularly prior to his execution, but now she joined the zealous ministrations of the Glovers, for John Careless, the brother of Mary, Robert Glover's wife, was even then languishing in the King's Bench Prison, in London, for holding heretical opinions. Careless had been a weaver in Coventry, and was originally confined in the City Gaol, but after being examined by Dr. Martin, he was sent to London. In the same prison was Archdeacon Philpots, and between the two a loving friendship appears to have sprung up. There is extant a long correspondence between them, which took place after the Archdeacon was imprisoned in the stocks in the coal-hole of the prison. In one of these letters Careless playfully alludes to his name. He says, "I will now, according to your loving request, cast away all care, and cast all my care upon Christ, who will care for me, and will be careless according to my name; for as soon as I had read your comfortable letter, my sorrows vanished away as smoke in the wind. I am sure the Spirit of God was the author of it." He kept up a correspondence with many other sufferers for conscience sake, but ultimately died in prison, in July, 1556, and was buried in a dunghill.

In the previous year, the brothers Glover appear to have been residing in Coventry, when the Bishop of Coventry and Lichfield (Dr. Banes) issued a warrant to the Mayor to arrest John Glover, who was the leader of his brothers. The Mayor of Coventry gave him warning, and John and William Glover escaped, but Robert being ill in bed could not move, so the officers found and seized him. As his name was not in the warrant the Sheriff who was with them would have let him go, but the officers persisted in detaining him until the Bishop came. Eleven days elapsed before Dr Banes arrived; in the meantime Robert Glover lay in prison refusing the offer of a friendly hand to be released on a bond. As soon as the Bishop arrived, Glover was questioned as to the true church, the number of sacraments, the mass, the confession of sins to a priest; but to these questions his answers were not satisfactory, either at Coventry or at Lichfield, where he was removed. He was remitted to the common gaol at Coventry to await a writ for his execution from London. Whilst in prison he was visited by his friend Austin Bernher, a zealous preacher of the time, and who subsequently appears to have resided at Southam. To Bernher we are indebted for an account of the faltering spirit of Robert Glover until the day drew nigh, when, in company with Cornelius Bongay, a capper, of Coventry, he went cheerfully to the stake and faggot on the 20th day of September, 1555. There is a touching letter of Robert Glover's extant, addressed to his wife, who received letters of condolence from Ridley, Latimer, and her brother Careless.

The fates of John and William Glover likewise

demand pity and commiseration. John injured his health from lurking about in woods. He several times narrowly escaped capture, for a search was made for him at the end of Mary's reign, as he had been excommunicated for his opinions. He died and was quietly buried in Mancetter churchyard. No service was read over his grave; no minister attended his funeral. Persecution did not cease with death, for the Chancellor of the diocese, Dr. Draicott, demanded that the body should be taken up by the vicar and cast over the wall into the highway. The vicar protested that it was impossible, as the body had been buried six weeks. He was ordered to do this after an interval of twelve months, and then the place where he was buried must be reconsecrated. In the meantime, he gave Glover a bill to read, pronouncing him a damned soul.

Robert Glover died at Wein, in Shropshire, whither he had fled for refuge nearly at the same time as his brother, and the body carried to the parish church, but the curate forbade the body being buried until he had heard from the bishop. In the meantime, a tailor, named Richard Morrice, attempted to inter the corpse, but was prevented by one Thorlyne. By the Bishop's order (Dr. Banes), dated 6th September, 1558, the body was removed in a dung cart, and was buried in a neighbouring broom field.

On the 18th September, 1577, Mrs. Lewis was

executed at Lichfield, after a long term of imprisonment and repeated examinations.

In Mancetter church, there are tablets erected to the memory of the Mancetter martyrs, by the late Rev. B. Richings. In the chancel of the church, Fox's "Book of Martyrs," and several religious books, are chained up for the use of the people.* Within a mile or two of the home of the Glovers is the birthplace of George Fox, the founder of the Society of Friends, and still further on the Leicestershire side of the street way is Wykin Hall, the residence of William Wightman, the last person burned at the stake in England for heresy. He denied the doctrine of the Trinity, and was executed at Lichfield, 1610. Fox was not born, however, until fourteen years after this event. By the roadside is an obelisk to his memory, erected by the efforts of the late Charles Holt Bracebridge, and on the hills above, at Hartshill, is one of the earliest of the Quaker chapels and also a long established Quaker school.

* There are chained books of divinity also at Wootton-Wawen church.

The Heiress of Canonbury.

THERE is no spot so difficult to find, and no place better worth seeing in the county of Warwick, than the old moated mansion of Compton Winyates. The greater part of the moat is now filled up, and the spot on which the old stables stood outside the drawbridge is now a verdant lawn, by the side of which the road winds which leads you to the hoary portal of the quaint and retired house. It is a place of intense quietude and stillness. Not a sound breaks upon the ear. It might be the palace of the sleeping beauty, for there are no signs of life discernible.

It is built in a recess or comb of the Edge hills, about equal distances from the villages of Tysoe and Brailes, whose handsome churches are the pride of the country side; indeed the church of Brailes, desolate as it now appears, is known as the cathedral of the feldon. In the quiet valley of the Vineyard, for so its name imports, the family of Compton have long been connected, and from it they have taken their name. Their name appears in deeds as early as the twelfth century, and, indeed, they seem to have held the estate under

Turchill, the Saxon sheriff, in the days of the Confessor. The Comptons have been a rising family. They appear as knights of the shire, and as coroners, for many years; but it was not until William Compton, who was left fatherless at the age of eleven years, that the family assumed a high position in the county. William Compton was a page to Henry, Duke of York, the second son of Henry VII. When the Duke of York became King, under the title of Henry VIII., William Compton became a Gentleman of the Bedchamber, and was advanced to various offices and trusts. He was knighted, was created Chancellor of Ireland, led the rear guard of the King's troops at Therouene, and he built a fair mansion on his paternal estate, bringing much of the material from the castle of Fulbrooke, on the north side of the Avon.

From whichever side you approach Compton Winyates, you cannot obtain a view until you are close upon it, and hence it is better known as Compton-in-the-Hole than by its proper title. It is a brick and timber building of singular construction. It is quadrangular in plan, with a projecting porch, and in its most picturesque form admirably represented by the accompanying engraving. The timbers have become dark with age, the bricks have lost their brightness, and the lighter mortar gives a hoary tone to the whole. In the gable to the right are the officers' quarters, and beyond are the barracks. The

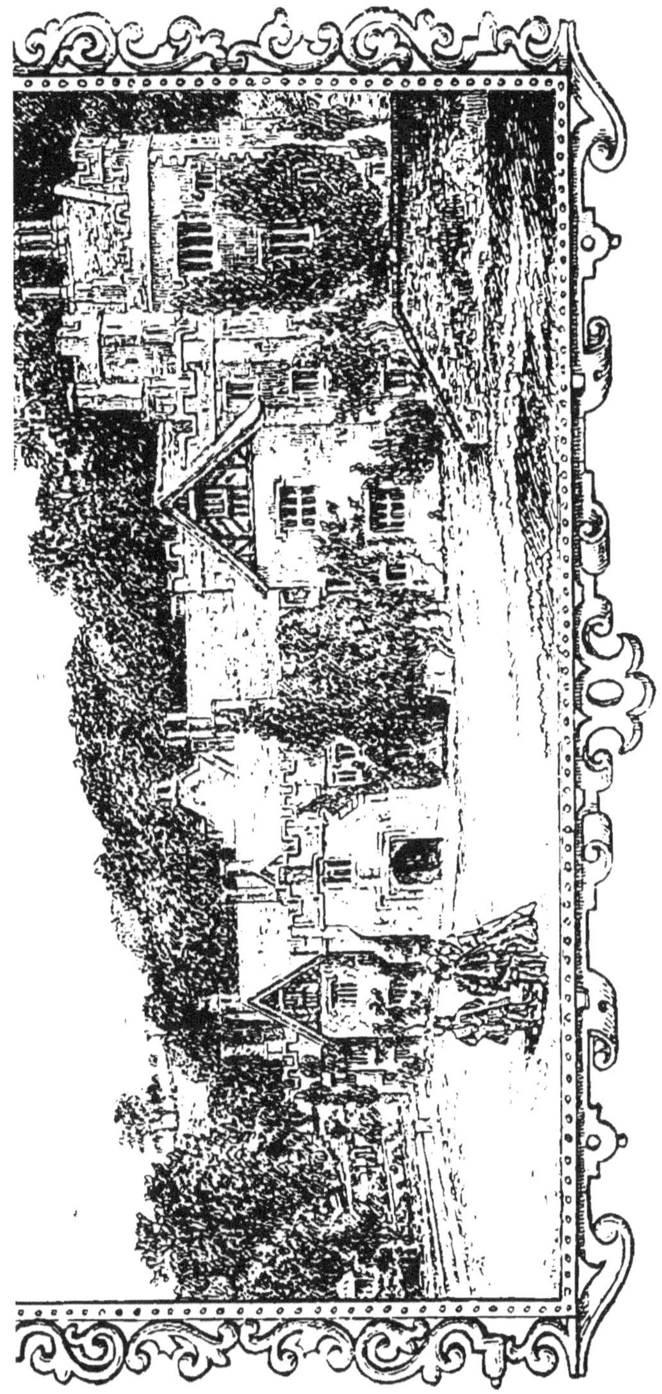

turret leads to the prison, the cell, and the outer walls, for Compton Winyates is a transition house. It is the last style of a fortified dwelling, for the garrison occupied but a slight portion of the building, with a separate entrance from the family and domestics. As you approach the time-beaten door, and raise the heavy knocker, you cannot fail to be struck with the old-fashioned escutcheons, the continued repetition of the Tudor badges on every panel and spandril; and when at length you enter into the quiet courtyard, a portly figure in a jaunty cap, slashed doublet, and baggy trunks would not much surprise you, for so appropriate are the surroundings. On the right is the room in which King Hal made merry. On the left King Charles slept the night prior to the fatal battle on Edgehill. Tudor knight or cavalier might even yet be peeping from the broad casements filled with small quarries and no little painted glass. Across he courtyard, with its cracked and time-worn flags, ou enter the great hall. The screen, which fences the uttery hatch and kitchen, supports the minstrels' gallery, hich yet remains. Its quaint carvings have attracted he notice of hundreds of visitors. Pieces of tapestry ang on the walls. The daïs, where the Comptons sat, ay be traced. There is the solar, but it leads to a suite f rooms, and a new and spacious staircase leads to the oms on either sides of the quadrangle. And what oms? Here is the ghost room, and there the secret chamber. In that spacious apartment, Tudor and Stuart princes have rested. Up that narrow staircase hunted priests have performed mass in the little chapel in the roof. But who were the Papists? There is a stately chapel on the ground floor, with its fine panel work disfigured by white paint. The white paint was added by "tidy John," a bygone Earl of Northampton, with a genius for neatness and whited sepulchres. The beautiful stained glass window of the chapel is gone, taken away bit by bit, when Compton was dismantled and the furniture sold a century ago. For years this fine mansion was a prey to the weather and every idle loon in the neighbourhood. There is a bit of the glass in Cherrington church, which affords an idea of its rich beauty when Dugdale saw and described it. The whole roof can be traversed silently. There are queer passages and queer rooms. It is a gigantic hiding place, and you are not sure as you lean against the fine cleft oak wainscoting that it will not open and land you in an unknown apartment beyond, of which no one has either the secret or the key. If the inside of the house is a study, the chimneys are a marvel. They are of brick, twisted, knotted, turned, fluted, billetted, capped, zigzagged, and ornamented in every conceivable form. What grotesque figures peep from the woodwork here and there! It is the very home of romance, and it has a romantic history —it was the married home of the heiress of Canonbury.

Sir William Compton had been dead sixty years when his grandson died in 1588, and Lord William Compton succeeded to the estates. At this period Elizabeth had reigned thirty-one years, and the memory of her famous visit to Kenilworth had hardly faded from men's minds in Warwickshire. In London the scions of many noble families were engaged in commerce, and making those princely fortunes which enabled them to found a family. Amongst the princely merchants of the time was Alderman Sir John Spenser, knight, who was an opulent clothworker, residing at Canonbury House, at Islington. Sir John had been more than once Lord Mayor, and had distinguished himself by his munificence and hospitality. When Henry Quatre sent the Marquis of Rosny, better known as the Duke of Sully, as his ambassador to England, Sir John entertained and lodged him in the most sumptuous manner at his own cost. His public spirit and generosity made him a great favourite with Elizabeth, and his great wealth—for he was reputed to be worth a million sterling—made him an object of wonder to the people. So great, indeed, was the repute of his riches, that a pirate of Dunkirk once came over with a crew of twelve men with a view of capturing rich Spenser as he rode to Canonbury House in the evening, and then hold him to ransom. Fortunately, Sir John stayed in the city the night this little plot was to come off, and thus frustrated the bold design of the piratical crew.

Elizabeth Spenser, the heiress of Canonbury, was the only daughter of Sir John, and was the object of many a young noble's devotions. She was the richest heiress of her time, and her father resolved that she should wed a sober citizen and merchant, and not one of the fly-blows of the Court. At Canonbury she was secluded from nobles and gentles of whatever degree, whilst her father was busy in the city. Elizabeth was a girl of spirit, and Lord William Compton a man of resource. They loved each other. As a baker's boy he gained admittance to Canonbury House, and one day, in the year of grace 1593-4, Sir John, on returning home, found that Elizabeth had flown. Concealed in a baker's basket, Lord William had carried her off, and Elizabeth Spenser was now Lady Compton.

Sir John was deeply irritated at his daughter's conduct. Time seemed only to make his resentment deeper. The intercession of friends only added to the sore sense of wrong, when suddenly Sir John received an imperative message to meet her Majesty at her palace of Greenwich. He at once prepared to obey the mandate, and he was speedily in the presence of his Queen. Her Majesty received him graciously, and bade him welcome. She explained to him that she wished him to stand sponsor with her to the first child of a young couple whose father had abandoned them. Sir John willingly consented, and still feeling his daughter's disobedience, promised to adopt her Majesty's *protégé* as his own. Her Majesty smiled her thanks, and said that the ceremony must be private, as befitted the condition of her poor little charge. Sir John bowed acquiescence, and the Court passed into her Majesty's private chapel, where the baptismal ceremony was performed, her Majesty giving the name of Spenser to the boy. The singularity of the incident, and the beauty of the child, affected Sir John, who at once proposed to make his new nameson his sole heir; and in order that he might not relent, asked her Majesty to accept his estates in trust for the infant, which he promised to settle irrevocably by deed.

Whether this generous offer was expected by the Queen or not, her eyes sparkled with delight as she accepted the promise, stating that she knew it would be faithfully kept. Then turning to a side door, she said, in a loud tone, "You may enter." The door opened, and Sir John beheld Lord Compton and his daughter, who at once knelt at his feet. The astonishment of Sir John was increased when, before he could speak, the Queen said:—"Sir John, the child whom thou has just adopted is thine own grandson! Take these (his parents) also to your favour; extend to them your forgiveness, and make this one of the happiest hours in a Queen's life!"

"Pardon! dearest father, pardon!" cried the weeping daughter. "Pardon"—continued she, taking the child from an attendant and raising it in her arms,—"pardon, for this child's sake!" Lord Compton also joined in the appeal, which Sir John could no longer resist. With a voice nearly inaudible by emotion, he exclaimed, "Heaven bless you, my children!" embracing them by turns; "I do forgive, with all my heart, the past; and I most sincerely thank her Majesty, who has brought about this event, and which shall ever be remembered as the happiest moment of my life!"

Thus is the story told of the elopement of the heiress of Canonbury, and her reconciliation with her father, who lived until 1609, and then fulfilled his promise of bequeathing his wealth to his daughter and his daughter's children.

It is said that the thought of so much wealth affected the brain of Lord William to such an extent that the Lord Chamberlain had for a time to administer to his affairs; but if this was the case, Elizabeth, his wife, was a woman of resource. She knew she was the inheritor of wealth, and she had a noble idea of spending it. This stately dame penned the following letter* to her husband:—

"My sweet Life,—Now I have declared to you my mind for the settling of your estate, I suppose that it were best for me to bethink and consider within myself what allowance were meetest for me . . . I pray and beseech you to grant to me, your most kind and loving wife the sum of £2,600 quarterly to be paid. Also I would, beside that allow

* Harl MSS.

ance, have £600 quarterly to be paid, for the performance of charitable works; and those things I would not, neither will be accountable for. Also, I will have three horses for my own saddle, that none shall dare to lend or borrow; none lend but I, none borrow but you. Also, I would have two gentlewomen, lest one should be sick, or have some other let. Also, believe it, it is an undecent thing for a gentlewoman to stand mumping alone, when God hath blessed their lord and lady with a great estate. Also, when I ride a hunting, or a hawking, or travel from one house to another, I will have them attending; so, for either of those said women, I must and will have for either of them a horse. Also, I will have six or eight gentlemen. And I will have my two coaches, one lined with velvet to myself, with four very fair horses; and a coach for my women, lined with cloth and laced with gold, or otherwise with scarlet and laced with silver, with four good horses. Also, I will have two coachmen; one for my own coach, the other for my women. Also, at any time when I travel, I will be allowed not only caroches and spare horses, for me and my women, and I will have such carriages as be fitting for all, orderly, not pestering my things with my women's, nor theirs with either chambermaids, nor theirs with washmaids. Also, for laundresses, when I travel, I will have them sent away before with the carriages, to see all safe. And the chambermaids I will have go before, that the chamber may be ready, sweet and clean. Also, that it is indecent for me to crowd up myself with my gentleman usher in my coach; I will have him to have a convenient horse to attend me, either in city or country. And I must have two footmen. And my desire is, that you defray all the charge for me. And for myself, besides my yearly allowance, I would have twenty gowns of apparel; six of them excellent good ones, eight of them for the country, and six other of them very excellent good ones. Also, I would have to put in my purse £2,000 and £200, and so you to pay my debts. Also, I would have £6,000 to buy me jewels, and £4,000 to buy me a pearl chain. Now, seeing I have been and am so reasonable unto you, I pray you do find my children apparel and their schooling, and all my servants, men and women, their wages. Also, I will have all my houses furnished, and my lodging chambers to be suited with all such furniture as is fit: as beds, stools, chairs, suitable cushions, carpets, silver warming-pans, cupboards of plate, fair hangings, and such like. So for my drawing-chamber in all houses, I will have them delicately furnished, both with hangings, couch, canopy, glass, carpet, chairs, cushions, and all things thereunto belonging. Also, my desire is that you would pay your debts, build up Ashby House, and purchase lands, and lend no money, as you love God, to my Lord Chamberlain, who would have all, perhaps your life, from you . . . . . . So, now that I have declared to you what I would have, and what it is that I would not have, I pray you, when you be an earl, to allow me £2,000 more than I now desire, and double attendance."

This letter had the effect of bringing Lord William to his senses, for it showed him that if he had a wife with money, she had a notion of spending it. Besides, he had his duties as Lord-Lieutenant to perform, and a great career was before him.

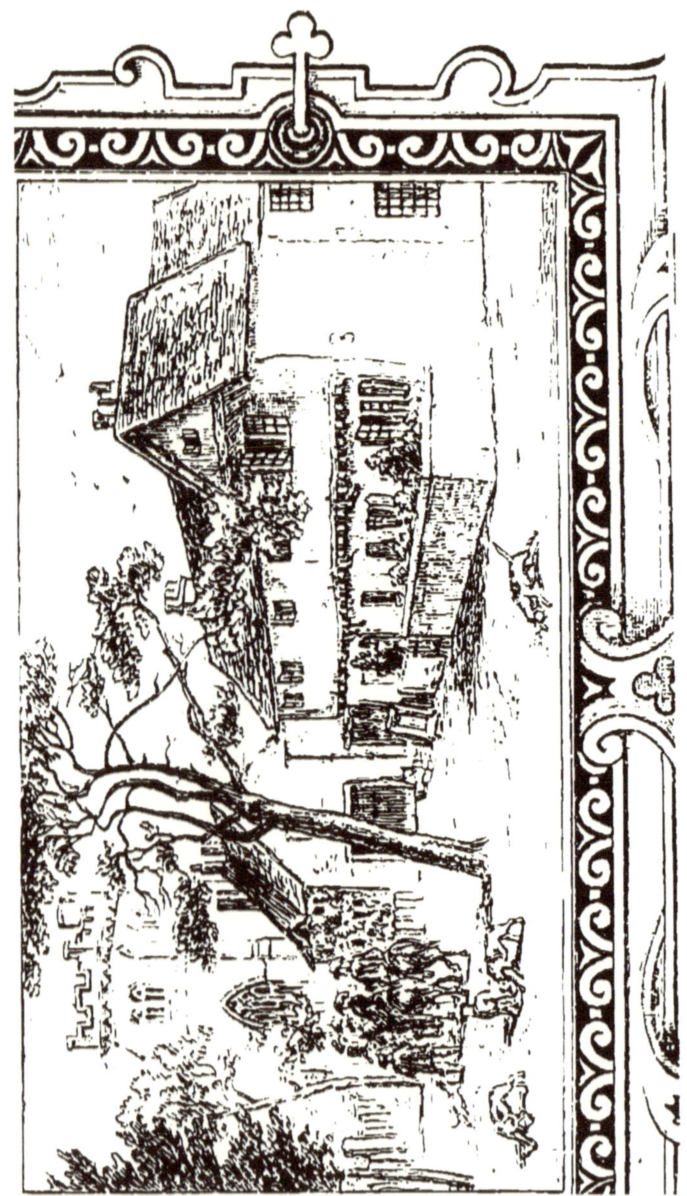

The Bloody Hunting Match at Dunchurch.

WHEN the sixteenth century was near its close, and it was known that good Queen Bess could not long survive, men's eyes turned longingly and wistfully towards her successor. The fêtes and junketings at Kenilworth were over. The proud Earl of Leicester, Robert Dudley, was dead; and his brother, the "good" Earl of Warwick, had only survived him a year. Kenilworth had fallen into the possesion of Sir Robert Dudley under the terms of his father's will, but he was absent from the country winning his spurs with the Earl of Essex at Cadiz; and with him were Carew, of Clopton, and Conway, of Ragley. The Shirleys had leased their ancient house to the Underhills, and were in Persia fighting the Turks; Shakespeare was buying property at Stratford; Michael Drayton was busy with his Polyolbion; Thomas Overbury was dreaming and calculating his chances in the great battle of life; whilst the studious Henry Ferrers, the antiquary, was collecting county pedigrees and other relics of the past, passing his time alternately between London and his old moated mansion at Baddesley Clinton. The more active spirits amongst the Puritans of the county sought employmen abroad, fighting for Protestantism in the low countrie whilst the Holtes, Grevilles, Harringtons, and Compton sought favour at Court, and waited patiently for th coming change, which they knew could not be lon delayed.

The members of the old faith, and they were many i Warwickshire at this period, brooded moodily over thei many wrongs. Many of them had been heavily fined a recusants, and they hoped that the coming change c dynasty would bring them some relief. They ha opened communications with James, and he had fe their hopes. They had seen his beautiful but unfortunat mother escorted across their shire by the leading count gentlemen,[*] on her last journey from Staffordshire t Fotheringay, and they longed for the time when at leas they could worship in their own way, freely, and i peace. There were, however, some amongst these stead fast believers in the old faith whose spirits chafed a delay. They could not wait, and were ever ready wit sword and dagger to take advantage of every opportunit to assert their claim to religious equality, and to do wha they conceived to be the bidding of the church, and th dictates of their priests. Amongst these restless me and ardent Catholics was Robert Catesby, of Lapwortl

* Sir John Harrington, Sir Thomas Lucy, Sir Fulke Greville, S Francis Willoughby, William Boughton, Edward Boughton, and Joh Shuckburgh (A.D. 1586).

a descendant of the great lawyer and faithful minister of Richard III., Sir William Catesby, who paid the penalty of his faithfulness to a losing cause two days after he was taken prisoner in the field of Bosworth, and whose body rests in the church of Ashby St. Ledger's, in Northants.

Robert Catesby appears to have been a gentleman of great force of character. He was tall and stately in his demeanour, his face, "noble and expressive"—a man of great possessions, not only in Warwickshire, but in Oxfordshire and Northants. His father, Sir William Catesby, who died in 1598, had been frequently fined and imprisoned for recusancy,* but Robert appears to have been a Protestant at one period of his life; and, indeed, it is upon record that all those engaged in the Gunpowder Plot were converts to the old faith, and that Catesby, his father, and his cousins, the Treshams, owed their conversion to Father Persons, Prefect of the Jesuits. Catesby appears to have been born at Lapworth in 1573, probably at his father's seat at Bushwood, which, though adjoining Lapworth, is in the parish of Old Stratford. There is no entry of his baptism either at Stratford or Lapworth, though the name of his servant and fellow-conspirator, Thomas Bates, appears in the register of the latter place.

* On the 15th November, 1581 (twenty-third Elizabeth), Sir William Catesby, Lord Vaux of Harrowden, and Sir Thos. Tresham, were cited before the Star Chamber for harbouring Jesuits in their houses.

That Catesby was at one time Protestant would appear from his having married Catherine, a daughter of Sir Thomas Leigh, of Stoneleigh, whose other daughter, Alice, married the clever, eccentric, and unfortunate Sir Robert Dudley, of Kenilworth, and became in subsequent years Duchess Dudley, whose pretentious monument,

BUSHWOOD, AS IT APPEARED AT THE COMMENCEMENT OF THE CENTURY.

erected in her life-time, yet remains in Stoneleigh Church. The mother of Catesby was a Throckmorton, of Coughton Court, an ancient Warwickshire family of some note, and she resided in the days of her widowhood at the old hall of Ashby St. Ledger's. In his ardent zeal for the Catholic faith, her son had joined the madcap Earl of Essex in the street fight with many other Warwickshire men, by which the discarded favourite sought to gain access to the Queen, and was wounded and captured in the fray. He only obtained his liberty by paying a fine of £3,000. Ever afterwards he was a plotter, a stirrer up of sedition, the bosom friend of Father Garnet, the Prefect of the English Jesuits, and the originator of that strange wild plot which gave rise to the "Bloody Hunting Match at Dunchurch."

The old Queen died at last—on the eve of Lady-day, 1603; and the news was conveyed to James I. by Sir Robert Carey, who appears to have been accompanied by his brother-in-law, who was a Warwickshire man, Thomas Berkeley, of Caludon, near the city of Coventry. When the news reached Warwick, the great Lent Assize was being held, and Sir Fulke Greville, of Beauchamp Court, threw up his cap and cried, "God save King James," and took immediate steps to proclaim the new king in the county town. The owner of Combe Abbey, Sir John Harrington, hastened to his seat at Exton, in Rutlandshire, to receive James on his progress from the north. Lord William Compton, of Compton Winyates, accompanied Queen Henrietta from Scotland to London, and was high in royal favour. George Carew, of Clopton, was made Governor of Guernsey, and was shortly afterwards made a peer. Harrington was likewise ennobled and entrusted with the education of the Princess

Elizabeth, the King's eldest daughter, at his mansion at Combe.

Whilst these honours were being distributed, Robert Catesby was a disappointed fanatic, a widower, and a brooder over his religious wrongs. The whole Catholic party were disappointed in James, but the Catholic party were divided into two distinct sections. The old English Catholics, like the Ferrerses and the Throckmortons, were disposed to obey the new order of things, and to wait patiently for better or more auspicious times. Those Catholics who followed the Jesuitical teaching of the day, and believed in Spain and the Vatican, were anxious to show how deeply they felt the hollow treachery of James, and the disappointment he had caused. It was a time of plots; and Robert Catesby was a plotter. He was in possession of vast estates, not only in Warwickshire, but in Northants and the adjacent counties. He possessed, however, all the wild unreasoning bigotry of a neophyte. He was stung by his heavy fine, he saw his relations suffering in pocket, in liberty, and in position, for the sake of the religion they professed, and as he passed to and from his lodgings at Lambeth, to his house at Moorcroft, near London Wall he could see St. Stephen's at Westminster, where the laws he suffered from were enacted; and gradually the idea grew that he could become the saviour of his religion by striking one blow at King, princes, and lords, when they met in Parliament assembled, and thus rid the country of Protestant ascendency. The idea was a wild one, but was not new. It had been proposed before; and the King's father had been destroyed by powder. Trains, mines, and powder, were familiar military instruments in the Low Country wars. They had been used for other purposes, and here was an opportunity greater than any before conceived to show the power of the vile brimstone, and the avenging hate of the Catholic people. It only required a strong will and helping hands, and these the great Warwickshire squire knew he could find. There was living with him at this time one Jack Wright, a master of fence, but a broken down squire from the north. He and his brother Kit could be relied on as helping hands, but active brains were required as well. There was Tom Winter, the younger son of a small Worcestershire squire, a fellow convert, a man of quick brains and active habits, who had seen some service too—he would doubtless do his bidding. Catesby was no common man; he was one of those who could command and impress his fellows with his peculiar influence. But Winter hesitated. Murder on so grand a scale startled him. He wanted to know the result in case they succeeded. He thought that something might be done by foreign help without so much destruction of innocent lives. These scruples were overcome after some delay and negotiations, and these four men, tainted with sedition, and suspected traitors, set seriously and earnestly to work to carry out their wild project of Catholic revenge and Protestant extermination. They had solicited foreign help; they had tried to enlist the assistance of the bitter enemies of England in aid of their religion and cause. When these plans failed, they began to perfect their plot without a thought of the resulting horror which must ensue if they succeeded. They had procured through Winter's mission to Sir William Stanley and Velasco, the aid of an experienced sapper, named Guy Fawkes, who had been a soldier in the Low Countries. He was a convert, too, and was well known to the Jesuit Fathers.

These were the men, and these were the means they proposed to employ to gain their ends. They proposed to mine under the throne, and when the King was surrounded by the nobles and princes on the occasion of opening Parliament, to fire the mine by means of a train and bury the King, Prince Henry, and all the magnates of the land in one common ruin. They further intended to seize Prince Charles, or, in default of him, the Princess Elizabeth, who was staying in the newly-built mansion of Combe with Lord Harrington. She was of royal blood, and was chosen to be the representative of Catholic rule in this broad land, and then to be married to some Catholic peer.

To carry out this idea of a mine it was necessary to

obtain possession of a building adjoining the Houses of Parliament. What house could they get? A cautious examination showed that there was a small stone tenement in Parliament Place, which seemed suited for their purpose. It leaned against the Prince's chamber, then forming part of the House of Lords. It was the official residence of one Whynyard, a yeoman of the wardrobe, and had been leased by him to the great Warwickshire antiquary, Henry Ferrers, or "Ferris," as he is called in the old histories and in the local dialect. When Bates brought this news to Catesby, the difficulty of obtaining possession seemed insurmountable. Ferrers was the neighbour of Catesby. It is only a couple of miles from Bushwood to Baddesley Clinton, and of course all Catesby's antecedents were known to Henry Ferrers. He would inquire what Catesby, a pardoned rebel, would require the house for, for though a Catholic family to the present day, the Ferrerses belonged to the English rather than to the foreign Catholic school. Evidently some fresh accomplice was necessary, whose character was free from suspicion and taint. This individual was found in Thomas Percy, a kinsman of the Earl of Northumberland, known in history as the "Wizard Earl." Percy had been a gallant in his youth, but was now a believer in the Jesuits, and had, moreover, married Jack Wright's sister. He felt himself slighted by the Court, and readily fell into the plot.

The house was taken in his name, and as he was one of the band of gentlemen pensioners, he readily satisfied Henry Ferrers as to his motive for requiring a residence near the Court; and on the 24th of May, 1604,* the agreement was signed, whereby the old antiquary received £20 for his lease, and the rent of £4 per quarter. Preparations were now made to commence the mine, but further help was wanted to take charge of the materials collected at Lambeth; and this induced the conspirators to admit Robert Kays, a reduced Catholic gentleman, into the plot. The mine was, after many fruitless attempts, abandoned, when it was found possible to obtain the cellars under the Parliament House. Here the conspirators stored their powder, and departed into the country to raise men and money.

A traveller from Warwick to Stratford-upon-Avon, after toiling up the hill of Coplow, is rewarded by a view of the extensive landscape which stretches across to the Edge hills on the south, and to Ilmington on the west. He will have Charlecote, Fullbrook, and Hampton Lucy pointed out to him, and his attention directed to the famous deer stealing exploits of Shakespeare. If he turns to the north for a moment, when he reaches the thir milestone, he will see a bye-road leading to a lone farm house pleasantly situated in the valley, amidst the undulating country of the red forest land of Arden. Th

* The original agreement is in the State Paper Office.

house is a modern structure of two gables, but it stands on the site of an ancient moated grange or manor-house, known as Norbrook. The site of the moat can yet be traced. This was the large and strong mansion house of John Grant, an accomplished but a moody gentleman.

REMAINS OF NORBROOK, PRIOR TO THE DEMOLITION.

who had been seduced by Essex's promise of religious toleration into joining his ill-starred street expedition. In the old Queen's time the persecuting spirit of the age had caused grief and lamentation within those moated walls, and Grant had become of a settled, melancholy disposition. He had married Tom Winter's sister, and in January, 1605, he accepted an invitation from Catesby, his old neighbour, to visit him at Oxford, in company with John Winter, of Huddington, his brother-in-law. Catesby wanted money. He had already sold his patrimonial estates at Lapworth and Bushwood to Sir Edward Greville, of Milcote, and more money was wanted to purchase the arms and equipment of the men necessary to seize the Princess Elizabeth, and to march on London when the great blow was struck. After some deliberation, these two country squires gave in their adherence and were sworn into the plot. The Lapworth serving man, Thomas Bates, who had seen the mine at Vinegar House, and whose suspicions must have been aroused was also admitted to a knowledge of the plot, and sworn to secrecy on the primer. He was the only one of the conspirators below the rank of a gentleman; and even he had suffered from the religious persecutions during Elizabeth's reign.

During the early part of the year it was found necessary to inform a larger circle of gentlemen of the existence of a plot than was at first contemplated. Power had been given to Percy and to Catesby to do this according to their discretion, with a view to obtain money and men. Thus Stephen Littleton, of Holbeach, and his younger brother Humphrey, were told that Catesby was raising a Catholic regiment of horse for service in Flanders with the Cardinal Archduke; and the promise of command in this regiment induced Stephen Littleton to raise a troop of horse and equip them for the service. Francis Tresham, of Rushton, Northants, cousin of Catesby, Sir Everard Digby, of Goathurst, Bucks, and Ambrose Rokewood, a great breeder of racehorses, of Coldham Hall, Suffolk, were induced to join Catesby, through the "great love" they bore him. The first promised £2,000; the second, £1,500; and the latter, horses, men, and money. Nothing, however, could be done until November; and after the disposition of the forces to be employed, the whole party, accompanied by the Jesuit fathers, went on a pilgrimage to St. Winifred's Well, in Flintshire.

The position of the conspirators in Warwickshire was as follows:—Grant's house at Norbrook was made the magazine and rendezvous of the conspirators. The site of the powder room to the east of the present house is yet pointed out. Catesby, after the sale of his property at Bushwood, appears to have made his mother's house at Ashby St. Ledgers his home. Wright's family were removed from Yorkshire to Lapworth, a good mile from Bushwood. Sir Everard Digby took up his residence at Coughton Court, the seat of the Throckmortons; the uncle of Catesby, the representative of the family, appears to have been a minor in 1605. Rokewood became a tenant of Clopton House, near Stratford-on-Avon, the seat of Lord Carew, who had married the heiress of the

Cloptons. Coughton is now standing in nearly the same state as it was at the plot, and the hall at Clopton is not much altered, though the house has been new fronted. On the eastern side of Warwickshire, at Shelford, John Littleton resided; and it was fondly hoped that he would join in the grand hunting match on Dunsmore, to which Sir Everard Digby had invited all the Catholic gentry on November 5, 1605, the rendezvous being the Lion Inn, at Dunchurch, from whence, on hearing of the blow being struck, they were to march on Combe, and seize the Princess Elizabeth.

There was much consultation, and much running to and fro amongst those interested in the plot, between the time of the pilgrimage and the time fixed for the blow to be struck. In these movements, Father Garnet, Ann Vaux, and Mrs. Brooksby, the daughters of Lord Vaux, of Harrowden, took a warm part. In the early days of November, the two ladies, Father Garnet, and Father Greenway were at Coughton.

In the centre of the flourishing village of Dunchurch, on the southern side of the open space leading to the church, is a long, low-gabled house with overhanging floors. The mouldings and general construction point it out to be of the Tudor era, though, from a date on the northern gable, it appears to have been repaired just prior to the Civil Wars. This was an old pack-horse inn, called the Lion. Mr. Matthew Bloxam was fortunate enough to identify this old house by means of some old maps as the rendezvous of the great hunting match, on Monday and Tuesday, the 4th and 5th of November, 1605; and thither Sir Everard Digby, John Grant, and his brother Francis, with his retainers and friends, marched. It was known that Rokewood had placed relays of horses along the road to London, and as the horses and the rider were the best, the news would not be long delayed when the blow was struck. The general feeling of those not in the secret was that of uncertainty. They knew that some movement was on foot, but what they did not know. We have a glimpse of the means employed to muster the gentlemen supposed to be well-affected to the conspirators. The Bull Inn, at Coventry, the site of the present barracks, in Smithford-street, in which Henry VII. was entertained the night after the battle of Bosworth, and in which Mary Queen of Scots, had been detained, was the scene of one of these gatherings. Humphrey Littleton, Robert Winter, Richard York, Stephen Littleton, and a person named Gorven were there, hoping to meet John Littleton from Shelford. John, whose hold of Shelford was not a secure one, did not come, and Winter went over next morning to tell him that his brother had had a quarrel, and wanted him at Dunchurch.

John replied churlishly, and would not go.* Winter then rode to Dunchurch, where he arrived about six o'clock. The news was not long in reaching him and his friends on that chill November eve, for he rode on with some of his companions to Ashby St. Ledgers, not farther, in a direct line, than five miles from Dunchurch.

The leading conspirators hovered about London until the time was at hand for the "great blow." On the 25th of October, Catesby was at White Webbs, a house taken really by Father Garnet, in Enfield Chase. The house taken by Percy in Parliament Place, called Vinegar House, was inhabited by Father Robartes, a Jesuit; Mrs. Gibbins, the porter's wife, being housekeeper. Tresham was in Clerkenwell. Guy Fawkes was at his lodgings in Butcher Row, near St. Clement's Danes. Tom Winter was at Montagu Close. Rokewood, Kay, and Kit Wright, were lodging with a Mrs. More, at St. Giles's Fields, and with them Percy was to stay when he returned to town with the Duke of Northumberland's rents. Jack Wright was at the Horse Ferry, Lambeth.

Lord Compton, the Lieutenant of Warwickshire, was in town. All was quiet and apparently unsuspicious about the Court. The Lady Elizabeth was still at

* John Littleton had been fined for going in the street broil of the Earl of Essex, and though his name is mentioned in the depositions, Dugdale states that he died in prison in the reign of Elizabeth. His nephew John is probably alluded to. (See ante, p. 227.)

Combe. Why should the conspirators suspect anybody or anything wrong? The famous letter was sent to Lord Monteagle on Saturday, October 26th, and if Cecil or any of the courtiers suspected any plot prior to this, they have left no evidence whatever to show it. On Monday, the 26th, Winter left Montagu House in search of Father Oldcorn and Jack Wright. On Wednesday, the 28th, Guy Fawkes visited the vaults, and found everything as he had left it. Still there was a suspicion of Tresham; and it was only on his solemn affirmation of innocence that the Northampton squire saved his life from Catesby's poignard, for he was suspected of having written the letter to Lord Monteagle. This was on Friday, and at one time it seemed as if the party was prepared for flight, but Percy returned to town, and laughed at the idea of the plot being discovered. Catesby spent Saturday in buying arms. Sunday arrived, and yet the conspirators could see no outward sign that their secret was known. The Jesuits, Oldcorn and Greenway, left on Monday for the country, with hopes of the successful result of the plot. Catesby and Jack Wright rode on quietly to Enfield Chase, where they were to sleep and then trot quietly on to Dunchurch in the morning, believing all was safe. Before midnight Fawkes was a prisoner and the town alarmed. It was then that it was seen that flight was the only chance of saving their lives; Fawkes might tell everything under the torture of the rack. In the early morning of Tuesday, the 5th, by various routes, the conspirators left London for the north. Rokewood was the last to leave. He started at eleven, and soon caught those who had started earlier. At Brick Hill he caught Catesby and Jack Wright, and beyond Fenny Stratford they met Percy and Kit Wright. Rokewood made the whole distance of eighty-one miles in less than seven hours. Percy and Kit Wright had to cast away their cloaks in that fearful race for life. They reached Ashby at six o'clock, just as Lady Catesby and her guests were sitting down to supper.

A few hurried words told that all was lost. The old hall supplied them with arms, and they rode hurriedly to Dunchurch—so hurriedly that one or more of them lost their way. At Dunchurch they found a large company assembled, and to them they could give but little hope. Morgan was there, Pierson, and Dimock. There were Sir Robert Digby, of Coleshill, and many other Catholic squires. It did not require any words to tell "all was lost," that the mysterious scheme had failed, and that every one must look for himself. Those who were not implicated in the plot, or otherwise compromised, began to depart to their several homes. One of the servants of the inn, George Prince, heard the words, "I doubt not we are all betrayed," spoken from one of the casemates of the inn, but what were the councils, and what the speech that night at the old Lion Inn, we shall probably never know. A smith, Bennette Leeson, of Ashby, says, that on the evening of the 5th of November some one came to his forge and asked the way to Dunchurch, offering "to contente him well if he would directe him thither," whereupon he went and rode before him. Presently there followed him some twelve horsemen, amongst whom was Mr. Robert Catesby. He "conducted them to Dunchurch, where they alighted at the sign of the Lion, at one Morrisen's house; and he walked their horses about for a quarter of an hour, and had two shillings for his pains. Bates, Catesby's man, came and entreated him to direct him the way to Rugby, which he did, and received twelve pence. At Rugby they met nine more men at the Bayliff's house, who were well mounted, and returned with them to Dunchurch, where they saw Catesby. They then, within a quarter of an hour of their coming, rode together Coventry way."

They now wanted money and men, arms and horses. They had resolved upon appealing to the Catholics for help, to make a stand against the King's forces. If Warwickshire and Worcestershire would not rise, the staunch Catholics of Wales would; and who could tell the issue of such a conflict? It was their only chance, though a desperate one, but, then, they were desperate men. On they rode across Bourton Heath, crossing the

Fosse way at Princethorpe, by the old encampment at Wappenbury, beneath the sombre shadow of Weston, and thence to Warwick through Lillington, halting at last at Norbrook. There were horses at Warwick; horses at the Castle, belonging to the King; horses at Mr. Benock's, the great trainer; and these were stolen in the night. But during that ride what thoughts must have passed through their excited brains! It was the time of the November meteors. If these "fiery shapes" met their eye, would it not seem like Heaven's judgment on their great premeditated crime? In the midst of their tribulation, they did not forget the anxious hearts at Coughton Court, where Fathers Greenway and Garnet, with Mrs. Brooksby and Ann Vaux, were waiting. Bates was despatched to them with a note, for no one else could be trusted who had a knowledge of the country lying between Alcester, Aston Cantlow, and Norbrook. We have a vivid description of the consternation of the two priests on the receipt of the news. There is an expression recorded of extreme caution on the part of Father Greenway, who afterwards went with Bates to Robert Winter's, at Huddington, where he met Catesby, and then went on to Hendlip Hall, where Garnet afterwards was captured. At Huddington, Tom Winter joined the party—Rokewood, Percy, and Morgan were exhorted to confess their sins, and make up their souls for death Father Hart, a Jesuit, absolved them, and the party then went northward, through Stourbridge, to Holbeach, in Staffordshire, where Stephen Littleton lived, and where the ruling spirits resolved to make a stand or die. On their road thither they seized a store of arms at Hewel Grange. Here came to them the Nemesis which had pursued them, for in drying the powder before the kitchen fire, which had been wetted in crossing the river, a live coal fell into the platter. Catesby, Morgan, Grant, and Rokewood were blown from their seats, and their faces scorched by the powder. The end was at hand. Sir Everard Digby, Bates, and Littleton left during the night. Robert Winter followed, but Tom Winter resolved to stand by his fellows and defend his compatriots to the last. At eleven o'clock in the day, Sir Richard Walshe, the Sheriff of Worcestershire, with the *posse comitatus* attacked the house. Tom Winter was shot through the right arm, Jack Wright and his brother Kit fell next, Rokewood was wounded, and Percy and Catesby were slain. Rokewood, Winter, Morgan, and Grant were taken prisoners, and Kay, Stephen Littleton, Digby, Tresham, Bates, and Robert Winter were also in custody. The plot was at an end, and the plotters were in the hands of justice.

In the meantime there was consternation in Warwickshire, and the written facts are somewhat in variance with those popularly received. Early on Wednesday morning, the 6th, whilst the conspirators were on their way to Huddington, Mr. Benock, the horse trainer, of Warwick, writes to Lord Harrington, at Combe, stating that he fears some great rebellion is at hand, for his private horses had been taken away by John Grant, of Norbrook, and asks what is to be done. Lord Harrington naturally thought of his charge, the Princess Elizabeth, and enclosed the letter of Benock to Lord Salisbury, and asks what is to be done if a rebellion takes place. Later in the day he writes to say that as the troubles were spreading, and being fearful of keeping the Princess in an unfortified house, he had sent her, to Coventry, under the care of Sir Thomas Holcroft (where the citizens were loyal) for greater preservation. We know from the town books that the citizens accepted the charge, called out the civic guard, and lodged the Princess with Mr. Hopkins in the Palace Yard, which yet remains. Early on the morning of the 6th, Warwick was in arms. Mr. Ralph Townsend, the Bailiff, was in readiness. The idea of cutting all the Catholics' throats is mentioned, but it was known that old Sir Fulke Greville was rousing up the country side, and taking arms from houses where the owners were absent, and munitions of war from the other. Sentinels were placed at all the fords and bridges. Two waggon loads of trunks, and furniture for houses, were seized at Barford. Mr. Combe, of Warwick, was an active magistrate. Sir Richard Verney, the Sheriff, and Sir

John Ferrers, of Tamworth, followed the conspirators. The Bailiff of Warwick lamented the absence of the Lieutenants of the train-bands in London, and mentions about fifty names as being with the party, whose total numbers did not reach sixty. From the many documents preserved, we know that early in September Rokewood took possession of Clopton, after a long parley with Robert Willson, who was in charge of the house, Grant and Winter vouching for Rokewood's intimacy with Lord Carew. Catesby, Sir Edward Bushell, Mr. Boise (who married Mr. Grant's sister), Mr. John Grant and his two brothers, Mr. Wright, Mr. Winter, Mr. Thomas (a kinsman of Mr. Rokewood's), Mr. Kay and his wife, Mr. Townsend, and Mrs. Morrison, a Lincolnshire gentleman's wife—Morrison was reported as having been staying at Grant's—were frequent visitors. On the Sunday after Michaelmas-day there was a great dinner, when many strangers attended; the practising of the great horses is mentioned, and also that Rokewood "lived on his penny." A cloak bag, containing "massing reliques," was captured by the Bailiff of Stratford. Mention is made of the capture of some of the conspirators in Snitterfield bushes, and the country people yet point out the spot. John Wright appears to have lived at Elsham, in Lincolnshire, for one of "his wenches" was brought by a William Kyddall, who afterwards went to London with Christopher Wright, and left, armed, on Monday. He was arrested on Thursday, at Barford. The young Mr. Grants—Walter, Ludovic, and Francis—denied all knowledge of the conspiracy. Mrs. Grant was arrested on the 13th, by Barth Hales, "a careful man in these uproars." She and her family appear to have been much respected, for the Sheriff's house was fired on the 15th to release them; and the Sheriff writes to Cecil to say that he will transmit his prisoners as soon as he could find fit men. The end was at hand. On the 23rd of November, Thomas Winter confessed. Grant confessed on the 17th January. The conspirators were hung; and Garnet shortly followed them to the gallows. Then came the grasping for the plunder. Amongst the numerous papers preserved in the Record Office, amongst those found by the Historical MSS. Commissioners, and amongst the Burleigh papers in the British Museum, the letters asking for a share of the effects of the conspirators are the most sad of all. The Sheriff (the Varney of Sir Walter Scott's novel of Kenilworth) asked for reward, but on July 11th, 1606, John Levingston and Mr. Hale received a grant of the goods and chattels of Sir Everard Digby, Grant, and Rokewood. On January 28th, 1607, Sir William Anstruther received a grant of the moiety of all goods belonging to Digby, Rokewood, Grant, Winter, Tresham, Catesby, Percy, and Garnet; and in November, 1608, one Ellis Rothwell presents a petition for certain rents to be granted to her out of the gunpowder treason

Thomas Lawley, the first man who entered Holbeach, desires to be remembered because he took Thomas Winter alive, and tried to revive Catesby, Percy, and the two Wrights. Out of this plot arose in some degree those agrarian disturbances at Hillmorton a few years later.

In May, 1607, large bodies of men, women, and children suddenly assembled in Warwickshire, Leicestershire, and Northamptonshire, to protest against the enclosure of hitherto open tracts on the estates of those conspirators whose lands had fallen into the hands of new proprietors, and on which the people had formerly right of pasturage. The feeling of the people was strong against enclosure. At Hillmorton they cut down hedges, filled up ditches, and laid open all enclosed fields which had been hitherto free of common. They termed themselves "Levellers," and placed themselves under a leader, named John Reynolds, whom they called Captain Rouch, but who was evidently a madman. The train-bands sympathized with the people, and it was only after a sharp skirmish with the regular troops, in in which Sir Henry Fookes, who led the foot, was "sore hurt," that the riots were put down. Reynolds was hung, drawn, and quartered. Many were condemned to death, though they neither committed "crime or atrocity," but acted in a mistaken sense of upholding their presumed rights.

T

Le Preux Chevalier.

On the Saturday preceding the great hunting match at Dunchurch, there was staying at Stoneleigh Abbey another disappointed man, who, in the popular opinion, was the embodiment of all that was chivalrous, learned, and honourable. At home and abroad, in the opinion of his countrymen and contemporaries, Sir Robert Dudley, knight of Kenilworth, was *Le Preux Chevalier*, the handsome, accomplished, but unfortunate son of Robert Dudley, Earl of Leicester. On the 2nd of November, 1605, he found himself disgraced, his mother dishonoured, and his prospects blighted. Nine years had elapsed since he had married Alice, the daughter of his neighbour, Sir Thomas Leigh, and at this time was the father of four daughters. The year 1605 was memorable to him, for the Court of Star Chamber had pronounced against his legitimacy on the 13th of May, and he had spent the intermediate time in vain endeavours to get the sentence altered.

The story of Sir Robert Dudley is the story of a hero of romance. He is the hero of Kenilworth, for the novel of Scott fades in interest when compared with his life, yet the scene and the actors are nearly the same. The very origin of his family is woven in mystery, for though his great grandfather, Edmund Dudley, was fiscal counsellor to Henry VII., and was reputed to be a descendant of the old lords of Dudley, cruel memories relate how Edmund's father, John, was a carpenter, whose only claim to his surname was that he followed his trade in the little town which had grown around the princely Castle of Dudley. Edmund had married one of the De Lisles, and when Henry VIII. ascended the throne, he was beheaded as a sacrifice to popular feeling because of his cruel imposts and exactions. When he died, his son John was only eight years old, yet he lived to be Lord of Dudley, Earl of Warwick, Duke of Northumberland, as well as the virtual ruler of the kingdom. When Edward VI. died, he endeavoured to raise his daughter-in-law, Lady Jane Grey, to the throne. This was an offence Queen Mary could not forgive, and he too, on the 22nd of August, 1553, forty-three years and four days after his father, lost his life and his head by the hands of the executioner. A few months before Queen Elizabeth ascended the throne, in November, 1558, the attainder against his sons, Ambrose and Robert, was removed. Ambrose had distinguished himself as a soldier, and in 1562 received his father's earldom, and was known as the "good" Earl of Warwick. Robert who was a polished and unscrupulous courtier, marreid

Amy Robsart, but the Queen had barely been on the throne two years ere the tragedy at Cumnor made him a widower. Amy Robsart died on the 8th of September, 1560, and in less than three years Lord Robert began to receive substantial marks of her Majesty's favour. On the 9th of June, 1563, he received a grant of the castle and manor of Kenilworth, and on the 27th of September, in the following year, was created Earl of Leicester, having been made Baron Denbigh the day previously. For twelve years after the death of Amy Robsart, Robert Dudley was the suppliant and grasping courtier of the Queen—dreaming of sharing the throne, refusing the hand of Mary Queen of Scots, passing his time in idle dalliance, in bold intrigues, or blustering insolence. His hopes of sharing the throne with Elizabeth were high in 1566, when Elizabeth visited Kenilworth for the first time. In August. 1572, she was again at Kenilworth, and in this year Robert Dudley again ventured on marriage with Lady Douglas Sheffield. There does not appear to be any reason to doubt the truth of this marriage at Asher, in Surrey. It was solemnized in the presence of witnesses by a lawful minister, and according to the forms of the Church of England. It was promoted by the Duke of Norfolk, but, for obvious reasons, the Earl of Leicester did not desire it to be made public. This was the marriage which Sir Walter Scott confounded with Amy Robsart; the issue of this secret marriage was *Le Preux*

Chevalier, Sir Robert Dudley. He was born at Shene (now Richmond), in Surrey, and at his baptism the Earl of Warwick and Sir Henry Lea were his godfathers, and Lady Dacres his godmother. Lord Leicester wrote to his wife thanking God for the birth of his son, "who might be their comfort and staffe in their old age," and subscribed himself "your loving husband." During the next three years Sir Robert was treated as the legitimate son of the Earl; but at the end of that time Walter Devereux, Earl of Essex, died, leaving Lady Lettice Knollys his widow. Captivated by the charms of this lady, Lord Leicester endeavoured to persuade his wife to disown her marriage, and offered her the then princely income of £700 per annum, if she would do so, in the Close Arbour of the Queen's palace at Greenwich, in the presence of Sir John Huband and George Digby. On her refusal, he terrified her with threats, and it was deposed that he offered her £1,000 to deliver up her son to Sir Edward Horsey, Captain of the Isle of Wight, who was present at the marriage, and, in fact, gave Lady Douglas away.

When, in July, 1575, Queen Elizabeth came to Kenilworth on her famous visit—when the "Princely Pleasures" were arranged in her honour—Leicester was perplexed with the rival claims and charms of Lady Douglas and Lady Essex. There is a mystery about the death of Walter Devereux, which Leicester's enemies—and he had many—attributed to poison, and fear of this fate probably induced Lady Douglas to remain silent when Leicester married the Lady Lettice Knollys, Countess of Essex. Rumours of Leicester's free and easy method of disposing of marriage ties had evidently reached Sir Francis Knollys, and this marriage was celebrated in his presence, and in the presence of witnesses, including a notary public. There was one child born of this marriage, the "noble imp," who died in his boyhood, and is buried in the Beauchamp Chapel, at Warwick. The marriage took place the year after the "Princely Pleasures," and Elizabeth, when she heard of it through the malicious interference of Mons. Simier, sent Leicester a prisoner to Greenwich Castle. During this period, and for seven years afterwards, *Le Preux Chevalier* resided with his mother, Lady Douglas; but when the boy was ten years of age, he was sent to school at Offington, in Sussex, and at the age of fifteen he was entered at Christ Church College, Oxford, as *comitis filius*, in the beginning of the year (1588) in which Leicester died. By the will of his father, which was made at Middlesborough, in the Low Countries, on August 1st, 1567, Ambrose, his brother, was left his heir, with remainder to his "base born" son, Robert Dudley. The young man was only seventeen years of age when he came into possession of Kenilworth Castle, and the manors his father bequeathed to him, by the death of the Earl of Warwick.

The spirit of adventure was strong in Robert Dudley. When he attained his majority, his first act was to equip an expedition to the South Seas, and he sailed for Trinidad on the 6th November in the *Bear*, a ship of 200 tons burden, with Captain Munck in the *Bear's Whelp*, and two small pinnaces. He parted company with his Vice-Admiral, and went alone along the coast of Spain to the Canaries, which he reached on December 14th. He had much sickness on board, but, capturing two small caravels, he maimed them, and sailed for the Island of Trinidad. In the account which Sir Robert wrote for Hakluyt's "Early Voyages," he describes his voyage, the native Indians, and the Carribean coast of Paria. Here he found a silver mine, and his crew entered one of the mouths of the river Orinoco. Here he was joined by one of his missing pinnaces, and after waiting for Sir Walter Raleigh, who did not come, he sailed for Bermuda, hoping to meet her Majesty's ships, to apprise them of a Spanish fleet. Here he met nothing but storms; but on his way home he fought a Spanish armada of 600 tons, until his powder was spent, and after narrowly escaping being wrecked on the Isles of Scilly in a fog he arrived home. He tells us that, though he and his fleet took, sunk, and burnt nine Spanish ships, including the one he fought on his way home, which subsequently sunk, he gained nothing by the adventure.

About this time he married one of the daughters of

Thomas Cavendish, the great navigator; but he seems to have died shortly afterwards, and Robert Dudley joined the army of the Earl of Essex in the expedition to Cadiz, and for his gallantry was knighted by the Earl, who was the son of Lady Lettice Knollys, titular Countess of Leicester, by her first husband. Later in the year he arrived again at Kenilworth, wooed and married Alice Leigh, and in September following his first daughter, Alicia Douglassa, was born.

Whilst Elizabeth was yet alive, he instituted proceedings to prove his legitimacy, with a view of claiming the earldoms of Leicester and Warwick. The titular Countess of Leicester was residing at Drayton Basset, her dower house, mourning the loss of her rash son, when she heard of these proceedings, which would render her marriage with Leicester null and void. She immediately filed a bill against Sir Robert for defamation, and when James I. ascended the throne, Lord Sidney, of Penshurst, who had married Mary Dudley, the sister of Robert and Ambrose, stopped the proceedings which had been taken at Lichfield, and caused all the depositions to be brought to the Star Chamber, where, after eighteen months' delay, judgment was pronounced against his claim, on the 13th of May, 1605, and the whole of the papers and depositions impounded and sealed up. Dugdale appears to have seen them, and they were quoted as late as 1824 before a Committee of the House of Lords, on a claim being made for the barony of De Lisle by the Sidneys, of Penshurst. In the course of these proceedings, the cruel manner in which justice was denied Sir Robert was plainly set forth.

Chagrined and disappointed, Sir Robert applied for and obtained license to travel in Italy for three years. He left his wife and children behind him, as well as envious hearts, for before his license expired he was recalled by writ of Privy Seal, which he could not obey, and his castle and all his lands were seized under the Statute of Fugitives for the King's use. In 1611, a forcible sale was effected for £14,500 to Prince Henry, the eldest son of James I., though it had been previously valued at £38,550, a sum admittedly below its value. Only £3,000 of this sum was ever paid, in consequence of the death of Prince Henry, and even this small sum never reached the hands of Robert Dudley, for the merchant to whose care it was entrusted failed.

From this time henceforth, Sir Robert Dudley was a stranger in the land of his birth. He settled in Florence, and though there are evidences of his desire to conciliate King James, these were unavailing; indeed, his book about bridling parliaments and establishing a despotism saw the light at a time when it was likely to do far more harm than good. He forgot and neglected Dame Alice and his children, and entered into an alliance with Elizabeth Southwell. He was the friend of Cosmo II. and the Duke of Tuscany, and busily employed himself in raising the then insignificant fishing village of Leghorn into a distinguished city and finely fortified port. In 1620, Ferdinand II., Emperor of Germany, raised him to the title of Duke of Northumberland, by diploma, for his distinguished services, for Dudley was the Admirable Crichton of his day. He composed a healing powder, known in Italy as the *Pulvis comitis de Warwick*—the Warwick powder—which was largely believed in. He published the "Catholicon," a popular medical work, of which no copy now exists. His great work, the "Del Arcano del Mare,"—the "Secret of the Sea"—was in six parts, and republished several times. In this work he illustrated the principle of "great circle sailing." He was one of the first to train dogs to set a partridge, and, indeed, the catalogue of his accomplishments would fill many pages. In 1630, Pope Urban VIII. gave him the power of creating nobles. When Lady Lettice died the manors of Long Itchington, Temple Balsall, and other property, were taken possession of by the Sidneys, of Penshurst, under an entail; but Sir Robert instituted proceedings to recover this property, given to him by his father's will, but died in 1649 before the question could be settled, for the country was embroiled in civil war. In the church of St. Pancras, in Florence, there is a carved shield bearing the bear and ragged staff, showing where he and Elizabeth Southwell, and many of their children, found a last resting place.

It must not be supposed that Dame Alice Dudley, his wife, and four daughters, were unprovided for. She had a jointure of £14,000 on the Kenilworth property; and, in 1621, an Act of Parliament was passed to enable her to sell this jointure in the life-time of her husband, as though she was a *femme sole.* She appears to have had possession of Dudley House, near Leicester Square, when she died. On the 23rd of May, 1645, Charles I. made her a Duchess, and her children were granted the precedence of duke's children. In 1660, the Chancery suit was revived for the recovery of the Long Itchington and Balsall estates by Dame Alice Dudley, and this suit was successful, and Charles II. confirmed her in the honour and title of Duchess. It was not till her husband had been in the grave twenty years, and more than sixty years after her desertion, that this good and noble woman died at her house in St. Giles-in-the-Fields, in the county of Middlesex. Her stately tomb, erected in her lifetime, still remains in the chancel of Stoneleigh Church, and an engraving of it, without the inscription, may be found in Dugdale.

The charities of the Duchess and her daughters yet remain. With £3,000 given by her eldest daughter on her death bed, the Duchess Dudley purchased an estate at Mancetter for the augmentation of six poor livings—Leek, Wootton, Ashow, Kenilworth, Monk's Kirby, and Stoneleigh—to the extent of £20 a year. To these churches she also gave the beautiful communion plate they still use. The youngest daughter, Lady Katherine Levison, founded the hospital for thirty-five poor widows and the schools which still exist at the highly interesting village of Temple Balsall, and charged her estate at Foxley, in Northants, with sufficient funds to repair, and keep in repair, the Beauchamp Chapel at Warwick in which her grandfather, Robert, Lord Leicester, and his brother Ambrose, are interred.

The Queen of Hearts.

THE story of the "Queen of Hearts," as the Lady Elizabeth Stuart, the eldest daughter of James I., was called in the latter part of her chequered career, is one of the most pathetic chapters of history. Born at Falkland, in Fife, on the 19th of June, 1596, we know but little of her early years, save that she accompanied her mother, Anne of Denmark, in her progress to England, after the accession of her father, James I., to the English throne, on the death of Queen Elizabeth, her great namesake. Her mother, notwithstanding her many weaknesses and foibles, was fond of her children, and it requires no effort of imagination to picture the parting of the mother and daughter at Dingley, in Leicestershire, on the 25th of June, 1603, when Elizabeth, according to the custom of the times, was separated from her family in order to be educated as became her rank, and instructed in sound Protestant principles. The gentleman to whom she was entrusted was John, Lord Harrington, Baron of Exton, in the county of Rutland, and at this period, in right of his wife, owner of Combe Abbey, in the county of Warwick.

Combe Abbey was one of the three great Cistercia abbeys of Warwickshire, the others being Merivale founded in 1148 by Robert, Earl of Ferrers, and Stone leigh, built by Henry II. in the year 1154. Combe wa intermediate in date, for it was built by Richard d Camville in the year 1150, and was largely endowe After being in possession of the monks for 389 years, a the dissolution of the religious houses it was granted b Edward VI. to John Dudley, Earl of Warwick, and o his attainder it reverted to the Crown, and became th property, by purchase, of Robert Kelway, a lawyer o some renown, whose only daughter, Anne, married S John Harrington, of Exton. Lord Compton had forme one of the escort of Anne of Denmark and the Prince from Scotland, so the Princess did not come to Wa wickshire an entire stranger to the principal inhabitan of the county. The Abbey itself had been adapted as place of residence, and its general aspect was preserv until a recent period.* In the sylvan scenery Combe, in the old manor of Smite, the Lady Eliz beth found a home and many friends. Lady Harrin ton appears to have been a woman of considerab ability, and her daughter Lucy was as versatile she was extravagant. Elizabeth's favourite compani

* The east wing has been recently pulled down and rebuilt on a mo extensive scale, from the designs of Mr. Wesfield. It is far from co plete.

was Ann Dudley, the niece of Lord Harrington. With Ann Dudley Elizabeth formed a lasting friendship. When the Lady Elizabeth became a resident at Combe, Lord Harrington appointed Master John Tovey, A.M., head master of the Free School, Coventry, to be his chaplain, and to assist him in the education of the Princess.* The life of this young girl seems to have been singularly happy at Combe, and she appears to have cherished the memory of the sylvan glades, the flower-decked ways, green meadows, and long stretches of soft purple landscape over the midland vale. She is described as showing excellent abilities at her studies; she was docile, quick of apprehension, and exceedingly affectionate. Her portraits at Combe have a soft dreamy look, but she was in early life vivacious and affable. Her graceful form she inherited from her mother, and from her father she derived a love of pageantry and show. She appears to have visited many of the county families, and on the 3rd of April, 1624, she made a public entrance into the neighbouring city of Coventry, where she was entertained in St. Mary's Hall, and presented with a silver cup, which cost the city £29 16s. 8d. On this occasion Master Tovey preached a sermon before her in St. Michael's Church. She rode to the Cross and visited the library at

* This gentleman was known for his uncompromising Protestantism. He died in 1614, after his return from abroad, it is said of slow poison, administered by the Jesuits.

the Free School, founded by Tovey two years before, and "gave some money to it." The attention to the Princess which this visit caused doubtless led to the powder-plot conspirators arranging for "the hunting match at Dunchurch," for Combe Abbey was defenceless; and as the Lady Elizabeth at the time of this visit was only eight years of age, it was thought that she might be educated in the Roman Catholic faith, and affianced to some nobleman of the same persuasion. On the 6th of November, Lord Harrington received intelligence of the rising at Dunchurch, and late in the afternoon he removed the Princess to Coventry for safety, and lodged her with Mr Hopkins, who lived at the Palace Yard, High Street, which still exists much in the same state as when the Princess lodged there. The citizens mounted guard, and there is yet preserved an account of the bows, pikes, black bills corslets, partisans, halberds, and gloves delivered to Mr Collyns, the mayor, and nine other citizens, from the city armoury on this occasion. When the disturbances were over, Elizabeth returned to Combe and resumed her studies. In 1609, she visited London with Lord Harrington and his family, and on this occasion she partook of the Court festivities, and witnessed several of the rude and brutal sports of the time, including lion, bear, and dog fights, at the Tower. There is little recorded of the after life of the Princess at Combe. She appears to have been serious and sedate, and her character imbued with thoughtfulness far beyond her years. She was only thirteen years of age when she addressed to Lord Harrington the following verses :—

"This is a joye—this is true pleasure,
If we best things make our treasure,
And enjoy them at full leisure,
Evermore in richest measure.

God is only excellent,
Let up to him our love be sent;
Whose desires are set and bent
On ought else shall much repent.

Theirs is a most wretched case
Who themselves so far disgrace,
That they their affections place
Upon things named vile and base.

Earthly things do fade, decay,
Contentations not one day;
Suddenly they pass away,
And man cannot make them stay.

All the vast world doth contain
To content men's hearts in vain,
That still justly will complain,
And unsatisfied remain.

Why should vain joys us transport?
Earthly pleasures are but short,
And are mingled in such sort,
Griefs are greater than the sport.

God, most holy, high, and great,
Our delight doth make complete;
When in us He takes His seat,
Only then we are replete.

Oh my soul, of heavenly birth,
Do thou scorn this basest earth;
Place not here thy joy and mirth,
Where of bliss is greatest dearth.

From below thy hand remove,
And effect the things above;
Set thy heart and fix thy love
Where thy truest joyes shall prove.

To me grace, O Father, send,
On Thee wholly to depend,
That all may to Thy glory tend;
So let me live, so let me end."

In the early part of the year 1612, Elizabeth, then i her sixteenth year, was introduced to her father's Cour on her education being completed. Here she seems · have won all hearts, though her stay was but brief, fc as young as she was, her marriage was the subject negotiation. The Elector Palatine appears to have be in every way a suitable match for Elizabeth, though l suit did not meet with the approval of the que mother, whose great ambition was to see her daughter queen. She even went so far as to try to dissuade l daughter from the match: "As you are the daughter a queen," she urged, "be also a queen yourself; thi how you will like to be called *Goody Palsgrave!*" Pa grave being the German title of the Elector Frederi Elizabeth waited patiently amid all this for the arri of her suitor before she gave a final answer.

On the 16th of October, 1612, Frederick embarked on board a splendid yacht for England, and the next day arrived at Gravesend. On the 18th he proceeded with a gay cavalcade on board a royal barge, and proceeded up the Thames, amid the acclamation of crowds of spectators. On passing the Tower he was greeted with a royal salute, and at Whitehall he was received by Prince Charles, then eleven years of age, the Prince of Wales being ill at the time. The Elector won the approval of the Court by his princely demeanour and courtesy, though his want of a regal crown was lamented. Apartments were assigned to him in St. James's Palace, and he had frequent opportunities of joining the Royal family. Elizabeth appears to have been much pleased with him, and at this time she was still under the protection of Lord and Lady Harrington. She invited him to a solemn supper, which was followed by a masque, then one of the popular entertainments of the Court. The joys and festivities of the period were overshadowed by the untimely death of Henry, Prince of Wales, to whom the Princess had been sincerely and affectionately attached. Her letters to her brother are models of tender affection and fine sensibility. The Prince Palatine showed how deeply he sympathized with the Royal family in their affliction; but the King liked not any melancholy humour, and feasting, junketing, and jolity were maintained, for, as King James said, "If he had lost one son, he had found another." The King heeded not the whispers that the Prince had died of poison, and that Robert Carr, Viscount Rochester, his favourite, was implicated. On the 27th, Elizabeth and Frederick were betrothed with great pomp, to the evident delight of the nation, who viewed this Protestant alliance with great favour.

The general feeling of the nation is expressed in the lines addressed by Sir Harry Wotton to Elizabeth, commencing—

> "You meaner beauties of the night,
> That weaklie satisfie our eies
> More by your number than your lighte,
> Like common people of the skies,
> What are you when the moon doth rise?"

The marriage took place on Valentine's-day, 1613 the marriage being hurried on by James, because of th lavish expenditure to which he was put by entertainin the Elector and his friends. We have contemporar records of the ceremony. One writer,* in describing th Princess, says, "Her vestments were white, the embler of innocency; her hair dishevelled, hanging down he back, an ornament of virginity; a crown of fine gol upon her head, the cognizance of majesty, being all ov beset with precious gems, shining like a constellatior her train, supported by twelve young ladies, in whi garments, so adorned with jewels, that her passage look

* Arthur Wilson.

like a milky-way." Whilst the Archbishop of Canterbury was performing the marriage we are told "some eruscations and lightnings of joy appeared in her countenance that expressed more than an ordinary smile, being almost elated to laughter, which could not clear the air of her fate, but was rather the forerunner of more sad and dire events." But these events were then in the unknown future, and were not thought of in the general rejoicings, the ringing of bells, and the firing of cannon. The city of London vied with the Court in celebrating the event, and ere two months had passed away, the Elector and his fair bride left the fireworks and the pastimes, friends and relations, to proceed to their future home at Heidelberg. These espousals had cost the King no less a sum than £140,000, and the Queen had called her daughter publicly "Goody Palsgrave." Lord Harrington received the privilege of coining copper money, to recoup him for the trouble and expense of educating the King's daughter, for the King was so impoverished that he had no other means of payment.

Ann Dudley and the Harringtons accompanied the Princess to Germany, and the party arrived at Flushing on the 28th of April, and in their progress to Amsterdam they were cordially received. Here the party tarried awhile, whilst Frederick hastened forward to make arrangements for the reception of his royal bride. The Princess and her suite in the meantime proceeded slowly up the Rhine in a splendidly decorated yacht, to the sound of music. Touching here and there, and everywhere received with demonstrations of joy, the beauty of that month of May must have ever remained a green and sunny spot on Elizabeth's memory. On the confines of the Palatinate she was met by her husband and his retainers, and along the route to Heidelberg she found herself the object of the people's love. Every person endeavoured to make her future home pleasant to her, but none more so than the dowager Juliana, who welcomed her at the gates of princely Heidelberg itself.

The Castle of Heidelberg must always be associated in the minds of English and Scotch with the memory of Elizabeth Stuart. It is grand even in its ruins; but it was magnificent in May, 1613. The British party were enchanted with it and the reception they received. Jousts, tournaments, and spectacles were held for their entertainment, and the German nobility showed how warm was their appreciation of the great English Princess. In a recess on the hills the Elector caused a garden in the English style to be made for the pleasure of Elizabeth, and over its portals the Royal arms of England can yet be traced.

For five years the sun of felicity beamed on this happy pair. Sons and daughters blessed their union. Religion graced their life, and every earthly wish seemed gratified. It was, however, a period of intolerance and bigotry. Men's passions and feelings ran high. Even in England men had been burnt for heresy. Scotland was the home of furious Presbyterianism. The Puritans were gathering strength in England. The fate of the Huguenots was not forgotten in France. The Netherlands were full of memories of papist persecutions, and Germany was the birthplace of Luther. Frederick himself was the hope of Protestant Germany. In his household Abraham Scultelus was established as chaplain. He was an austere and a rabid disciple of Calvin, and he prophesied day by day that "under Frederick's banner truth would spread and take root over the whole German Empire; by his interposition, all were to be reclaimed from idolatry to the pure faith of the Gospel." At this time Germany was convulsed with the disputed succession to the crown of Bohemia, to which the Archdukes of Austria, as Emperors of Germany, claimed a prescriptive right. The Emperor Ferdinand II. had just succeeded his father, the Emperor Matthias, a rigid Catholic, when the smaller German Protestant States resolved to elect a prince of their own persuasion to the vacant throne, and they offered it to Frederick, the Elector Palatine. His mother dissuaded him from accepting the perilous honour, but Elizabeth had high notions of kingly dignity and of Protestant supremacy. Her mother had inculcated in her mind the wish to be a queen. Years after it was remembered against her that, when her husband hesitated to accept the crown of Bohemia, she exclaimed, "Let me rather eat dry bread at a king's table than feast at the board of an elector." It was a wild and romantic wish, too soon, alas! to be realized.

The succeeding events belong not to Warwickshire, but to European history. The result was the inauguration of what is known as the Thirty Years' War. At Prague, the capital of Bohemia, Scultelus stirred the smouldering fires by preaching against Lutheranism as well as Popery. Thus, at a time when all should have been united, Protestants were divided amongst themselves. A year after entering Prague the war commenced, and Frederick saw himself deserted by his friends, his hereditary estates overrun by the Spaniards. He made a gallant attempt to save himself and his kingdom on November 8, 1620, beneath the walls of Prague; but he had not only enemies without but treachery within. Elizabeth became almost heroic in her misfortunes. She forbade the hopeless defence of the city, and retired with her husband, derisively called the "Winter King," to Breslau, in Silesia. Shortly afterwards, in the strong castle of Küshin, Prince Maurice was born, when kingdom, palatinate, electorate, rank, station, high hopes, and grand designs were lost. Notwithstanding the touching letters which Elizabeth wrote to her father; notwithstanding the indignation of the people of England; James I. neither gave encouragement or help to his only daughter. He left her to her pitiable fate. Deserted, betrayed, and neglected, the royal fugitives left Germany and took refuge in Holland. She was attended by Ann Dudley—who had been married to Count Schomberg, killed at Prague—by a young English volunteer named Hopton, and a few cavaliers, about eighty in number, as a guard. Elizabeth's conduct in misfortune was admirable; while Frederick seemed to melt under adversity. The death of his promising eldest son, Henry Frederick, under distressing circumstances in the Zuyder Zee, crushed his spirits, and he never held up his head again.

In the struggles which ensued, we find the names of enterprising young Englishmen mixed up with such historic names as Tilly, Wallenstein, and Gustavus Adolphus. When the Swedish hero was slain at the battle of Lutzen, Frederick was dying at Mentz. On the 17th of February, 1629, in the thirty-sixth year of his age, he breathed his last, and found a grave in the now eventful town of Sedan. His unfortunate Queen then devoted herself to her family. Her eldest surviving son, the selfish and arrógant Charles Louis, who ultimately succeeded to the Palatinate, showed a heartless disregard of his mother. Her other children were sources of anxiety to her. The English civil wars interrupted the small annuity she received from England, and the Queen of Bohemia became little better than a pauper begging her bread. Thus was she punished for having resolved to be a queen. She had drunk misfortune to the dregs.

In the meantime, her early home at Combe was undergoing strange vicissitudes. Her old friend, Lord Harrington, had died on his way home from Heidelberg on the occasion of her wedding. His son did not long survive him, and Combe and its lordships fell to the inheritance of her old friend Lucy Harrington, who had married the Earl of Bedford. Lucy was the friend of Ben Jonson, and the cynosure of the literary genius of the period; but her extravagant liberality was so great that she had to sell Combe Abbey in 1622 to Elizabeth, the widow of Sir Thomes Craveń, Lord Mayor of London, whose descendant, Lord William Craven, held it for many years.

Lord Craven, the owner of the mansion in which she had spent her youth, generously and chivalrously devoted himself to her service. Whilst her sons, Prince Rupert and Maurice, were fighting and shedding blood almost within sight of Combe, the lord of the abbey was her faithful friend. There is a touching tenderness in this romantic attachment, for though the "Queen of Hearts" had the art of captivating all strangers who were brought in contact with her, she had no pleasure or comfort with her children. The eldest and the most promising of her thirteen children was drowned in the Zuyder Zee, three died young, and Charles Louis inherited a portion of the Palatinate, and neglected his mother. The wild and thoughtless Princes, Rupert and Maurice, were a portion of their time but little better than pirates after the battle of Naseby. Edward, the fourth son, abjured Protestantism and became a Roman Catholic. Philip, the fifth son, slew a defenceless man in the market place at the Hague, and fled to France, where he became a soldier of fortune, and was slain in the Civil Wars. Edward was married, but became a Roman Catholic. Her daughters, too, gradually deserted her.* The able and intellectual Elizabeth left her mother to reside with her aunt, the Electress Dowager of Brandenburg. Sophia, the youngest daughter, was received by her brother at Heidelberg. Henrietta Maria was espoused, in 1651, by Ragotski, Prince of Transylvania, and died shortly afterwards. Louisa cruelly deserted her mother without warning, and entered a convent in France. Thus the Queen of Bohemia became childless and desolate, and in her old age, broken in health and spirits, she accepted an invitation of her nephew, Charles II., to come to England. She arrived at Margate on the 17th of May, 1661, and proceeded to the mansion of her friend, Lord Craven, in Drury Lane, then on the out-

* Miss Berger, in her "Life of the Queen of Bohemia," gives a long and interesting account of the daughters.

skirts of the metropolis. She returned only to die. She was neglected alike by Cavalier and Puritan. She left all her wordly possessions—a few pictures and a few books—to Lord Craven. Nothing is known of her decease, but in a contemporary chronicle occurs this brief notice, "On the 13th of February, 1662, died the Queen of Bohemia—a princess of talents and virtues not often equalled, rarely surpassed." Though she died in obscurity, Elizabeth Stuart received a royal funeral, and her remains were interred in Westminster Abbey on the 1st of March, 1662.

Though Elizabeth, when young and when old, was under the protection of the Lords of Combe, she was the ancestor of kings and queens. Her son Rupert survived her, as Governor of Windsor Castle, till 1682. Charles Louis died in 1680, but his son only survived him five years. His daughter, Charlotte Elizabeth (who had been principally brought up by her aunt Sophia, and well educated), in 1671, at the age of nineteen, became the second wife of Philip, Duke of Orleans, the only brother of Louis XIV. of France, whose first wife was Henrietta, daughter of Charles I. Charlotte's son became the noted Regent of France during the minority of Louis XV. She lived till 1722, when she died at St. Cloud. From her Louis Philippe is lineally descended. Had they been Protestants, the family of Orleans would rightly have occupied the throne of England.

Elizabeth's youngest daughter, Sophia, was the only one of her children, who had issue, who remained a Protestant. Four years before her mother's death, she had married Ernest Augustus, the titular bishop of Osnaburg. The match was not a brilliant one, but by a succession of deaths, her husband became the Elector of Hanover. In 1660, she gave birth to George Louis, who succeeded his father in 1700. Death and fortune had gradually cleared the way between her and the English throne. By an Act of Parliament, passed in 1708, the crown of Great Britain was secured to her, and to her descendants, being Protestants, to the exclusion of all other claimants. Like her mother and grandmother, Sophia longed to be greeted with the title of queen. She hoped to survive Queen Anne, but it was not to be. She died three months before Anne, and her son ascended the throne as George I. Thus, through this unfortunate lady, so intimately connected with Combe Abbey, our present Royal family claim descent through the Stuarts, the Tudors, and the Plantagenets, to the throne of England.

Combe even now teems with memorials of the unfortunate Queen. Her likeness and the likenesses of her husband, sons, and daughters, beam from the walls and corridors. Though the west wing has been altered and the east rebuilt, there yet remains the cloister in which she must have played and studied, rooms in which she dwelt, and the gardens in which she wandered.

Many of the old trees, which now rear their hoary heads aloft were there in her day. The armour hangs in St. Mary's Hall, Coventry, where she feasted, and though desolate, Palace-yard is still in being. The Queen of Hearts has a green memory among the glades of Combe.

* * * * * *

In the early part of the present century, Combe had another lady, named Elizabeth, whose romantic autobiography has been published to the world. Elizabeth Berkeley married Mr., afterwards Earl of Craven. She was the mother of seven children, and her portrait, which hangs at the head of one of the smaller staircases, shows her to have been a beautiful woman. After living with Lord Craven for thirteen years, they separated, and she went a tour, and found a home at the Court of the Margrave of Anspach. She visited with him, and on the death of Lord Craven, married him, and came to England. Queen Charlotte refused to receive her at Court. Her husband disposed of his principality to the King of Prussia, and bought Brandenburgh House, Hammersmith. In 1806 the Margrave died, and the Margravine went abroad, and died at Naples in 1828. She wrote many plays and poems, but her autobiography is more interesting, from its reminiscences of Warwickshire and the neighbourhood. There are few localities which can claim so intimate a relationship with two German principalities as the old Abbey of Combe.

The Swan of Avon.

On the banks of the placid Avon, the river over which the loving willows droop and kiss the surface of the stream with their earliest catkins and grey leaflets, where the "mary-buds ope their golden eyes" to greet the sun of spring and the cuckoo flowers fringe the brooklet which rushes to hide itself in the greater stream, the "Swan of Avon" first saw the light. The crown imperial raised its coronet above "the pansies freaked with jet and the streak'd gillivers" which Dorcas scorned, and in the meadows the bold oxlips raised their freckled cups over the "violets dim," and the "pale primroses that die unmarried" to form the birthday garland of Warwickshire's greatest son.

The old river ran smoothly by the slopes of Copdock and through the meadows of Charlecote as of yore. The big leaves of the water lilies had not found a resting place on its bosom, when its face wreathed in smiles as it passed through the many-arched bridge, then just finished, and received on its bosom the reflection of the church, which was to be for many ages the shrine of the poetic pilgrims of the world. It washed the shores of the weir brake ere it received the rays of the unclouded sun at Luddington's ford, as it went on its way to Hillborough and Bidford, where it was ever to be associated with the name of Shakespeare in tradition and in story.

Elizabeth had been Queen of England some five or six years, and the people had begun to breathe freely and think freely under the new freedom which had succeeded the black clouds of Mary's reign, when, on a bright April morning in the year 1564, a well-to-do burgher of Stratford-on-Avon, residing in Henley Street, was greeted with the news that he was the father of a male child. It was an event which gave no small delight to the gentle mother, for, though she had borne two female children during the six or seven years of her wedded life, her tender nurslings, Joan and Margaret, had either died in infancy or survived at most but a few months. There was joy, therefore, in the house of John Shakespeare when his eldest boy first saw the light which forced its way through the chequered quarries of the birth-room. The lark sang at heaven's gate the joyful news, and the flower buds shook their bells in the spring winds. Hope was young, and the gentle mother, whilst she pictured forth the glorious future of her boy, shrunk somewhat with dread as she thought of his dead sisters, who lay in the cold churchyard, with naught but the company of the big elm trees and the idle ripple of the Avon to soothe their last long sleep.

The well-to-do burgher, John Shakespeare, if he did not share the raptures of the mother, thanked heaven that Mary had her wish, and that he had an heir to the prosperity which had blessed his labours during the twelve years he had resided in Stratford. He had worked hard it is true, but then he worked at first with a view to provide a home for the sweetheart waiting for him in the sylvan nook at Wilmcote; but now he was married, and his wife's fortune had helped him on in the world until he was a prosperous trader, though careless of many matters which the Court of Aldermen deemed of importance.

In his dreams, John Shakespeare must have thought now and then of his early days, when tilling the small farm at Snitterfield, which his father, Richard Shakespeare, rented from Robert Arden, of Wilmcote. From that upland village his eye must have wandered over the extensive Feldon, diversified by wood and watered by the Avon. He could see the fringe of hills which marks the Oxfordshire boundary, as well as the heights of Ettington and Ilmington on the west. As he strolled along the lane to Welcombe, he could see the spire and towers of Stratford, by the side of the silvery Avon, over the tufted and bushy dingles which lay between. It was not more than three miles across the table-land to Pathlow, and from thence could be seen the tree-embosomed homestead of Wilmcote, which seemed so cosy in the valley beneath, between the Alne and the Billesley hills. When the evening sun set behind the heights of the ridgeway which overlooks the old Roman town of Alcester, how his loving footsteps carried him along this walk night after night, for at the first homestead at the entrance of the hamlet of Wilmcote dwelt Mary Arden,

MARY ARDEN'S HOUSE, AT WILMCOTE.

the daughter of his father's landlord. The house ye exists in a bower of greenery. The apple trees nestl by the side of the gables and peep in at the window and the cawing rooks inhabit the tall elms which shac it from the early morning sun.

Robert Arden, of Wilmcote, was a yeoman of gent

blood. He could trace his descent from Alwyn and Turchill, who were Sheriffs of Warwickshire when the Confessor reigned and the Conqueror ruled the land. He had married a second time to a widow named Agnes Hill, when John Shakespeare came courting his daughter Mary, who, for her part, did not look unfavourably on the energetic youth. If the Ardens were of gentle birth, the Shakespeares had fought at Bosworth, and there were many of them settled in various parts of the county, and along the Watling Street Road. It was with a stout heart and stalwart hope that John Shakespeare went forth to make a home for his beloved, and, though he married Mary Arden in the year 1557, it was not until the 23rd of April, 1564 (old style), that her son William was born in the old house in Henley Street.

If we turn to the tall vellum-bound parchment register of the parish of Old Stratford, in the church of the Holy Trinity, we find, amongst other entries, this significant line—

Gulielmus filius Johannes Shakspere XXX

On the 26th of April, 1564, then, William, the son of John Shakespeare, was baptized. As it was the common practice of the period to baptize the children three days after birth, it is presumed, and the presumption is borne out by tradition, that William Shakespeare was born on St. George's-day, 1564. It is strange that the day of England's patron saint should see the birth and the death of England's greatest son.

When the summer days merged into winter, it is easy tc imagine that the bereaved mother's feelings were wrough into the highest pitch of anxiety for the safety and lif of her son, as the dreaded plague had found its way tc Stratford, and was decimating its inhabitants. Whethe in answer to his mother's prayers, or that the gifted chil was destined to be spared, the plague passed by the Henle Street household, and left William Shakespeare to grov up a fair-haired, hazel-eyed boy. When Willie ha reached five years old, his father became the chief magis trate, or High Bailiff of Stratford. The household in tl meantime had been increased by another son and daughter, and at this time (1569) Gilbert was thre years old, whilst Joan was an infant.

John Shakespeare was evidently prospering in lif though his business was a miscellaneous one. He combine with his trade of a glover that of a woolstapler and dealer in farm produce. In the course of trade he migl occasionally slaughter an ox or calf, but it is doubtful he regularly carried on the trade of a butcher or fleshe Although in 1848 the house in which he lived present the appearance of a squalid butcher's shop, in 157 when John Shakespeare bought it, it was a substantial dwelling... From the views which have been preserved of it, skilled heads and careful hands have been enabled to restore it to its ancient appearance.*

SHAKESPEARE'S BIRTHPLACE, AS IT APPEARED BEFORE THE RESTORATION.

In the year (1575) in which John Shakespeare bought his house, Queen Elizabeth paid her famous visit to

* The house was purchased by Mr. Peter Cuningham on the 16th of September, 1847, when it was put up for sale by Mr. George Robins. The price, which was a little over £3,000, was raised by public subscription, and the house was placed under trustees on behalf of the nation. On the faith of a legacy of £2,500 from John Shakespeare, of Worthington, Leicester, the trustees commenced to repair the house, under the direction of Mr. Edward Gibbs, architect, in 1856. The legacy was afterwards withdrawn, and the trustees had to find the money by other means.

Kenilworth Castle, where the whole country side assembled to see the pomps and pageants provided for the entertainment of the Queen. William was now eleven years old, and it is more than probable that he accompanied his father to Kenilworth, and there saw some of the sports and the festivities which greeted the Queen during the time of her visit. It was a bright and prosperous time with the father, though there were troubles looming ahead—troubles which in three years' time made the Court of Aldermen exempt John Shakespeare and another alderman from paying the full levy of 6s. 8d. for equipping "three pikemen, two billmen, and an archer," on account of poverty. In the same year he was excused from paying towards the relief of the poor, and in the next year he was a defaulter to the extent of 3s. 4d. towards armour for the levy. No longer prosperous, he is obliged to mortgage his wife's estates at Ashbie, near Wilmcote, and the next year he sells his interest in his property at Snitterfield. Things are evidently going bad in Henley Street, in spite of the assistance which his eldest son could give him, for, notwithstanding the vagueness which enshrouds the career of William Shakespeare, it is too probable that he early left school to engage in some handicraft, trade, or profession; but whether as lawyer, glover, or butcher, assisting his father, or relieving him of the charges for board and raiment, there is no record to prove. This was a sad time to think of, and we may excuse some of the vagaries attributed to the poet-boy when we picture the avaricious creditors, the narrow means and gloomy prospects of the home of Shakespeare, when the year 1580 dawned in Stratford. It has been surmised that the records of debt and poverty preserved arose because John Shakespeare had gone to live outside the borough boundary, where the court was powerless to pursue him, but the "Swan of Avon" was in all probability "cradled into poetry by wrong, and learned in suffering what he taught in song."

In these times, how he must have welcomed the "coming of the players," who, year by year, visited Stratford, from the time of his father's bailiwick to the time when he himself "fretted and strutted his little hour upon the stage!" During this period, too, the soft passion had changed his being. In his rambles by the sunny Avon, or in the "daisy-pied" meadows, or in the tree-embowered lanes, he had met with Ann Hathaway, the daughter of a yeoman residing in the neighbouring hamlet of Shottery. He wooed and won. Late in the year he married her. William Shakespeare was only in his nineteenth year when he and two neighbours from Shottery went with his sweetheart to Worcester, to enter into a bond for the security of the bishop in licensing "William

Shagspere and Ann Hathway" to be married after only one proclamation of banns. This bond is dated November 28, 1582, and is preserved in the Consistorial Registry at Worcester. Where the marriage took place is not known, but evidently at some village church. From the fact of the registers of Luddington being destroyed, it is surmised that the wedding took place there. This church has disappeared, but

LUDDINGTON OLD CHURCH.

Captain Saunders has preserved a view of it, which is here reproduced.

Six months after their marriage a daughter was born, who was christened Susanna on the 26th of May, 1583. Hamnet and Judith, twins, were baptized on February 2nd, 1585. These formed Shakespeare's family. Hamnet died in his twelfth year, Susanna married Dr. Hall, a physician of Stratford, and Judith became the wife of Thomas Quiney. The marriage and the married life of Shakespeare have been the theme of a thousand theories and probabilities, but these facts only have come down to us. At Shottery, the paternal home of Ann Hathaway still remains, and like the home of Shakespeare, was a timber-framed structure—a panelled house with the panels filled with "dab and wattle"—or, in other words, basket work covered with rough plaster. This cottage, with its rustic garden and ancient well, gives us an idea of what it was like in Shakespeare's time, when he sat with Ann Hathaway in the old oak settle and conjured up the glowing ideas which are embodied in Juliet, Olivia, Rosalind, Imogene, and other heroines familiar to us. It is one of the very few relics of Shakespeare's time it is possible to recall in its original state.

The personal history of Shakespeare is a blank from his marriage to his appearance in London. He appears to have resided in Stratford for some four years after his marriage, but, in 1589, his name appears as one of those who shared the profits of the Blackfriars Theatre in London. In 1597, he was rich enough to purchase New Place, at Stratford. In the same year his father tendered the redemption of his mortgage. In the year before, an application was made to the Herald's College by John Shakespeare for a grant of arms, and the application was acceded to in this year. In the year following, permission was given to impale these arms with those of Arden, his mother. Between 1604 and 1608 he retired to his native home, and died at New Place on the supposed date of his birth, April 23rd, 1616. His burial is thus recorded in the register of Holy Trinity Church,

1616
Aprill
25 | Will Shakspere gent X

and on his gravestone in the chancel, beneath the monumental bust erected to his memory, are these remarkable and well-known lines :—

> "Good frend for Iesus sake forbeare
> To digg the dvst encloased heare
> Bleste be Y^E man Y^T spares thes stones
> And cvrst be he Y^T moves my bones."

His will, made the year before his death, commences thus :—

"In the name of God, Amen, I, William Shackspeare, of Stratford-upon-Avon, in the countie of Warwick, gent., in perfect health and memorie (God be praysed), do make and ordayn this my last will and testament in manner and forme following: that is to say, first, I comend my soule into the handes of God my Creator, hoping, and assuredlie beleeving, through thonelie merites of Jesus Christe, my Saviour, to be made partaker of lyfe everlastinge; and my bodye to the earth, whereof yt ys made."

To his daughter Judith he left a considerable sum of money, and his "brod silver and gilt bole." To his daughter, Susanna Hall, he left the bulk of his property, including New Place, the Henley Street estate, and the house in Blackfriars. To his granddaughter, Elizabeth Hall, he bequeathed his plate. To the poor of Stratford he bequeathed £10. His sister Joan (who had married William Hart, a hatter,) at this time occupied the house in Henley Street, in which the poet was born, and he very considerately left it to her, for her natural life, under the yearly rental of 12d. He also left her all his wearing apparel. To Hamlett Sadler, William Reynoldes (gentleman), Anthonye Nashe, Mr. John Nashe, and to his "fellowes, John Hemynges, Richard Burbage, and Henry Condell, he left xxvj*s*. viij^{d}· a peece to buy them ringes." A sword was left to Thomas Combe. To his godson, William Walker, he bequeathed xx*s*. in gold. To his wife he left his "second best bed, with the furniture."

William Shakespeare's will is written on three sheets of brief paper, thus necessitating three autographs. The last signature, "By me, William Shakspeare," is written in the middle of the third sheet. The second signature stands thus—

Much comment has arisen with respect to the bequest to his wife, a bequest that was not unusual at that period, for the wife was provided for by dower, yet it is as strange and as vague as all the records of the poet.

It is not for this that we keep the memory of William Shakespeare green in our hearts. We cherish the few material relics which are left to us. We like to be reminded of the things which surrounded him in the life, but in his will he did not devise his choicest treasures and priceless jewels to anyone. He left them free to all mankind, and mankind accepted the heritage.

The house he bought with his savings, and in which he died, has passed away, but Lear and Hamlet remain to us. Doubts may be thrown on his life, but we have Juliet and Miranda. Ariels may whisper to blundering Calibans of drinking bouts and deer stealing; Trinculos and Stephanos swallow stories of holding horses at play-house doors, of merry meetings at taverns, and *liaisons* with the Dame Quicksy, of roadside inns; but Shakespeare rests with his wife and daughter in the chancel of the glorious old church whose shadow falls on the bosom of the Avon. Yet the sweet "Swan of Avon," the friend of Raleigh, of Ben Jonson, of Southampton, the countryman of Drayton and Overbury, the honoured of queens, the pet of kings, the creator of kings and queens, was a Warwickshire man, of whose life we know so little, but whose works will live for ever.

Meddlers may colour and recolour his monument, and tell us that his life is made up of outside fragments. There is a fitness in this vagueness. It makes our faith and wonderment the greater. The very book in which his baptism and death are registered is a subject of doubt. We turn to the entry of his wife's death, and the same uncertainty prevails. We read

1623.
AUGUST 8. { MRS. SHAKSPEARE,
ANNA UXOR RICHARDI JAMES.

Did Ann Hathaway marry again? Hamlet's mother did. We go to the rolling hills of Northamptonshire and seek the grave of his only grandchild, but can find it not. Loving hands and eyes have searched for it; but, like all the personalities of the poet, all is vague and dim.

We remember with pride that he was gentle and was loved; that he was honoured by the great; that his life, though overclouded by legends and myths, was begun and ended in Warwickshire. The "Swan of Avon" was a Warwickshire man, and no one should forget that the name of the "poet of all time" was

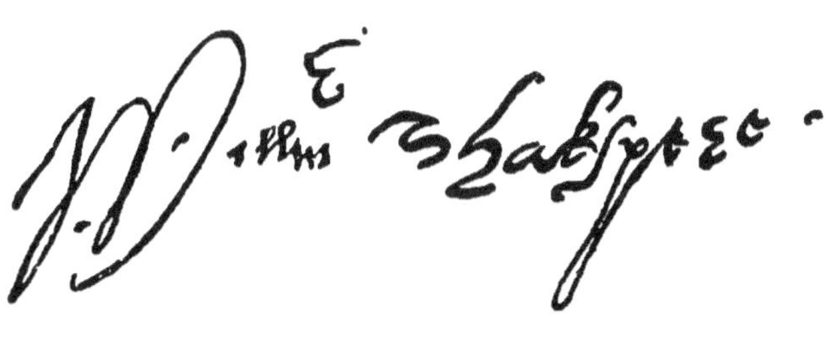

The Captain, Lieutenant, and Ancient.

WHEN Shakespeare was but lately dead, when the country was disturbed by the disputes between Charles I. and his Parliament concerning ship money and tonnage and poundage, three travellers visited Warwickshire who have left us a vivid and interesting description of the country in the Lansdowne MSS. (British Museum). They are described as the "Captain, Lieutenant, and Ancient" of the military company at Norwich, which city they left on August 11th, 1634, and passed through twenty-six counties, and to them we are indebted for a picture of Warwickshire, at the time when William Dugdale was preparing his famous history. The first place described in Coventry, where our travellers say:—

"Here wee rested very quietly and contentedly, and in the morning address'd o'selves to a stately fayre church, wch n. compare wthout organs wth many cathedralls, though none itself, both for largenesse, tightsomenesse, fayrenesse, and neatnesse, wch hath as fayre and lofty a spire as any in this kingdome, built, as they credibly reporte, by 2 mayds at a small charge. In this church there are some fayre and ancient monuments, and amongst the rest these are of emmency.

"Sir Thomas Berkley's tombe, of black and white marble, onely sone of Henry Ld Berkley and his Lady Katherin, sister to Thomas D., of Norfolke, and his sones.

"The Ld Swillington's tombe, himself in armour, in freestone, and his two wives.

"The 2 sisters fayre, gravestone in brasse, somewhat defaced, that built the fayre high steeple in that church.

"Neere adjoyning to this church stands another fayre one, wch hath a spired steeple, and these two, wth another little one seldom used, containe the whole city.

"This city as it is sweetly situated on a hill so it is beautify'd wth many fayre streets and buildings, and for defence thereof it is compassed wth a strong wall nigh 3 miles about, wth a whole jury of gates, and many offensive and defensive towers, graced and much beautify'd wth a fayre, lofty 6 square crosse, though not altogether soe richly guilded as that vnparralell'd one in Cheapside, yet wth as curious and neat worke and carvings cut in stone as that of lead. A fayre large hall there is over against their fayre church, wth a stately ascending entrance, the vpper end adorn'd wth rich hangings, and all about wth fayre pictures, one more especially of a noble lady (the Lady Godiva), whose memory they have cause not to forget, for that shee purchas'd and redeem'd their lost infringed liberties and ffreedomes, and obtain'd remission of heavy tributes impos'd upon them by vndertaking a hard and vnseemly taske, wch was to ride naked openly, at high noone day through the city, upon a milke white steed, wch she willingly performed, according to her lord's strict injunction. It may bee very well discussed heere whether his hatred, or her love exceeded. Her fayre long hayre did much offend the wanton's glancing eye.

"The civill governm^t is discreetly ordered and wisely administred by a generous and prudent mayor, wth his 12 discreet brethren, 2 sheriffes, and 10 aldermen, clad in scarlet, wth a fayre sword and cap of maintenance, 5 maces and other officers, and an hon^ble, grave, and learned recorder [Sir Edward Cooke] to grace and preserve her ancient liberties. As this precious place is placed in the middle of this famous island, soe doth she verefy and make good the old proverb, 'in medio consistit virtus,' for she wants nothing, either of pleasure or profit, participating largelie of them both; ffor both the sweet situation of the city and generous condition of the people (some whereof the margent is graced wth the mentioning)* invited heere a longer stay, but wee were call'd away to visite that famous castle of Guy of Warwicke.

"In our way thither, in the middle thereof, wee were detayn'd one houre at that famous castle of Kellingworth [Kenilworth], where wee were vshered vp a fayre ascent into a large and stately hall, of 20 paces in length, the roofe whereof is all of Irish wood, neatly and handsomely

* Sir Thomas Porter, Sir George Bray, and the Lady Littleton.

framed. In it is [are] 5 spacious chimneys answerable to soe great a roome. We next view'd the great chamber for the guard, the chamber of presence, the privy chamber, fretted about richly with coats of armes, and all adorn'd wth fayre and rich chimney peeces of alabaster, blacke marble, and of joyner's worke in curious carv'd wood; and all those fayre and rich roomes and lodgings in that spacious tower not long since built and repayr'd at a great cost by that great ffavorite of late dayes [Robert Dudley, Earl of Leicester]. The private, plaine retiring chamber where in o^{r} renowned Queene, of ever famous memory, alwayes made choise to repose her selfe. Also the famous strong old tower, called Julius Cæsar's, on top whereof we view'd the pleasant large poole, continually sporting and playing on the castle, the parke, and the fforest contigious thereunto. But one thing more remarkable then any we had yet seen was the sight of the massy, heavy armour of that famous and redoubted warrior,* whom we next hastened to.

"In o^{r} way thither and wthin a mile of Warwicke, wee saw an old decayed chappelle, now prophan'd in being made a wood house; there we found his statue, full 3 yards in length and answerable to his armour: there also we saw, close by the river side, in a rocke, his cave, where in (leaving the world's cares) he retired and liv'd a hermit, after all his brave and warlike atcheevm^{ts}, and there ended his days."

"Neerer to the towne (of Warwicke) and in the high road stands his leaning crosse: and soe we entered that old shire, Bayliffe Towne, which for a fayre and stately castle may compare with most in England. It is most sweetly and very pleasantly seated on a rocke very high, upon that pleasant river (the Avon) that divides the shire in twaine: whether ye sumptuousnesse of the building wth the richnesse of the ffurniture, the pleasantnesse of the seat, or the strength of the brave, ancient, high towers, wth her owne defensive situation, exceeds, it is hard to be determined. At o^{r} first ascending entrance, wee pass'd over a large bridge and then through a strong double gate into a fayre court leaning on either hand, a strong and lofty defensible tower, namely, Julius Cæsar's on the left and Guy of Warwicke's on the right."

"This castle is seated on the sayd river Avon. By it a second Eden, wherein is a most stately mount, wch overtops and commands a great part of her owne and some part of 4 adjacent neighbouring shires; and the whole hill and declining brow is so planted and furnished wth beech, birch, and severall sorts of plum trees, as it is most delightful and very pleasant to ascend.

* Guy, Earl of Warwick.

"By this large and pleasant peece of ground, wch is adorned wth all kind of delightfull and shady walkes and arbors, pleasant groves and wildernesses, fruitfull trees, delicious bowers, odoriferous herbes and fragrant flowers, betweene the river and the high rocky foundation of the castle, on the south side thereof, there are many rare and curious fish ponds, all made and hewn out of the solid rock of freestone, like cisterns of lead, wch are levell wth the river, and supply'd wth great store of good fish.

"This sumptuous, stately building, this most pleasant garden, and these delightfull fish ponds were made thus rare and excellent at the cost and charges of that worthy and famous knight, the late owner and inhabitant Sir Fulke Grevill, Lord Brooke. And as at the last castle we met with the high armour of that warrior Guy of Warwick, for his body, so heere we saw that for his horse, his fearfull sword and dagger, the large rib and tooth of the wild boare, wch they call a dangerous beast, that frequented the woods, the hills and the rockes thereabout, wch he encountered wth all and slew, if report passe for credit.

"After having viewed the seat of Sir Thomas Puckering, called the Priory, wee then heard of the rare monumts that one of the two churches there in the towne afforded. Thither therefore we hastened, and we found them as [illegible] reported. First is the Ladye Chappell, built by Richard Beauchamp, Earle of Warwicke, Aº 1464, in the time of Henry VI., the glasse windowes whereof are richly and curiously painted.

MONUMENTS.

"In the middle of the sayd chappell is a fayre and rich monument, hereon lyeth the sayd Earle, all in armour, double gilt, about wch tomb is placed the engraven statues of the same worke of 14 earles, countesses, lords, knights, and ladies of that family. At his head there is a [illegible] wth a helmett; at his feet the beare muzzled and a gryphon. This monument for its largeness may compare wth any in that famous chappell at Westminster.

"In the same chappell is another fayre rich monument erected there 1588 for Robert Dudley, Earle of Leicester, and his Countesse. A [illegible] of there is for Ambrose Dudley, E. of Warwicke, his brother, 1589, and Robert Dudley, who dyed at 3 years of age. In the middle of the chancell lyeth Thomas Beauchamp, E. of Warwicke, in his coat of maile, sword and armour; his Countesse by him, both in fayre alabaster—hee a wild beare, the muzzled beare; shee a lambe, as ye gentle lambe ly couching at their feet.

"In another chappell, on the other side of the quire and chancell, wch was sometimes the counsell house, wch is in a manner round wth 10 seats of ffreestone about it, is a very fayre, rich, and lofty tombe, for that Honble Ld Sir Fulke Greville, Lord Brooke, built exceedingly stately, wth 10 fayre pillars of touch [*i.e.*, touchstone] and 6 of alabaster, 2 arches of the rich table, all of blacke excellent stuffe, and curiously wrought and polished, and amongst inscriptions about it engraven this—'Sir Fulke Grevill, servant to Queen Elizabeth, councillor to King James, and ffriend to Sir Philip Sydney.' This now is called by his title Brooke's Chappell.

"In the church is an ancient plaine monument of Tho. Beauchamp, E. of Warwicke, Ad 1402, and Margeret, his Countesse. He was father to the Earle that built the chappell.

"Another monument there is in the sayd church of Thomas Ffisher. Esq., and his wife. This gentleman built the neat pryory there: hee was sometimes steward to the noble Duke of Norfolk.

"The next day we marcht out vnder a long strong arch'd gate, hewne out of a rocke, over wch is a fayre chappell, and were for Worcester; anc in the way we met wth a seat and parke, a ladyes (Snotfield, the Lady Hales), and likewise the seats of 2 honorable persons, by Austei Market, Beechley [ye Ld Brookes and the Ld Conweys]; and anothe seat of a worthy and generous knight, the then High Sheriffe, Si Symon Clarke, and soe crossed over a small swift streame [the Arrow] At Coak Hill, 8 miles from Worcester, wee left the last shire (Worcestei shire) and came into the next, for there the two shires parted: clos whereunto is the house and parke of a gentleman of a very ancier ffamily (Mr. Fortescue), aud wthin a mile of the city the seat of a honble judge, Speechley, Judge Barkley's.

"In that dayes travel wee came by Stratford-upon-Avon, where i the church in that towne there are some monuments, which church w built by Archbishop Stratford. Those worth observing, and which w tooke notice of, were these—

"A monument for the E. of Totness and his lady, yet living.

"The monument of Sir Hugh Clopton, who built that strong sto bridge of 18 fayre arches over ye river. He was Ld Mayor of Londo

"A neat monument of that famous English poet, Mr. Wm Shakespea who was born heere.

"And one of an old gentleman, a batchelor. Mr. Combe, vpon whc name the sayd poet did merrily farn vp some witty and facetious verse wch time would not give vs leave to tacke up."

Cavaliers and Roundheads.

THE leaven of Puritanism was scattered far and wide through Warwickshire by the teachings of Thomas Cartwright, the elder Clarke, and Fenn, during the latter part of the sixteenth and during the early part of the seventeeth centuries. In the towns the teachings of the Puritans became popular, and not a few gentlemen listened to the cold and austere preachers who made their way into the reformed pulpits and enunciated the doctrines of Calvin in their most uncompromising aspect. The teachings of the Puritan divines were made tenfold more pungent by the example of the levity of the Court and the symptoms of general corruption apparent. They had seen the fatuous James I. promoting one favourite after another to the highest offices of State, and making their favour the only avenue to honour, distinction, and State employment. The poisoning of Sir Thomas Overbury in the Tower was not forgotten in his native county, and though Carr was succeeded by George Villiers, Midland born, the son of a poor knight of Brooksby, in Leicestershire, from him they could hardly look for better things. Long before

Y 2

George Villiers was created Duke of Buckingham his mother had married for her second husband Sir Thomas Compton, the somewhat craven-hearted, poor-spirited brother of the first Earl of Northampton of that name, the sister of the Duke was married to the head of the old house of Feilding, of Newnham-Paddox, and a patent of nobility had followed the alliance. These events happened whilst the Captain, Lieutenant, and Ancient were traversing the country. Sir Fulke Greville, "the servant of Queen Elizabeth, the counsellor of King James, and the friend of Sir Philip Sidney," was assassinated by his servant in 1628, after repairing, restoring, and beautifying the Castle of Warwick. In the following year the Duke of Buckingham was also slain by the knife * of an assassin at Portsmouth. The new owner of Warwick Castle, Robert, Lord Brooke, was a notorious Puritan. On the site of the present orangery in the grounds of the castle there was a Presbyterian chapel, formed of an old timber-framed, panelled house. Here the Lord Brooke listened to the discourses of Samuel Clarke the younger until he gave him the vicarage of Alcester. Coventry was the very hotbed of violent religious zeal. The inhabitants had cordially received William Prynne when he went through Coventry in 1637, on his way to Caernarvon

* The double expanding knife or dagger used by Fenton is preserved at Newnham. It is engraved in Ireland's "Views of the Avon."

Gaol, and had appointed Puritan preachers in the churches under their control. Richard Vines was preaching in the east against prelacy and priestcraft, at Weddington and Caldecote, and the fruits of his teaching were soon seen in the iconoclastic tendencies of his patron, Colonel Purefoy.

On every hand there were signs of a gathering storm. The action of the King with respect to ship money, tonnage and poundage, and the Royal prerogative stirred the country to the very dregs. The ruling spirits of the Midland shires were not inactive. In a small retired room, situated in the upper story of Broughton Castle, Lord Saye and Sele received the leaders of the discontented spirits and debated on the course to be adopted. Hither came Lord Brooke, Richard Knightley, of Fawsley, whose eldest son had married Hampden's daughter. Hither came Pym and Hampden himself, and bye-and-by Lord Essex and the Earls of Warwick and Bedford, to confer on the state of the realm. At one time so much did they despair of their country and the popular cause that they formed the design of emigrating to America.

The famous Parliament of 1640 gave the malcontents an opportunity for which they had been waiting, and on the 28th of February, 1642, the great breach between the King and Parliament took place in Warwickshire. The King issued his commission of array to the Earl of

Northampton, and the Parliament appointed Lord Brooke as their lieutenant to put in force the ordinance of the militia. Whilst in other counties the townspeople and burghers sided with the Parliament, the country gentry, as a rule, took the part of the King.

Long before the King could obtain arms, men, or money, there were overt acts of rebellion and outrages in the Midland shires. At Edgbaston, and in the neighbourhood of Coventry, zealous partizans made excursions on their own account, and even in Warwick the signs of hostility were not wanting, whilst Charles was irresolutely wandering about from place to place.

As early as June, 1642, whilst Sir William Dugdale was demanding in the King's name stores of ammunition or the surrender of castles, Colonel Purefoy, on Wednesday, the 14th of June, broke down the Cross in Warwick market-place and defaced the monuments in St. Mary's Church.

It was known that the magazines of the county were at Coventry, of which city the Earl of Northampton was Recorder, and the train-bands, as early as Monday, the 11th of July, preferred a request to Lord Brooke that he would remove the magazines to Warwick. Two hundred volunteers enrolled themselves in the county town for this purpose, rejoicing in the Parliamentarian Lord-Lieutenant. On this day Lord Brooke, accompanied by 100 horsemen and many wagons, went to Coventry and brought away the magazines of arms. At Stratford-on-Avon large crowds met Lord Brooke with the train-bands, and 400 men joined his regiment. On the 16th of

THE ARMY BEFORE COVENTRY.

June 300 men, in addition to the train-bands, met at Warwick, but no arms were forthcoming. On the following Monday there was a rumour that Lord Northampton and 300 horse would oppose the Parliamentary ordinance at Coleshill. Altogether, Lord Brooke mustered 1,700 men with arms, in addition to large numbers without.

In the meantime, Lord Northampton had not been idle. Many of the old manor houses were repaired and fortified. Kenilworth was garrisoned, as were also Astley, Maxstoke, Compton Winyate, Aston Hall, Coughton, Milcote, Wormleighton, Shuckburgh, Charlecote, and many other places; but they were early abandoned as points of defence, and left to the tender mercies of the most venturesome of the local Puritanic leaders. Amongst those who espoused the cause of the King were the Lord Northampton, the first Earl of Denbigh, the Earl of Chichester, Lord Craven, Sir Charles Adderley, Sir Simon Clark, Sir Clement Fisher, Sir Henry Gibbs, Sir Thomas Holt, Sir Thomas Leigh, Sir John Repington, Sir Richard Shuckburgh, Sir Hercules Underhill, and many of the country gentlemen, whilst the inhabitants of the town ranged themselves on the side of the Parliament, supported by Lord Brooke, Lord Feilding (afterwards the second Earl of Denbigh), Sir Edward Peto, of Chesterton, Colonel William Purefoy, of Caldecote Hall, Mr. Abbott, of Caldecote, and many of the Presbyterian ministers; thus, as in the instance of Lord Denbigh and his son, members of the same family fought on opposite sides.

Warwickshire being in the very centre of England,

and containing within itself the royal stronghold of Kenilworth, was naturally the scene of the earliest exploits. Early in August Rugby had been the scene of a Cavalier excursion; and the same month King Charles marched out of Leicestershire with a body of horse, hoping from the assurance of Lord Northampton that he might obtain admission to Coventry and possession of the ammunition therein stored. His troops appeared to have made Dunsmore Heath their rendezvous, and then to have marched on Coventry; but the citizens were not to be cajoled or gained over by promises. They were pleased to see his Majesty, but they would not permit his Cavaliers to enter their gates in force. A guard of 200 might be permitted, but no more. This was on the 18th of August. On the 19th he planted his cannon against the gates, and thus the Civil War began in earnest, for the King declared he would lay the city in ruins for the affront he had received. The citizens manned the walls, repaired the breaches, sallied out from the city with two pieces of ordnance, and attacked the Cavaliers, forcing them to retreat. During this attack Charles stayed at the house of Sir Thomas Leigh, of Stoneleigh, though popular tradition points to the now demolished mansion of Fletchampstead, the seat of the Leighs, as the abode of the King.

During this period Sir William Dugdale was despatched to remove the troops and ammunition from Kenilworth, but, notwithstanding his celerity, he was attacked near Curdworth by the men of Coventry and Birmingham, but succeeded in joining the King in Leicestershire.

During the attack on Coventry, Lord Brooke had been collecting forces at Northampton, and it was resolved to reinforce Coventry, and fortify and strengthen the garrison at Warwick. On their way the parliamentary forces met the mounted Cavaliers near Southam, and a skirmish ensued, in which the Royalists had the worst of it. The battle and pursuit seems to have continued as far as Marton, for during the restoration of the church many bullets were found in the walls and signs of fire on one of the church aisles.

The King withdrew his forces into Leicestershire, and on the 25th of August set up his standard at Nottingham; but Warwickshire was yet to be the scene of bloodshed and of romance.

The Siege of Caldecote Hall.

ON the lowlands which extend between the Watling Street Road and the heights of Tuthill and Hartshill, on the east bank of the river Anker, is Caldecote Hall. The house is now an ordinary modern structure, though there are many signs of the old manor house to be seen. When the strife between King and Parliament broke out it was the residence of Colonel Purefoy, the parliamentary representative of the borough of Warwick, an ardent Puritan, who was the patron of Richard Vines, one of the leading Puritan preachers of the day, and who was vicar of Caldecote at the time. The men belonging to the Caldecote estate were drawn off to defend Coventry and to reinforce Lord Brooke, when the King raised his standard at Nottingham, on the 25th of August, 1642. On the 28th, being Sunday, Colonel Purefoy appears to have visited his home, little suspecting the hasty march of Prince Rupert and his Cavaliers to Warwickshire. Perhaps, next to Lord Brooke, Colonel Purefoy was at this time the most conspicuous leader of the Puritan party in Warwickshire, and his capture would have done much to dispirit the opponents of the

King in the Midlands. The following description of the attack on Caldecote Hall is taken from the oral traditions preserved in the family of one of those engaged in the defence, whose grandson was alive in 1844.

"We had," he says, "heard that the King had tried to seize the castle at Hull, and that he had sent his nephews, Prince Rupert and Prince Morris (Maurice), wild, devil-may-care fellows, harum-scaruming through the country, frightening honest folks and setting them against the King. Well, the King collected a parcel of gentlemen and troopers and came to Coventry, but the citizens would not let them enter the city. They did not care if the King came, but they would not have the riff-raff of the country. The King got in a mighty rage, and went to Stoneleigh, and sent his cannon to batter the gates down. This put us in a great quandary, for we could hear the thunder of the ordnance, and there were rumours that the Cavaliers had forced the gates and were burning the city. We could see from the top of the church tower the smoke, but whether it was from the powder of the culverels or the fire of the houses we could not tell. Colonel Purefoy had come over to the manor from Warwick Castle to see his son-in-law, Master George Abbot, who was also a Parliament man, to concert with him about the raising of more men to join my Lord Brooke, who was at Northampton, and to see if more provision could not be sent to Sir Edward Peto, who was in command of the Castle at Warwick, and who expected to be besieged. I recollect the time well, for it was on Sunday morning, the 28th of August, in the year of grace 1642. Then I went up to the top of the tower to see if I could see anything of Coventry spires and the fire, for I was anxious about my father. My uncle Robin and three men had come over with the Colonel, but there were but nine men altogether, including the Colonel and Master George, about the house, and some of these men had wives in the village. I, as I have said, went up the tower to look towards Coventry, but I could see nothing but a little smoke. I was looking at the river Anker, which shone so bright in the sunlight, and thought how nice it was, when I saw the river move as I thought. I looked again, and then I saw it was the steel jackets of a lot of soldiers coming winding and glistening on the road like a silver serpent coming along. I looked again and saw they were soldiers, but not the men of our regiment, but I thought of the devilskin Prince, of whom uncle Robin had told me. I nearly flew down the steps, for I was young then, and found the Colonel and Master George walking together with the Rev. Richard Vines, the preacher, in the front of the house facing the river. I told him what I had seen. The Colonel patted my head and said I was a good boy, but Master Vines talked of the depravity of the human heart, and the sin of looking from the tower on the Sabbath. Master George's eye struck fire. He told me to go with the Colonel into the hop garden and hide him there. I knew where he meant, for we had contrived a snug hiding place in the middle of the garden, and had covered it with old hop poles. People called that cowardice afterwards, but we knew that the King's men wanted the Colonel, for he had spoken boldly in Parliament against the ship money and the King's exactions. There were, at this time, only eight men inside the house, for we had not time to call the villagers, who did not know that the Colonel was come home. Master George said that all the men who were worth anything were away at Warwick and Coventry. So the bells went tinkling for church as usual, for the Colonel would not have them taken away, though Master Vines said they were an invention of the evil one and a relic of papistry.

Dame Purefoy (our mistress) and Master George called us together, and she said that the King's men were coming, but they had resolved to resist them and prevent them coming into the hall. It was an old fashioned house then, for the Colonel had not begun the alterations you see now. We got the good feather beds and placed them at the windows, and barricaded the doors. The mistress told Dolly, the cook, to make up a fire and bring the pewter spoons and plates to melt down for bullets, for we had some powder and several guns but no bullets. Master George showed the women servants how to load the guns, so that the men might watch the outside. Almost before we had all the guns loaded we could hear the clattering of the horses' hoofs on the road. Good Lord, what a row they made, and though it was the Sabbath-day, they were singing snatches of profane songs. Master George had stationed himself with the four men at the great entrance just opposite the courtyard, but the mistress and I were at the porter's wicket at the side; the old steward and uncle were in the upper rooms. While we were waiting my heart went pit-a-pat, but I did not feel much frightened. We did not know which way they would approach; but we heard the halt of the troopers, for there were eight or nine troops of horse—several hundred men altogether. Then a trumpet sounded, and several officers and men came to our wicket. My mistress asked who they were and what right they had to disturb godly people on the Sabbath-day. They demanded entrance for Prince Rupert in the King's name to search for a rebellious subject who had been levying war against the King. My mistress told them to be gone as marauders. They said they would have admittance, and were about to force the door, when the dame lifted up one of the guns and said "God forgive me," pulled the trigger, and fired. I peeped out and saw that one of the officers had fallen. There was a scream, a groan, and a scuffle, and immediately afterwards a volley of bullets were fired against the wicket. Master George, on hearing the shot rushed to that side of the house, and we fired all the guns at the windows and loopholes. We saw the godless troopers drop one by one, and the rest ran away. We then drew a long breath, whilst the women loaded the firelocks again.

"We could see some consultation going on, and immediately a series of shots were fired at the windows. We did not mind that. The glass was shattered about the room. Master George conjectured that they were about to attack the courtyard entrance, and stationed us all there. He was right; for shortly afterwards the court gates were burst open, and the troopers rushed at the hall door with battering poles. 'Now then,' shouted Master George, 'steady, take good aim,' and we all fired. Down dropped two or three officers and several of the soldiers. We had spare guns and we fired again. Then the women handed us the reloaded arms, and we fired a third time before they cleared out of the courtyard. We all thanked God, and some of us thought that they had gone after so warm a reception. Master Abbott knew better. He said that they would try to make a diversion. We did not know what he meant, but soon found out. Some straw was brought to the front and fired, and when the flame and smoke were at the highest the Cavaliers again made a rush at the hall door. Again we fired, but though we did some execution, it was not so much as before. They came on again, but our powder began to run short. The soldiers now fired the stables, and Master George said we should be obliged to give in. The dame said it was perhaps for the best, and just as the Cavaliers, headed by Prince Rupert himself, were preparing for a last attempt, the dame flung open the door, for the flames had nearly reached the manor house, and cast herself at Rupert's feet, and besought him not to injure the hair of the heads of a few poor women. The Prince and the officers could not believe that we had so few souls and so many women. Before he said aught he had the house searched for the Colonel, and when he really found the bird was not there, he gave us all our lives, but wanted Master George to accept the command of troop of his horse, but Master George said he could not conscientiously do so. The soldiers wanted to sack the house as they had done others, but the brave Prince would not let that be done. He said we had acted bravely, and he knew how to respect brave men and women. They then took up their wounded, and went off in the direction of Coventry. The villagers from Weddington, Mancetter, and the neighbourhood came, and we soon extinguished the fire. We all laughed at Dolly, who was lamenting over her broken and melted platters she had polished so bravely.

When night fell, the Colonel came in, and before morning was off towards Northampton."

In Vicar's "*Magnolia Dei Anglicani*," a somewhat similar account is given of this stirring incident. The officers killed were Captain Mayford, Captain Shute, and one Captain Steward, and fifteen men.

In Caldecote Church, which adjoins the house, there is a monument to Mr. George Abbott, erected by his mother-in-law. The inscription runs thus :—

"Here lieth the body of George Abbott, late of Caldecott, in Warwickshire, Esquire, whose eminent parts, virtues, and graces, drawn forth to life in his exemplary walking with God, his tenderness to all the members of Christ, who frequently fled to his charity in their wants, and counsel in cases of conscience. His exact observation of the Sabbath, which he vindicated by his pen, and on which August 28th, 1642, God honoured him in the memorable and unparalleled defence of this adjoining house, with eight men (besides his mother and her maids) against the furious and fierce assault of Princes Rupert and Maurice, with 18 troops of horse and dragoneers. His perspicuous paraphrases of the books of Job and Psalms, his judicious tracts of public affairs then emergent, his known integrity in public employments, rendered him one of a thousand for singular piety, wisdom, learning, charity, courage, and fidelity to his country, which he served in two Parliaments, the former and the present, whereof he died a member February the 2nd, 1648, in the 44th year of his age. This monument was erected to his memory by his dear mother and executrix, Johan Purefoy, the wife of Colonel William Purefoy, his beloved father-in-law, the 28th day of August, Anno Domini 1649."

The Capture of the Standard.

ONE of the least known, but one of the most gallant of the Warwickshire Cavaliers who joined the army of the King was Captain John Smith, of Skilts. His old home yet stands on the south-western edge of the county, where it commands a fine view over the Arden and over Worcestershire. Early in the disturbances he was in command of a troop of horse at Rugby, and took an active part in disarming the Roundheads there, and at the puritanic village of Kilsby, where he met with a stout resistance, and shed, it is believed, the first blood in the Civil Wars. His great deed was the recapture of the King's standard at the fight of Edgehill.

Between the skirmish at Southam and the battle of Kineton the rival commanders had not been idle. Lord Northampton had made a dash at Warwick Castle, but had been repulsed. The commander of the garrison, Sir Edward Peto, of Chesterton, had hung wool-packs outside the gatehouse on great hooks (which yet remain) to protect the walls from Lord Northampton's cannon. On Guy's Tower he hung out, instead of the red standard, a winding sheet and a bible to show he was ready to die for his faith. Parliament trembled for the safety of this stronghold, but ultimately Lord Northampton withdrew his troops, and both parties prepared for the first trial at arms in force.

Troops had been raised on all sides. Lord Brooke's purple-coated Warwickshire regiment was early in the field; Hampden's green coats were not behind; Holles's red coats followed, so that in the course of a month the Earl of Essex, as Commander-in-Chief for the Parliament, found himself in command of a formidable army. He crossed Warwickshire in the month of September, on his march to Worcester, where he rested to watch the King's movements, who was raising troops at Shrewsbury and Chester.

The King evidently felt the importance of marching on London, and striking a blow at the head quarters of Parliament before the Earl of Essex could intercept him. According to the "*Iter Carolinum,*" he left Shrewsbury on the 12th of October, 1642, and proceeded to Bridgenorth; from whence, on the 15th of that month, he went to Wolverhampton; thence, on the 17th, to Bremichen (Birmingham), to the mansion of Sir Thomas Holt, Aston Hall; on the 18th he went to Packington, the house of Sir Robert Fisher; on the 19th to Killingworth (Kenilworth). Whether the castle was then garrisoned by the forces of the Parliament or abandoned by them, whether for the night he took up his abode in the castle or else where, the writer of this *iter* does not inform us. Lord Clarendon, however, states that it was "a house of the King's, and a very noble seat." He was now with his army between the two hostile garrisons of Coventry and Warwick Castle. On the 21st of October he proceeded with his army to Southam, probably marching by way

HOUSE IN WHICH CHARLES I. SLEPT AT SOUTHAM.

of Chesford Bridge, Cubbington, and Offchurch. At Southam, the house in which he slept yet remains. From hence he issued a proclamation to his troops. On the 22nd of October he proceeded to Edgcote, Prince Rupert taking up his quarters the same night at Wormleighton, at a fine Tudor mansion belonging to the Spencer family. There is an anecdote related by Dr. Thomas of Mr. Richard Shuckburgh, of an ancient family in Warwickshire, the possessor of the Shuckburgh estates in this county in the time of the Civil Wars, as in no way inferior to his ancestors, and then goes on to say, "As Charles I. marched to Edgcote, near Banbury, on the 22nd of October, 1642, he saw him hunting in the field, not far from Shuckburgh, with a very good pack of hounds, upon which, it is reported, that he fetched a deep sigh, and asked who that gentleman was that hunted so merrily that morning, when he was going to fight for his crown and liberty; and being told that it was this Richard Shuckburgh, he was ordered to be called to him, and was by him very graciously received, upon which he went immediately home, armed all his tenants, and the next day attended him on the field, where he was knighted, and was present at the battle of Edgehill. After the taking of Banbury Castle and his Majesty's retreat from those parts, he went to his own seat and fortified himself on the top of Shuckburgh Hill, where, being attacked by some of the Parliament forces, he defended himself till he fell with most of his tenants about him, but being taken up and life perceived in him, he was carried away prisoner to Kenilworth Castle where he lay a considerable time, and was forced to purchase his liberty at a dear rate." There is in the church of Upper Shuckburgh a monumental bust of this Warwickshire worthy and staunch Royalist, representing him, not unlike the portraits of Charles I., with a moustache and piked beard, according to the fashion which then prevailed.

The rear of the King's troops was commanded by Prince Rupert, who took up his quarters at Wormleighton House, and occupied with his pickets the highlands of Burton, Warmington, and Arlescote. The King was at Edgcote, and the outlying pickets overlooking the vale of Red House saw the camp fires of the troops of the Earl of Essex, who had left Worcester on the 14th of October, and had marched along bad roads and miry lanes in a line nearly parallel with the King, but in profound ignorance of his whereabouts. Hampden and Lord Brooke were about a day's march in the rear of Essex, for they had crossed the Avon at Stratford on the 18th.

The King had decided to halt for the Sunday, but hearing of the vicinity of the parliamentary army, he ordered his troops to extend to the westward and occupy the oolitic bluffs which here form the fringe of Warwickshire, to stop the advance of Essex and his troops. This order was not given till three o'clock in the morning. The distance was only five miles from the head-quarters of the King at Edgcote, and the appearance of Prince Rupert's Cavaliers on the Edge-hills about eight o'clock was the first intimation that the forces of Essex had that the King was so near them.

Standing at the Round Tower, which has been erected near the artificial ruins which now crown the summit of the Edge hills between Ratley and Radway, we can see the whole of the position occupied by these rival English armies. The whole of the green lane between the Round House and the Sunrising was lined with troops. The right of the King's forces rested on Bullet Hill, beneath the old British camp at Nadbury, above Arlescote, and the left at Sunrising, where the road comes up from Stratford. No better position could have been chosen. The King's forces were numerically superior to those of the Parliament, for he had some 15,000 or 16,000 men and the Parliament about 2,000 less. The King's strength consisted of cavalry. The Parliament, though not weak in cavalry, were stronger in trained infantry.

Those who have visited the battle-field will be told how the King breakfasted at a cottage at Radway immediately below the Round House, and a small mound some four hundred yards west of Radway Church is said to be the spot from whence the King surveyed the parliamentary forces. Lord Lindsay, the King's general, counselled delay, but the impetuous Prince Rupert overruled the experienced soldier. The King rode at the head of his troops and addressed the men spiritedly. Lord Lindsay dismounted, and taking a pike in his hand led the troops into the plain. His prayer is said to have been, "O Lord, Thou knowest how busy I must be this day. If I forget Thee, do not Thou forget me. March on, boys!" It was late in the afternoon of Sunday the 23rd of October, 1642, whilst the bells of the churches had hardly ceased to sound for divine worship, ere the artillery roared, the foremost lines advanced, and the battle had begun.

The conflict did not last long. Prince Rupert charged with headlong fury and carried all before him, and had he not paused to plunder the wagons of the enemy in Kineton streets, there would have been another tale to tell; but he had been used to the wars of Germany, and forgot in pillage how his presence might be needed elsewhere. The King's infantry was hard pressed by Lord Essex, Sir Edward Verney, the standard-bearer was killed, and Ensign Young seized the trophy and delivered it to Lord Essex. He gave it to his secretary, Chambers, who, exulting in the prize, waved it round his head, and accompanied by six troopers was carrying it from the field, when Captain Smith, who had been stationed with his troop on the left wing, after charging several times, found himself alone with one Chickley, a groom, the rest of his troop following the pillage of the routed rebels. "As these two," so says the historian, "were passing on towards our army, this mirror of chivalry espied six men (three cuirassiers and three arquebusiers) on horseback, guarding a seventh on foot, who was carrying off the field a colour rolled up, which he conceived to be one of the ordinary colours of his Majesty's Life Guards, and therefore, seeing them so strong, intended to avoid them. Whilst he was thus considering, a boy on horseback calls to him, saying, 'Captain Smith, Captain Smith, they are carrying away the standard!' He would not suddenly believe the boy, till by great asseverations he had assured him it was the standard; who forthwith said, 'They shall have me with it if they carry it away,' and snatching an orange scarf from a parliamentary soldier, he desired Chickley, if he saw him much engaged, in with his rapier at the footman (Chambers) that carried the banner (who was then secretary to Essex, the rebels' general), saying, 'Traitor! deliver up the standard' and wounded him in the breast. Whilst he was bent forward to follow his thrust, one of those cuirassiers with a pole-axe wounded him in the neck through the collar of his doublet, and the rest gave fire at him with their pistols, but without any further hurt than blowing off some powder into his face. No sooner was he recovered upright but he made a thrust at the cuirassier that wounded him, and run him through the belly, whereupon he presently fell, at which sight all the rest ran away. Then he caused a foot soldier that was near at hand to reach him up the banner, which he brought away, with the horse of that cuirassier.

Immediately comes up a great body of his Majesty's horse, which were rallied together, with whom he staid, delivering the standard to Master Robert Hutton, a gentleman of Sir Robert Willyes's troop, to carry forthwith to his Majesty. The next morning King Charles sent for him to the top of Edgehill, where his Majesty knighted him for his singular valour." He subsequently, with a small party of horse, brought off three brass pieces of cannon that stood about the left wing of the rebels' army in the battle. This worthy knight banneret, on the 29th of March, 1644, was mortally wounded in an engagement at Bramdean, near Aylesford, in Hampshire, and died the following day at Andover, and on the 1st of April his body was interred with military honours in the south-east corner of the chapel on the south side of the choir in Oxford Cathedral.

Evening came on, and some thousand dead Englishmen lay on Kineton field. The Cavaliers had retired to the Edge hills at the critical moment of the battle. Both sides claimed the victory, but Essex, instead of renewing the attack, retired to Warwick, and in the morning the King's troops moved to Banbury. Both sides made mistakes, but when a parliamentary soldier climbed that night to the beacon tower on Burton Dasset Hill and fired the beacon, it flared the news to the country side, and from thence to London, that the men of the Parliament had met those of the King and had not been worsted.* The moral effect of the fight was that of a parliamentary victory.

Whether, as Lord Holles stated, Cromwell saw the fight from the tower of Burton Dasset Church, and fled in terror we shall never know; but the parish clerk of Tysoe, who ran from church with the congregation to see the fight, and the village tailor, who received a mortal

THE KINGSMILL MONUMENT AT RADWAY.

wound as the reward of his curiosity, are a part of history. It is related that a Roundhead gunner saw a Cavalier officer on a white horse: as the Royal army ascended the hill he fired at him with his field piece, struck him on the thigh, and mortally wounded him. He died, and was buried in the churchyard of Radway.

* The light was seen at Ivinghoe, in Buckinghamshire, and on the beacon there being fired it was seen at Harrow-on-the-Hill, and the news thus reached London. This beacon tower is engraved on page 199 ante.

Here, twenty-eight years afterwards, his mother, Lady Bridget Kingsmill, erected a monument to his memory. In Jago's poem of Edgehill there is a view of this monument preserved; but only the mutilated remains of the figure now exist. These are preserved in the tower of Radway new church. By the side is this inscription :—

"Here lyeth, expecting ye second comeing of our blessed Lord and Saviour, Henry Kingsmill, Esq., second son to Sr Henry Kingsmill, of Sidmonton, in the county of Southampton, Knt, who, serving as a captain of foot under his Matie Charles the First, of blessed memory, was at the battell of Edge Hill, in ye year of our Lord 1642, as he was manfully fighting in behalfe of his King and country, unhappily slain by a cannon bullet, in memory of whom his mother, the Lady Bridget Kingsmill, did, in the forty-sixth yeare of her widowhood, in the year of our Lord 1670, erect this monument. 'I have fought a good fight, I have finished my course, henceforth is laid up for me a crown of righteousness.'"

The burial place of the troopers is now marked by a plantation on Battle Farm. The field is now enclosed, and the positions of the army of Essex are difficult to make out.

* * * * * *

Some nine months afterwards, the field, on which Captain Smith had won his spurs, was the scene of another historical event. On Monday, July 10th, 1643, the Queen Henrietta Maria arrived in the Midlands to assist the King. On that day she left Walsall and went to King's Norton, where Prince Rupert (who in April had attacked and taken the town of Birmingham) met her. On Tuesday, the 11th, she went to Stratford-on-Avon, and lodged at New Place, the house where twenty-seven years before Shakespeare had died. In the neighbourhood many traditions of the foraging of her troops are preserved. On Thursday, the 13th, she proceeded on her way to Wroxton Abbey, and when on the field of Kineton, King Charles met her, and in honour of that event what is known as the Kineton medal was struck. The medal in question is very rare. On the obverse are seen Charles and his Queen, seated on chairs, their right hands united; they are represented trampling upon a dragon. The King is in armour; over his head is the sun, over his consort is the moon and the Pleiades. The legend is *Certius pythonem juncti* (when united they will more certainly destroy the dragon). On the reverse is an inscription in twelve lines, recording the occasion of the auspicious meeting in the vale of Kineton, on the day before-mentioned, and the defeat on the same day of Waller's army in the West. During the autumn and winter of 1642, the King's party in the West had gradually gained ground, and on May 16th, 1643, defeated their opponents under the Earl of Stamford in a sharp encounter at Stratton, in Cornwall. To support the Royal cause in those parts the Marquis of Hertford and Prince Maurice were sent with a force, and having joined the local partisans of the King, they proceeded towards the subjection of Somersetshire. To check this party Sir William Waller was entrusted with a complete army; and, after several skirmishes, an encounter took place upon Lansdown Hill, near Bath, without any decisive issue, but with considerable loss on both sides. But Lord Wilmot inflicted a decisive defeat at Roundway, near Devizes, at the very day and hour that Charles and Henrietta met on Kineton field.

The Heiress of the Puckerings.

Whilst King and Parliament were struggling for supremacy, the interesting] old house known as The Priory, at Warwick, became the inheritance of a young lady whose romantic career attracted great attention even in those stirring times. The house, which is now the seat of Thomas Lloyd, Esq., was originally built in the eighth year of the reign of Elizabeth, on the site of the old Priory, by one Thomas Hawkins, who obtained the soubriquet of "Fisher" from the fact of his father having sold fish at the Market Cross at Warwick. Fisher had been servant to John Dudley, Duke of Northumberland, and by his talents and integrity had raised himself up in favour until he became possessed of a vast amount of property, much of which had been alienated from the Church at the Reformation. In the curious record of the doings of the Corporation of Warwick, known as the Black Book, there are many entries relating to this extraordinary man, who died in 1576, the year following the visit of Queen Elizabeth to Kenilworth. His son Edward, then thirty years of age, succeeded him, and his estimated rent rol was no less than £3,000 per annum. This enormous wealth he quickly dissipated, for in less than four years he had sold this fair seat and the lands about it to Serjeant Puckering, the Lord Keeper of the Great Seal. He attempted to cheat my lord keeper by a fraudulent conveyance, and though he escaped the penalty of his crime through the intervention of Robert Dudley, Earl of Leicester, he ended his days miserably as a prisoner in the Fleet.

Sergeant John Puckering was the Speaker of the House of Commons (circa 1585). It was he who recommended that the sentence against Mary Queen of Scots should be carried out. He was knighted in 1594-5, and died a year afterwards, leaving a son, Thomas Puckering, as his heir, at Warwick. This gentleman was renowned for his taste, education, and refinement. He had travelled much, and was for several years the representative of Warwick in Parliament. He died in 1636, leaving one daughter, Jane, to inherit his name and lands. She was the last of the Puckerings.

Dugdale simply tells us that Jane Puckering was weak in body, and had been attended by some misfortunes, which, for the sake of brevity, he omitted to mention. But there are preserved in the Record Office, and in the journals of the House of Lords,* some touch-

* Lords' Journal, iv. 158.

ing particulars concerning this "Heiress of the Puckerings." On the 10th of February, 1640, Lady Puckering, the widow of Sir Thomas Puckering, Knight and Baronet, presented a petition to the House of Lords on behalf of Jane Puckering, her only child. In this petition she points out that the executors of her husband's will have got into their hands large sums of money belonging to his estate; but as they have failed to make composition with the King as directed by the will for the wardship of the heiress, she has been taken away from her mother, and awarded to Sir David Cunningham, an entire stranger to the family, but nearly related to one of the executors, "who is to have the estate if the child fail." The unfortunate heiress was at this time only ten years of age. She was sickly and lame, and the mother pleads that the child requires more care than can be expected from strangers, and petitions that she may have the custody of the child on repaying to Sir David Cunningham the money he has expended. She also prays that the executors may give an account of the proceedings, and that the child may be brought before the House of Lords in order that they may see how unfit it would be for any one but her mother to have wardship of her. In the course of the following month the House of Lords considered Lady Puckering's petition, and made several orders thereon; but whatever disposition was made of the young lady, she shortly afterwards again became the object of cupidity and sinister designs.

When about sixteen years of age whilst she was walking in Greenwich Park, in the autumn, a man named Joseph Walsh seized her, hurried her on board a boat, took her to a ship lying in wait, and carried her a prisoner to Dunkirk, then the haunt of a number of lawless pirates, and here Walsh announced that he had married her.

This barefaced abduction excited considerable interest. The few State papers preserved belonging to this case show the energy which the Parliamentary Council of State used in her behalf. We learn from the unpublished calendar the following facts, but the petition itself does not appear to have been preserved.

"1649, Oct. 15. Whitehall. Council of State to Sir Thomas Walsingham and Col. Blount. The enclosed petition, setting forth a foul fact committed at Greenwich, in seizing upon and carrying away Mrs. Jane Puckering, having been presented to us, we desire you to use all means for the recovery of the gentlewoman, and punishment of the offenders; and in order thereto, to examine the whole business upon oath, and return the examinations to us, that further course may be taken by writing letters beyond sea or otherwise. You are also to take order that those guilty of that fact be secured, in order to be proceeded against according to law. [I. 94, p. 488; 63, p. 140.]

"1649, Oct. 20. Council of State. Day's Proceedings. 18. Mrs. Magdalen Smith to have a pass for Flanders, to seek Mrs. Jane Puckering, as also letters of favour to the parliamentary agents there, to give her assistance in regaining Mrs. Puckering. Mr. Frost to confer with the Spanish Ambassador, and desire his letters for Flanders for the same object, as also for the surrender of the offenders, who carried her away contrary to law.

"1649, Nov. 5. Council of State to Col. Popham. We have been moved by some friends of Mrs. Puckering, lately stolen from Greenwich, and carried violently into Flanders, that a ship might be sent to Nieuport, to receive her on board, and bring her to England; you are therefore to order a ship of considerable force (as there is a party there that will endeavour to engage the pickeroons thereabouts to rescue her), to go to Nieuport in Flanders, and there receive her and her company, and carefully bring her over to England. The captain must give her and her company the best accommodation the ship will afford. [I. 94, p. 517.]

"1649, Dec. 10. Council of State. Day's Proceedings. 16. To write Mr. Thelwall to press for the delivery of Mrs. Puckering, that she may be sent to England."

From other sources we learn that she was not delivered into the hands of the authorities until 1650, when Parliament passed an Act to authorize the Lords Commissioners to inquire into the alleged marriage with Walsh, for Jane was heiress to great possessions in Warwick, Leamington, and elsewhere. The Court declared the alleged marriage void, and in the following year Jane married Sir John Baled, and died in childbirth January 27, 1652.

Sir Henry Newton, the nephew of Sir Thomas Puckering, succeeded to the estates. He was a staunch Royalist, who encountered Cromwell himself. He was so heavily fined that he had to sell his paternal estates at Charlton, near Greenwich, but he lived until January 22, 1700. The estate then passed to Lady James Bowyer, and after her decease to Captain Grantham, whose profuse hospitality obliged him to sell the Priory, which was then purchased by Mr. Henry Wise, of Brompton, the ancestor of the Wises of Woodcote and Shrublands.

For Faith and Conscience.

THE cause of Parliament was triumphant in Warwickshire long before the battle of Naseby and the second Lord Denbigh ruled over the Midlands, after the death of Lord Brooke at Lichfield. At Hopton, Lord Northampton had died of his wounds. At the capture of Birmingham the first Lord Denbigh had been wounded and was in a fair way of recovery, when his servant let him fall on the floor, and thus opened his wounds afresh. The whole history of the Civil Wars does not contain a more touching episode than the letters of the Feilding family during the struggle. The first Countess Denbigh beseeches her son to continue loyal, but he fought on the side of the Parliament at Edgehill. The letters of the second Lord Denbigh and of his wife are preserved at Newnham still.

There are two episodes preserved in the original but unpublished MMS. of Dugdale, which show the sufferings of the established clergy, and the indignities they had to undergo at the hands of the dominant party. The Rev. Gaius White, of Packington, and the Rev. Samuel Wilks, the vicar of Wappenbury, suffered with the Rev.

Francis Holyoke, of Southam, for their attachment to Church and King.

On the anniversary of the battle of Edgehill, or, as Dugdale puts it—

"'In the year 1643, on Sunday, October 22nd, the minister of Stonely (about five miles from Warwick), being in the pulpit, where he laboured to move his auditory to relieve their poore, especially in these dayes when he could not goe abroad to beg of others, one Bowyer, a trooper of Sergeant-Major Pouts, with two or three more of his fellowes, came to the church doore and discharged a pistoll. Afterwards they entered the church, where, having heard a little of the sermon, this Bowyer openly told the preacher that he lyed, calling to him in the pulpit three or foure times. The minister replyed that the church was no place for such unusual language; whereupon thease youths went into the churchyard and discharged their pistols against the window near the pulpit, hoping thereby to have murthered the preacher, to the great affrightment of all the people.' This is the statement given in one of the diurnals of those troublous times, the *Mercurius Anglicus* (for the forty-fifth week ending November 11th), under the influence of the King's adherents; but, as the Parliamentarians have not denied the fact, there can be no doubt of it. The *Mercurius Britanicus*, a publication on the other side of the question, thus comments upon the statement in its thirteenth number, 23rd: 'Anlicus tells us of one Mr. Stonely (confounding the name of person with that of the place), a prelaticall minister, how Master Bowyer, a Parliament trooper, affrighted him in the pulpit with the shot of a pistoll. Anlicus, indeed it was a pity, I must needs confesse, for your ministers are not so often in the pulpit, that they need not be shot out again, and it was more the pity that Master Stonely was so used, because I understand by some of his parishoners the good man had not troubled the pulpit sixe weekes before; and they say he now sweares, since he cannot be quiet he will not come in the pulpit in hast. I ever thought there was something that made the clergy so tender of coming there, but I never knew a reason till now. But suppose Master Bowyer discharged a pistoll at the church walls, could not Master Stonely discharge his duty in the church for all that. This miserable quibbler ends, as usual, with an invective against the establishment, or, as he terms them, malignant clergy.'"

The old fortified house known as Astley Castle was

taken by the parliamentarians early in the disturbances, and preserved under the circumstances detailed by Dugdale as follows :—

"In the time of the late . . . (sic.) the manor house was made a garrison by the Parliament, and one Goodere Hunt, a shoemaker in Coventre, constituted Governour thereof; for, beside a large and deepe mote yt it hath, the walls thereof are imbattled, it having had the reputation of a castle, upon wch occasion one . . . . . Burton, the then vicar of Filongley (near at hand), having been a fierce instigator of ye people to take armes for ye Cauk (as they termined it), and therefore fearing to be disturbed at his habitation by some of ye King's ptye, likewise himself to this strongholde for protection, where he became in the nature of a chaplaine to ye soldiers, and preacht in the church of Astley, under the protection of yt garrison. Whilst he continued there some of ye King's forces of Ashby-de-la-Zouch (in Leicestershire) were taken prisoners and brought to Astley, who one day espying an advantage by ye Governour's absence, and the weaknesse of those yt were then left in ye house, made their escape, wherein this Burton, endeavouring to resist them, received such a knock yt he shortly dyed, for whose buriall, his companions making a grave in the chancell hapned to digg upon the beforemenconed coffin of lead, where the Marquesse he body lay, wch as a special booty they took up, and converted the lead into bullets, turning out the bones and dust of that noble person into ye open churchyard (wch since, by the care of the said Mr. Chamberlayne, were again buryed), laying the body of yr seditious priest in his roome. From this Thomas, Marquesse Dorst. is Henry, now Earle of Stamford, Lord Grey of Groby (by his second sonne John Grey, of Pirgo, in Essex) descended."

In 1655 was published a catalogue of the lords, knights, and gentlemen who had compounded for their estates in Warwickshire.

This contains a list of perhaps the greater part of the Royalist nobility and gentry in the different counties in England, with the several sums at which each was assessed. The local names are arranged alphabetically.

Those of the county of Warwick are as under :—

	£	s.	d.
Adderley, Sir Charle[illegible]m, Warwichshire	407	10	0
Broth, Edw., of Edrington, Warwickshire, Gent. ..	59	10	0
Brown, Hen., of Tiso, Warwick	3	6	8
Clark, Sir Sym., of Broom, Warwickshire, Bar. ..	800	0	0
Court, John, of Ulnhall, Warwickshire, Yeom. ..	64	18	0
Clark, Matth., Oxhill, Warwick	15	0	0
Dugdale, Will., Shewstock, Warwickshire, Gent. ..	168	0	0
Fisher, Sir Clem., Packington, Warwickshire, Bar. .. with 30 p. an. settled	840	13	4
Fisher, Fran., of Parkington, Warwickshire, Gent. ..	422	13	0
Fisher, Tho., of Parkington, Warwickshire, Gent. ..	559	16	7
Gwillin, Peter, of Southam, Gent.	113	6	8
Grosvenour, Fulke, Morhall, Warwickshire, Esq. ..	856	10	0
Grosvenour, Gowen, Sutton Cofield	81	0	0
Glover, Robert, Mancetter, Warwickshire, Gent. ..	75	0	0
Gibbs, Sir Hen., and Thomas, his son, of Huntington, Warwick	517	0	0
Halford, William, of Halford, Warwickshire, Gent. ..	98	0	0
Harbech, Thomas, Colleshall, Warwickshire	24	0	0
Holt, Sir Thomas, of Aston Com., Warwickshire, Baron	4401	2	4
Lucy, Spencer, Charlcot, Warwickshire, Gent.	3513	0	0
Leigh, Sir Tho., Sen., of Stone Leigh Com., Warwickshire, Knight	4895	0	0
Mather, John, Mancetter, Warwickshire, Gent. ..	43	10	0
Northampton, Earl James .. .. with 2701 per annum settled	1571	18	4
Parker, Edmund, Hartshil, Warwickshire	239	0	0
Philpot, John, Lighthorn, Warwickshire, Clerk	73	0	0
Palmer, Giles, of Compton, Warwickshire, Gent. ..	1236	13	4
Rogers, Matthew, of Claverdon, Warwickshire	20	3	0
Repington, Sir John, of Annington, Warwickshire, Kt... with 601 per annum settled	408	0	0
Raleigh, George, of Farnborough, Warwickshire, Esq. .. with 50 pounds per annum settled	289	7	6
Underhill, Sir Hercules, and William, his nephew, of Idlicott, Warwickshire, Knight	1177	8	4
Warner, George, of Wolston, Warwickshire, Esq. .. 361 per annum settled for his life	860	0	0

The Stars and Stripes.

"ARGENT, two bars gules. on a chief of the first, three mullets of the second." Such were the arms allowed by the Herald's College; such were the arms emblazoned in the windows of Seckington Church as the heraldic insignia of the house and family of Washington.

In the time of Henry VIII. Laurence Washington, of Wharton, in Lancashire, left his native village to push his fortune in London. He had every inducement to do so, for his mother's brother was an alderman and merchant in the great city. Laurence entered himself as a member of Gray's Inn, but under the advice of his uncle, Sir Thomas Kitson, he forsook the law to become a merchant of the staple in the town of Northampton. During the fifty years which had elapsed since the battle of Bosworth Field, commerce had extended with gigantic strides; on every hand it was growing, and afforded an opportunity for the young and adventurous, which the scions of many noble houses were not slow to avail themselves of. Not only was wealth to be gained, but unknown countries to be explored, and the fabled riches of Ind and Cathay waited but to be secured by the merchant adventurers. Many a noble name is associated with that of Sir Thomas Gresham as the founders of the Royal Exchange, and it is not a matter of wonder that Laurence Washington left the law and addressed himself to the wool trade, then the great trade of the Midlands.

In Northampton Laurence Washington found a home, by the advice and assistance of his uncle, and entered largely into the wool trade. In 1532 he was Mayor of Northampton, and when the dissolution of monasteries occurred, he had no difficulty in procuring a grant of the manor of Sulgrave and other estates which had formerly belonged to the monastery of St. Andrew's in the town in which he lived.

To Sulgrave then the successful merchant retired, and erected a fair manor house as the seat of his family. He lived until the 19th day of February, in the twenty-sixth year of the reign of Queen Elizabeth (1583-4), leaving a family of seven daughters and two sons—Robert, who inherited the family estates, and Laurence, who appears to have followed his father's original profession of a lawyer. This must have been the Laurence Washington, of Gray's Inn, who purchased on the 24th day of February, 1582-3, lands at Whitacre inferior, in the county of Warwick—lands which he resold six years after to the poor Leicestershire squire, George Villiers, of Brooksby, whose son was destined to become famous as the

"Steenie" Duke of Buckingham, the favourite of James I. and companion of King Charles.

Robert Washington succeeded to the family estate at Sulgrave, and married Elizabeth, the daughter and heiress of Walter Light, of Radway. He had many

HOUSE OF WASHINGTON, AT BRINGTON.

kinsmen, who, like the Spencers, of Wormleighton and of Claverdon, had made fortunes in the wool trade, and had intermarried with members of the family of Sir Thomas Kitson. Sulgrave is only some eight miles from Wormleighton, and barely twice that distance from

Althorp, the Northamptonshire seat of the Spencer family.

It was a matter of common remark that the descent of the alienated Church property never reached the third generation in a direct line, and Sulgrave proved no exception to the rule. The seventeenth century had but just dawned when ruin fell on the family of Washington, and Sulgrave was to know them no more.

In many of the church windows on the Northamptonshire borders the familiar red bars and mullets attest the importance of the family; but it is at Great Brington, some half a dozen miles from Northampton, that we must seek the signs of the Washingtons. In this village, on the very edge of Althorp Park, is a plainly built but substantial stone house, which bears over the doorway, on a stone tablet,

"THE LORD GEVETH, THE LORD TAKETH AWAY;
BLESSED BE THE NAME OF THE LORD.
CONSTRUCTA 1606."

In this house Laurence Washington found a home when his prospects were sad and his home bereaved of his dear ones, for Lord Spencer remembered the claims of blood and kindred, and gave a welcome and a shelter to the ruined man. In 1610 the estate at Sulgrave was sold, and with the relics of his fortune Laurence left Brington and the house to his brother Robert, who lived and died therein. Robert appeared to have rented the windmill of Lord Spencer, and though a frequent visitor at Althorp, did not occupy the position which his elder brother and his children did.

There appears to have been considerable friendliness between the families of Villiers, Duke of Buckingham, and the Washingtons—one of them married Buckingham's sister—and to the good offices of the latter more than one of Laurence's children received the honour of knighthood. They appear to have been on very familiar terms at Althorp, for their names appear in the account books as visitors there and at Wormleighton two or three times a year, until the Civil Wars broke out and the Washington's took the side of the King. At this time Laurence Washington, the grandson of the original grantee of Sulgrave, was dead and buried at Brington. His epitaph records that he died on the 13th of Decemher, 1616. His brother Robert died on the 10th of March, 1622, whose wife Elizabeth died on the 19th of the same month in the same year.

The sons of Laurence were Sir William, of Packington, county Leicester, and Sir John, of South Cave. The latter had married Mary, daughter of Sir Philip Curtis, of Islip, and he died in January, 1624, leaving three sons, Mordaunt, John, and Philip.

Of the part they took in the Civil Wars we know but little. We know that they frequented the old hall of Wormleighton, which yet remains, though it is said to have been burnt down in the Civil Wars. It was here that Prince Rupert slept the night before the Edgehill fight. Here may be seen the relics of the "Star Chamber," the Clock Tower, and the Tudor Hall.

In 1657, John Washington and his brother Laurence, disgusted with the Commonwealth and the existing state of things, left England with one at least of his sons for Virginia. He took with him the insignia of his race, the mullet and the bars of his shield, and the spread eagle of his crest.

When a century later the great grandson of John Washington was a colonel under General Braddock, and led the revolted colonists through the War of Independence, the new empire of the west required an ensign to distinguish it among the nations of the earth. What could be more appropriate than the red striped bars of the Washington family arms, with the star-like mullets borne in chief? The out-of-the-way village of Seckington has lost the coat which once shone in the windows of its church. A great nation has found it, and for each stripe and each star there is a state, while the nation have taken the eagle from the coronet and, made it like the bird of Jove—ready to soar aloft.

The King's Preserver.

WHETHER, as his enemies remarked, Cromwell had made a compact with the evil one or not, it is remarkable that many of the greatest events of his career occurred on the 3rd of September. It was on this day, in the year 1650, that he defeated the Scots at Dunbar. It was on this day, in the following year, he won what he called "the crowning mercy" of the battle of Worcester, and made Charles II., young and ambitious, if not heroic, a fugitive and a wanderer. He left Worcester after the fight was over by St. Martin's Gate. A few Cavaliers lingered behind to divert the victorious Roundheads from immediate pursuit, when Charles found himself with David Leslie and the Scottish cavalry, which had done such scurvy service during the fight. Even amid the clatter of the horses' hoofs the murmur of the city could be heard, for in street and home the inhabitants were being pillaged and, if combative, slaughtered. At Bradbourne Bridge the King waited for a few minutes to let his few faithful adherents come up, and then with heavy hearts they turned their horses' heads towards the north.

It was a true mid-autumn evening, and as the troop glanced behind them they could see the purple Malverns throwing the shadows of evening over the vale as the sun set behind them. Clouds of smoke, and a dismal crash ascended from the "faithful city," whilst beyond the landscape was dotted by points of fire: for many miles along the slopes of "sandy-bottomed Severn." It was the last sad glance of civil warfare, only to be renewed in England by the son of the young King who was now fleeing from it.

Long experience had told the party that it was wise to avoid the towns. Droitwich was therefore left on the right hand. They passed the ford of the Salwarp at Hensford Mill, and at the Mitre Oak turned off for Hartlebury, and thus avoided Stourport. The party, who had long left Leslie and his horse behind, now skirted the valley in which Kidderminster lies, and proceeded by Chester Lane and Greenhill to Broadwaters. The fine views were lost to them in the gloom of the evening as they passed up Black Hill to Sion Hill, over what is now Lea Park, to Kinfare Heath. The manifest dangers of the heath induced the party to venture through Stourbridge, even at the risk of arousing any stray troops of militia which might be quartered there. A sudden dash dispersed the few parliamentarians who attempted to oppose their progress, and the party found themselves on the road to Wordesley and King Swinford. The party, after leaving Wombourn, entered Brewood Forest, where Charles had determined to seek shelter, for in this remote locality, then all forest land, the Giffards Lords of Chillington, had two hunting lodges inhabited by faithful followers named Penderel. The houses had been constructed by the Giffards in troublous times as hiding places for proscribed Papists and their priests. In White Ladies or Boscobel the King, it was certain, would find shelter, if not perfect security.

The grey streak of morning could be perceived in the east ere Charles Giffard, Colonel Carlos, and two or three faithful nobles and soldiers stood with the King before the picturesque house known as White Ladies. The ruins of a Cistercian Priory adjoined the house, and formed a picturesque scene. At this house, after a hasty meal, Charles was disguised as a forester with leathern jerkin and trunk hose. His long hair was cropped and his hands sooted; all his regal insignia was stripped off; his retinue departed, some to seek safety in disguise, others to join General Leslie, in the hope of being able to reach Scotland and safety. Yet within a few hours Leslie was a prisoner, his troops scattered, and many of Charles's friends in the hands of their enemies.

Charles remained all day concealed in a coppice at Brewood. In the evening, under the name of Will Jackson, he supped with one of the Penderel's, before he tried to cross the Severn by Madeley Bridge, in order to escape to France by way of the Welsh ports. On arriving at Madeley House, inhabited by Mr. Woolfe, a Cavalier, the King found the fords and bridges guarded, and after a few hours rest returned to Brewood, and on the morning of the third day after the Worcester fight sought refuge at Boscobel. It was on this day that the King and Colonel Carlos remained concealed in a large oak near the house. The next day they had another narrow escape, and in the evening they left Boscobel for Moseley. On the road thither the King had a narrow chance of capture. After a brief stay at Moseley, during which the house was searched and the celebrated priest catcher, Southall, nearly found out his hiding place, he left at night for Bentley Hall, in Staffordshire, where he was lodged in the servants' apartments under the name of Will Jones,* a groom.

Bentley Hall was a plain stone building with step gables, of which no portion now remains; but in September, 1651, it was the seat of Colonel Lane, a distinguished Cavalier officer who had fought at Worcester. His name is better known in history as the father of Mistress Jane Lane, his beautiful daughter, to whose courage and devotion the King, after the Penderels owed his life and preservation from his enemies. Jan

* In the various accounts which have come down to us these names are used indiscriminately.

Lane had been introduced to the King at Worcester, and had there expressed her ardent desire to assist the King against his enemies. Within a brief week her desire was granted, and she became the preserver of the King's life.

When the troubles which led to the Civil War broke out, Sir Robert Fisher, of Packington, was lord of the manor of Leamington Priors, and a devoted Royalist. King Charles I., in his progress through the country to levy troops a few days before he attacked Coventry, on the 18th of August, 1642, stayed at Packington, and the next day at Kenilworth. Nine years had elapsed, and his son, Sir Clement Fisher, had succeeded to his honours at Packington and Leamington. Sir Clement was in the prime of manhood, and was the betrothed husband of Jane Lane when the fugitive King arrived at Bentley House.

A project had been conceived by the King's friends which Jane Lane had promised to carry out, if the King was willing, which opened up a means of escape from the Midlands, if not from a southern or western port to France. The brother of Jane Lane had procured a pass from Captain Stone, the Puritan Governor of Stafford, for his sister and her groom to proceed from Bentley Hall to Abbott's Leigh, near Bristol, the residence of Mr. Norton, a relative of the family. It was originally designed that Lord Wilmot should act as the groom, but the plan was changed, and the King reluctantly consented to take his place.

On the following morning, after reaching Bentley, the disguised King left the house with Jane Lane on a pillion behind him. It was not an uncommon fashion for ladies to travel thus until the commencement of the present century. Mr. Petre, who had married Jane Lane's eldest sister, accompanied the pair with his wife, while Colonel Lane and a servant or two followed some distance behind. Bentley Hall was situated near Bloxwich, a line drawn from that place to Boscobel, and from that retreat to Madeley, and from Madeley to Bloxwich, a district some twenty miles in breadth from east to west, and some six or seven miles broad, represents the scene of the eventful week which Charles was leaving behind him for ever. The first stage was Great Packington, some twenty miles across Warwickshire, where the party were expected by Sir Clement Fisher to dine, and their course lay slightly to the east of Birmingham. They reached the high road between Darlaston, Wednesbury, and then struck off into one of the numerous byeways which traversed the country towards the Great Barr, passing through what is now known as the King's Vale, which runs in the hollow beneath the clump of trees known as the King's Standing. They were now on the borders of Warwickshire, close to Erdington, and in this neighbourhood the horse on which the King rode cast a shoe, and on taking the horse to the village blacksmith Charles chatted with the smith whilst the horse was shod, and in him he found an outspoken Republican who plainly told the King what he should like to see done, and Charles concurred, saying if the King was taken he deserved hanging more than the rest, on which the smith told him he spoke like an honest man. From Castle Bromwich the road was lonely enough until they reached Packington, where a warm welcome awaited the party. After partaking of some refreshment, Jane Lane and the King, accompanied by Mr. and Mrs. Petre, passed on their way to Long Marston, where it was proposed to pass the night at the house of Mr. Tombs, a relative of Colonel Lane's.

The whole character of the scenery now changed. The country was traversed by still lanes. Green trees were on every hand. Passing through the quiet village of Hampton-in-Arden, they had a glimpse of the great forest land spread out before them. The quaint house of Wharley, at Estcote, first met their gaze. They went from hence along the hill tops to Knowle, leaving the old preceptory and church of Balsall on their left. From Knowle their route was by Lapworth, until they again struck the high road from Birmingham to Oxford at Lapworth Bridge. The road to Stratford was now straight before them. At Henley-in-Arden, the party stopped to bait their horses, when they learnt that a troop of horse had preceded them on their way to Stratford. At Wootton Wawen, two miles on the road, they were stopped by the troopers, and for the moment it seemed that the capture of the King hung on the balance. On production of the pass they were permitted to go on their journey. At Bearley Cross they hesitated at the route they should pursue. They knew that the bridges over the Avon were strictly guarded, and the possibility of a ford higher up the Avon seems to have been debated, for Stratford was the well-known head quarters of parliamentary troops. They, however, passed forward along the heights of Pathlow, where there was another road branching off to the wished-for river. On arriving within a mile of Stratford, they perceived some troopers ahead of them. It was this that induced them to retrace their steps for some distance, when they turned to the south until they reached the road to Warwick, between Ingon and Snitterfield. They then, when near the Oak now called the "King's Oak," in King's Lane, turned their horses' heads again towards Stratford Bridge, which they were thus enabled to approach, without entering the town or encountering the troopers.* Though it is not known precisely how Charles crossed

* In a privately printed work of Mr. Frederick Manning, of Byron Lodge, Leamington, this route and all the places associated with Charles's escape are accurately depicted.

the Avon, there is no doubt the production of the pass would satisfy the guard at the bridge and enable them to pass on to Long Marston.

Their progress appears to have aroused some suspicion, for some troopers followed them to the old house at Long Marston, which still exists, and on their appearance being noted, the cook in the kitchen set Charles to wind up the jack, but seeing his awkwardness, struck him with the basting ladle, adding some not very complimentary remarks just as the soldiers entered the kitchen. This disarmed any suspicions they might have, and in this old house the remains of the jack are still preserved.

On the following day they proceeded, viâ Campden and Stowe-on-the-Wold, along the Cotswold hills to Cirencester, where they passed the night, and the next day passed on to Abbot's Leigh, where they arrived safely. When we consider the roads, the distance traversed each day seems very great, though the need was great to cross the hostile shire of Warwick and the troops which patrolled the county round Worcester and the vale of Evesham.

Disappointed of a vessel at Bristol, the fugitive monarch proceeded to Castle Carey, where he was sheltered by Colonel Wyndham. At Lyme he hoped to obtain a ship to France, and the King, Miss Coningsby, and Colonel Wyndham started for Charmouth, where Captain Ellesdon had engaged a bark to convey a runaway bridal party to France. All preparations were made for the voyage, but the skipper, one Lumbry, confided the secret to his wife, who not only threatened to betray him, but locked him in his room, so that he could not fulfil his engagement. In the meantime Charles and his faithful friends during half the night paced up and down the beach vainly expecting the boat. Disappointed, but not hopeless, the King next made for Bridport, with the hope of escaping to the Channel Islands, and took shelter in the out-of-the-way village of Broad Windsor. The joyful tidings were at last brought that Lord Wilmot had been successful in procuring a ship. The King, therefore, proceeded to Brighton, put up at the George Hotel, were they were introduced to Captain Nicholas Tattersall. There they remained up all night, and at four o'clock the next morning set out for Shoreham, from whence they set sail at seven o'clock the same evening. Next morning the King and his followers landed on the coast of Normandy, and after being mistaken for thieves at Rouen, reached Paris in safety. On the same day, just six weeks after the crushing defeat at Worcester, Lord Derby was beheaded in his own town of Bolton.

Jane Lane lived to become Lady Fisher. Her portrait still adorns the walls of the re-edified Packington Hall. Her grandniece, the daughter and heiress of another Sir Clement Fisher, married Heneage, the second Earl of Aylesford, and thus the present owners of the manor of Leamington became Lords of Packington and possessors of the estate of the Fishers. When the Restoration took place, Charles thought of rewarding his faithful Cavaliers and friends by bestowing on them a new order of knighthood, to be called "The Royal Oak." In a MSS. of Peter le Neve, Norroy, King at Arms, dated 1660, the following names of intended knights, with the value of their estates, are given :—

Middlemore, Edgbaston	£2000
William Combes, Stratford..	800
William Dylke, Maxstoke Castle	800
Richard Verney, Compton	600
Thomas Flint, Allesley	700
Thomas Boughton, Lawford	800
Edward Peto, Chesterton	1800
William Wood	800
John Bridgman	1000
John Keyte, Camden	1000
— Seabright, Reppington	1000
— Jennings, Broomshaw	1000
— Sheldon, Bedley	2000
Captain Geo. Rawley	700

The Bottle of Laurel Water.

THAT portion of the borough of Warwick known as the Saltisford, where Messrs. Webb and Barron's brewery now stands, has been the scene of many exciting events. In modern days the last lion fight of England took place on this spot,* when bull dogs were set to bait tame lions for the gratification of brutal tastes and the winning of a few bets. On the second day of April, 1781, it was the scene of an event which marked the end of a tragedy of another kind. Though it was not yet seven o'clock there was a large crowd assembled. There was a gallows erected, and down the hill there came from the gate a mourning coach followed by a hearse, and the Sheriff's officers dressed in deep mourning. Every now and anon, as the coach moved slowly on, the head of a handsome man was seen from the window of the mourning coach, beseeching the prayers of the people for him. On arriving at the scaffold much ceremonious punctilio took place between himself and the

* In Hone's series of Every Day Books there is an account of the fight between bull dogs and "Nero" and "Wallace," two of Wombwell's lions on this spot.

Sheriff, Captain Wren, as to which should alight first, though it was customary for the malefactor to do so, and this the Sheriff demanded with an expletive which need not be repeated. There then alighted from the carriage a well-built, handsome man, dressed in deep mourning, who ascended the ladder at the foot of the scaffold and prayed for a considerable time. He then in an audible voice addressed the spectators in these terms: "That he was then going to appear before God, to whom all deceit was known: he solemnly declared *that he was innocent of the crime for which he was to suffer!* That he had drawn up a vindication of himself, which he hoped the world would believe, for it was of more consequence to him to speak truth than falsehood, and had no doubt but that time would reveal the many mysteries that had arisen at his trial, and prove that he fell a sacrifice to the malice and black designs of his——." After praying some time he let his handkerchief fall, the drop fell, and all that was mortal of Captain John Donnellan was swinging in the morning air. He was executed thus early because the executioner had that morning to go to Washwood Heath to execute Hammond and Pitmore for the murder of Mr. Berwick, a butcher, of Birmingham.

Though nearly a century has elapsed since Captain Donnellan was executed, and though his story has been the theme of novel writers, of compilers of guide books, of lawyers and medical jurists, the romantic story of the Irish adventurer and his crimes have not lost their interest, though Lawford Hall, the scène of the Laurel Water tragedy, has long been levelled with the ground.

In June, 1777, the Dowager Lady Boughton, of Lawford Hall, near Rugby, went with her daughter to Bath to "drink the waters" and indulge in the frivolities and gaieties described by Christopher Anstey in the "New Bath Guide." At that juncture Bath was popular and the inns were full. The Warwickshire ladies seemed likely to have no more easy accommodation for the night than a couple of chairs in the coffee-room afforded. At this timely juncture a young and handsome young officer, with a smooth tongue and pleasant manner, staying at the inn, heard of their dilemma, and with a gallantry highly commendable, insisted on surrendering his bedroom to the ladies. Charmed with his politeness and manner, the ladies not only accepted his offer, but invited him to breakfast the next morning. Captain John Donnellan met his fate and its consequences at that inn.

Who could resist the plausible but unfortunate soldier. As a subaltern of the 39th Regiment, he had been foremost among the English assailants of Masulipatam, the capital of Golconda, when it was taken by storm from the French. He, for the consideration of 800 rupees, undertook to sort certain bales and chests from the loot which had been claimed by native merchants. For this he had been deprived of his commission, and had returned to England, where he was placed on half-pay, and now, by gambling, fortune hunting, and other impostures of the day, he sought advancement in life and a future livelihood. He had been master of the ceremonies when the new Pantheon was opened in 1772. Miss Boughton had never seen such a man. He wooed and won. An elopement followed, but the rage of her family was appeased when the generous Irishman agreed to abandon all share in his wife's fortune. A year after his marriage he came with his wife to reside at Lawford Hall, where his brother-in-law, Sir Theodosius Boughton, was brought from Eton, to begin life as a Warwickshire squire.

The character of Sir Theodosius was not a pleasant one. He had literally "wallowed in vice" at Eton. He was wilful, sickly, and quarrelsome, and though only twenty years of age on August 3, 1780, he seemed to have ruined his constitution by debauchery. He was in constant squabbles, from which he was glad of the assistance of his experienced brother-in-law to extricate him. Yet it was known that Sir Theodosius detested Captain Donnellan, and hated him with a hate that seemed like a presentiment of the fate in store for him.

The brotherly interest which Captain Donnellan took in the young baronet was shown in a variety of ways. He had spoken doubtfully of his health. Before August, 1780, he had suggested to Lady Boughton that "something or other might happen." He had warned her, too, against drinking out of the same cup, as the young squire was being salivated, and in the habit of mixing poison for rats. In a conversation with Mr. Newsom, the rector of Newbold, the gallant Captain had told some stories respecting the health of Sir Theodosius, and in reply to a remark of the rector, had said that he did not think the young man's life worth one year's purchase. This was on Saturday, the 26th of August. On the Tuesday following, Samuel Frost, one of the servants of the house, brought over some medicine, composed of rhubarb, jalap, spirits of lavender, nutmeg water, and syrup, which had been prepared by Mr. Powell, surgeon, of Rugby. The lad delivered the medicine, which was in a two-ounce bottle, to Sir Theodosius himself on the staircase, and at six o'clock Frost accompanied the young baronet out fishing.

It was a pleasant time of the year, the fruit was ripe in the gardens, and Mrs. Donnellan accompanied her mother during a walk in the gardens for an hour, and on their return to the hall at seven o'clock they met the Captain. who said that he had been down to see the fishing, and in vain tried to persuade his brother-in-law to return, as he might catch cold with the night air and the heavy dew. Captain Donnellan then had a basin of milk, his usual supper, and retired to bed. At nine o'clock Sir Theodosius came in, tired, but apparently well, had a little supper, and went to bed after arranging with his mother to send Sam Frost to a Northamptonshire gentleman, named Fonnereau, with a net for some fish, as he expected some friends the following day.

At six o'clock the next morning, in obedience to a summons from Sam Frost, who wanted some straps for the fishing net, the young baronet jumped out of bed and gave them to the boy. At seven his mother came in to give him his rhubarb draught, and she found him very well. He told her where the draught was to be found, and he asked for a bit of cheese to take the taste out of his mouth. She read the label on the bottle to satisfy him it was the right draught—"The purging draught, for Sir Theodosius Boughton." She poured out the liquid, remarking it smelt like bitter almonds. Some of it was spilt on the table in attempting to shake the contents. The boy ate a bit of cheese and laid down on the bed, remarking how nauseous the draught was.

In a few minutes he began to struggle; there was a gurgling in his throat; but directly afterwards he seemed inclined to sleep. His mother then left him, but on looking in a few minutes later, to her horror, she found him in unusual agony, his teeth clenched, and froth oozing from his mouth. He was evidently dying. In her agony she rushed down stairs, called the coachman, William Frost, to ride for Mr. Powell, as her son was dying. There was only one horse in the stable, for the Captain had gone to Newnham Wells to drink the waters.* Just then the Captain rode up, and the coachman leaped on the mare and rode off to Rugby.

The Captain had made some remark to the coachman which the other did not hear, and he then went up stairs and coolly asked Lady Boughton what she wanted. She told him what had happened, and that the medicine would have killed a dog if he had taken it. He asked where the physic bottle was. She pointed to two bottles, one which had been emptied on Saturday, and the one that morning. Donnellan took up the last bottle and began to pour water into it, shook it, and emptied its contents into a basin of dirty water. This aroused the suspicions of Lady Boughton, who cried, "You ought not to do that. What are you at? You should not meddle with the bottles." In spite of this the Captain served the other bottle the same,

* The wells at Newnham. "Anno Christi 1579. The three wells at Newman Regis, in this county, were found out in Whitsun week by one Clement Dawes, who, having received a great wound in his arm by a hatchet, by washing it in this water, within a few days space it was perfectly whole. One special effect of this water is that it turneth wood into stone. At Newman Regis is a fountain whose waters are very sovereign against the stone, green wounds, ulcers, and imposthumes; and being drunk with salt loosens, but with sugar binds the body."—Clarke's "Geography," p. 173, misprinted. London, 1671.

and then mixing the bottles together, asked Sarah Blundell to remove the water and the bottles. Her ladyship interfered, when the Captain requested that the dirty linen in the room might be removed. He remarked that the stockings might be wet and occasion the boy's death, but Lady Boughton, on feeling the stockings, found that they were not damp, nor had they been so.

The proceedings of the Captain were very strange. He requested the gardener to kill a couple of pigeons to put to the boy's feet, and have them ready when the doctor came. When the gardener took the pigeons into the house the young baronet was dead. In the few still hours of that dark morning he remarked to his wife that Lady Boughton had taken notice of his washing the bottles out. He called the coachman to vouch that he only went out of the house when he rode to the wells. When the doctor came he was told that the young man had died in convulsions after taking the medicine, but no suspicions were mentioned of the contents of the bottle.

The Captain in the course of the morning wrote to Sir William Wheler, of Leamington Hastings, the guardian of the boy, this studious announcement of his death.

"Lawford Hall, August 31st, 1780.

"Dear Sir,—I am sorry to be the communicator of Sir Theodosius's death to you, which happened this morning. He has been for some time past under the care of Mr. Powell, of Rugby, for the complaint which he had at Eton. Lady Boughton and my wife are inconsolable they join me in best respects to Lady Wheler and yourself.

"I am, dear sir, with the greatest esteem,

"Your most obedient servant,

"JOHN DONNELLAN.

"To Sir William Wheler, Bart."

In the meantime ugly suspicions were afloat in the servants' hall, in the kitchen, and in the stables. It was remarked that the young baronet had died of poison. Then Sarah Blundell remarked how queer the Captain had behaved. Then Sam Frost declared that the young squire could not have died from wet feet, for he never got off his horse the night before. Then it was found that Captain Donnellan had never been near the fishers. Then the gardener remembered that it was late when he came for the two pigeons, and how he had exulted in being master of Lawford Hall. These suspicions were not long in flying round the country, and though on Sunday Sir Theodosius was soldered up in his leaden coffin, and on Monday everything was prepared for the funeral, and the tenants had assembled, the interment was not to be as yet. In the midst of the preparation Dr. Powell brought a letter from Sir William Wheler to this effect—

"Leamington, September 4th, 1780.

"Dear Sir,—Since I wrote to you last I have been applied to, as the guardian of the late Sir Theodosius Boughton, to inquire into the cause of his sudden death. Report says that he was better the morning of his death, and before he took the physic, than he had been for ma weeks, and that he was taken ill in less than half an hour, and died two hours after he had swallowed the physic; and it will be a great satisfaction to Mr. Powell to have his body opened, and I am sure it must be to you, Lady Boughton, and Mrs. Donnellan, when I assure you that it is reported all over the county that he was killed either by medicine or poison. The county will never be convinced to the contrary unless the body is opened, and I beg of you to lay this matter before Lady Boughton in as tender a manner as possible, and to point out to her the real necessity of complying with my request, and to say that it is expected by the county," &c.

Captain Donnellan was equal to the occasion. He wrote to the careful guardian assenting to the proposal, and at once wrote to Dr. Rattray and Mr. Wilmer, of Coventry, to perform the *post mortem* examination. These gentlemen came late, as well as another letter from Sir William Wheler. A want of frankness was exhibited, and ultimately the doctors departed without opening the body, but each with a handsome fee. On being told that the examination was only for the satisfaction of the family, they recommended immediate burial. This was communicated in ambiguous terms to Sir William Wheler, and the funeral was fixed for the next day.

In the meantime Dr. Bucknill, of Rugby, offered to make the examination, and on the following day Sir William Wheler wrote requesting that Mr. Bucknill and Mr. Snow, of Southam, should open the body Here again prevarication and delay ensued, and ultimately the body was buried at seven o'clock at night without being opened.

If Captain Donnellan thought that all inquiry was over he was much disappointed. The scandal was too notorious to be thus allowed to pass by. The rector of Newbold and Lord Denbigh stirred Sir William Wheler to renewed action, and on the Saturday following the funeral an inquest was held at Newbold. The body was opened by Mr. Bucknill in the presence of Dr. Rattray and Mr. Wilmer, and the acrid flavour of laurel water was detected by Dr. Rattray. The inquest was adjourned till the 14th of September, when the Captain wrote to the coroner for all the information he could collect, and informing him of the careless way in which Sir Theodosius used poisons and left them about. In spite of these asseverations, and his protestation of injured innocence, the coroner's jury returned a verdict of "Wilful murder" against the Captain, and he was removed in custody, first to Rugby, and from thence he was taken, by way of Coventry, to Warwick Gaol, where he was kept chained and in close confinement until his trial.

The *Coventry Mercury* of this period shows how strong the feeling was which existed. Some evidently thought that wrong was being done to an innocent man, and various motives were assigned and misrepresentations made until November 4th, when all notice ceased till the trial, which took place at Warwick on March 30, 1781, before Mr. Justice Buller.

At the trial all these facts were deposed. A number of doctors gave their opinion that Sir Theodosius came by his death through drinking laurel water. A treatise on poison had been found in the locked-up room in which the accused kept his still, with the leaf turned down at laurel water. The lies he had told, and all the prevarications he had made, his boasting, smooth-faced hypocrisy were all laid bare by the keen counsel employed against him. The net of circumstantial evidence was drawn close around him.

The principal witness for his defence was the celebrated anatomist, John Hunter, who thought that Sir Theodosius might have died from epilepsy, and, without proof of the poisoning, declined to believe the laurel water theory of the prosecution. Then the Captain gave an account of his own time to show non-access to the medicine, which was entirely at variance with Lady Boughton's evidence. He stated that he was walking with his child in a field near the house when Sam Frost brought the medicine, and then went into the front garden, when Lady Boughton asked him to help her gather some fruit. He found the fruit above his reach, and then he went to ask Sam Frost to bring a ladder. After Lady Boughton had seen a carpenter named Matthews and a Mr. Dand, Donnellan went with the carpenter to Hewitt's Mill, and on his return he found Lady Boughton cross because her son was stopping out so late. Mrs. Donnellan asked her husband to change his shoes and stockings, which were wet, but he declined, saying that he was tired. He took his milk, and went to bed. He accounted for his actions in the morning by stating that he wanted to accompany Lady Boughton for a ride, but as she said she could not come for a quarter of an hour, he rode to the wells in the meantime. He had done his utmost to produce the very bottle when required by Mr. Caldecote, the solicitor for the prosecution. He had nothing to gain by the death of the baronet, as he had given up all claim on his wife's fortune. On the contrary, Sir Theodosius had promised him the living of Harborough and of Newbold when he came of age, and he was at the time preparing himself for holy orders in consequence.

All his evasions and explanations were in vain. He was found guilty and condemned to death. In Warwick Gaol he accused Lady Boughton of poisoning both her husband and son, and advised his wife to fly from a roof where so many people had died suddenly. On Sunday, the 1st of April, the day before his execution, his last act was to sign and depose to a declaration of his entire innocence and defence of himself, and called upon his solicitors, Messrs. Inge and Webb, to publish it. That defence and the shorthand notes of the trial were published, and the *Coventry Mercury* of June 4, 1781, contains some sharp queries addressed to Donnellan's solicitor, Mr. Webb, who is said to have made a considerable sum through the publication.*

After the death of Captain Donnellan his wife assumed the name of Beecham, and subsequently married Sir Egerton Leigh. Donnellan's two children, a boy and a girl, were kept in ignorance of their parentage, and went by the name of Beecham, until the son, who was intended for the church, was reproved at a ball at Northampton by a tradesmen, for what he thought improper conduct towards a lady. The young man resented the interference of a mere tradesman, when the latter replied that at least he was as good as the son of a murderer. Stung by this remark, the young man made inquiries as to what was meant, and then learnt for the first time who his father was. It preyed on his mind so much that he destroyed himself. The daughter of Donnellan died young.

The daughter of Sir Egerton Leigh and Mrs. Donnellan became Mrs. Boughton Leigh, of Brownsover, and at the death of Sir Egerton, his widow, and the widow of Captain Donnellan, became the wife of Barry O'Meara, the well-known surgeon who attended the first Napoleon at St. Helena.

In 1790, Lawford Hall was sold by Sir Edward Boughton to the Caldecotes. It was then pulled down

* A skilled and experienced solicitor who has read the original papers, preserved in the Staunton collection of Warwickshire antiquities, says the perusal left no doubt of Donnellan's guilt.

as a thing accursed, but some of the outbuildings were preserved for farm purposes. A rude view of it is given in Ireland's "Views on the Avon," and Mr. Matt. Bloxam, F.S.A., has a good drawing of it, made from surveys and measurements, which has been engraved.

The Princess Olive.

As late as the year 1866, the Judge Ordinary of the Court of Probate and Divorce, Sir J. P. Wilde, was engaged in hearing a case which was brought before him by a petition, filed in August, 1865, under the Legitimacy Declaration Act, which is one of the romances of historic Warwickshire, or one of the most remarkable cases of delusions and self-deceit on record.

In order to get a clear idea of the story then told, it is necessary to carry the mind back to the time when Garrick was organizing the first great Shakespearian festival at Stratford-on-Avon. At that period there was living at Warwick a family of respectability named Wilmot, who were house painters by trade. They had some claim to blue blood, if their story is true that they descended from the witty Earl of Rochester, of the later Stuart era; but in 1772 the family consisted of Mrs. Wilmot, her son Robert, and his wife, Hannah Maria. There was another son at Oxford who had some pretensions to scholarship, for in 1769 he became a Doctor of Divinity. He was born in 1716, and at sixteen years of age he had been sent to Oxford, where he took his

M.A. degree in 1748. He was a fellow of his college, and ostensibly a bachelor. In 1782, he became a rector of Barton-on-the-Heath, in the south-western part of the county of Warwick, a place famous for being the birthplace of Sir Thomas Overbury. Though Dr. James Wilmot was presumably a book-worm and a bachelor, he had been the actor in more than one marital drama, which might materially affect the succession to the British crown, if he was not the grandfather of the rightful heiress himself.

It was, however, years after the worthy doctor was dead that he was said to have married a Miss, or rather the Princess Poniatowski, whose brother was subsequently elected King of Poland. This alleged marriage took place about the time James Wilmot became a Master of Arts, for we are told that on the 17th of June, 1750, he had a daughter born whose name was Olive. How the doctor managed to keep his marriage secret no one can tell; but as he is alleged to have privately married George III. to one Hannah Lightfoot prior to the time the King married the Princess Charlotte Sophia of Mecklenburg Strelitz, on September 8, 1761, he must have been an adept at keeping marriage secrets.

In 1767 the doctor, with his new fledged divinity honours, became connected with the family of Lord Archer, of Umberslade, and is said to have visited at that nobleman's house, in Grosvenor Square, with his daughter Olive, then a handsome young lady of seventeen summers. At Lord Archer's house they met the young Prince Henry Frederick, then twenty-two years of age, and created that year Duke of Cumberland. The young Prince was smitten with the charms of the niece of King Poniatowski. He wooed and won. The marriage was celebrated at Lord Archer's house on the 4th of March, 1767. For four years their felicity was unbounded, but in 1771 his Royal Highness the Duke of Cumberland married publicly Lady Anne Luttrell, daughter of the Earl of Carhampton, and widow of Mr. Christopher Horton, of Catton, county Derby. The marriage gave such offence to George III. that the Royal Marriage Act was passed the following year. The daughter of the doctor, first wife of the Duke, found refuge, however, at her grandmother's house at Warwick, and on the 3rd of April, 1772, gave birth to a daughter, which was christened Olive by her grandfather on the same day. On the 15th of the same month, in the same year, Robert Wilmot, the house painter, had a daughter christened Olive at the church of St. Nicholas, and for forty years these Olives were not known asunder, for the doctor did not acknowledge his supposed granddaughter. He only recognised his niece. For forty years Olive—the Princess Olive, as she called herself—was kept in ignorance of her high lineage.

This was the more curious, as it is alleged that on the

day following her birth she was rebaptized by the King's command as Olive, daughter of the Duke of Cumberland. This second baptism was not, however, entered in the parish register, but was placed on record by a certificate signed by Dr. Wilmot, his brother Robert, and John Dunning, afterwards Lord Ashburton. This certificate was confided to the sacred care of the Earl of Warwick, as well as the following document, which was afterwards put in evidence :—

"GEORGE R.

"We are pleased to create Olive of Cumberland Duchess of Lancaster, and to grant our royal authority for Olive, our said niece, to bear and use the title and arms of Lancaster, should she be in existence at the period of our royal demise.

"Given at our Palace of St. James, May 21, 1773.

"(Witnesses)

"CHATHAM.
"J. DUNNING."

The Duke of Cumberland died in 1790, and in the following year Olive married John Thomas Serres, the son of Dominic Serres, and he followed the profession of a portrait and scene painter. It was not until after the decease of George III. that Olive Serres was made acquainted with her high lineage, but in the meantime she had practised as an artist, and, in 1806, obtained the appointment of landscape painter to the Prince of Wales. In 1805, she had published a novel called "St. Julian," and even in 1806 she had another volume ready, consisting of poetical miscellanies, which she termed "Flights [illegible] An opera followed, called the "Castle of [illegible]ogether with a volume of "Letters of Advice to her Daughter." In 1813, she advanced the theory that her late uncle, Dr. Wilmot, was the author of the "Letters of Junius," but that was quickly disproved. This was four years before she was apprised of her royal descent, and that Dr. Wilmot was not her uncle but her grandfather. She was, to use her own words, "the said Olive Serres, having been informed of her proper position in life shortly after the demise of his Majesty King George III., and being (as she had foundation to believe) the legitimate daughter of Henry Frederick, Duke of Cumberland, fourth and youngest brother of his said Majesty, assumed the honour, title, and dignity of a Princess of the blood Royal; styled herself 'her Royal Highness Olive, Princess of Cumberland,' and adopted the royal arms, livery, and seals, in like manner as made use of by other junior members of the Royal family."

In September, 1820, not long after succeeding to the throne, George IV. issued his command, through Lord Sidmouth, that the certificate of marriage between his uncle, the Duke of Cumberland, and the elder Olive Wilmot should be "proved and authenticated." This was done: it was duly authenticated before Lord Chief Justice Abbott (afterwards Lord Tenterden); and the lady in question was told—apparently, however, only verbally—by her solicito[illegible], that his Majesty "had been graciously plea[illegible]owledge her Royal Highness as Princess of Cumberland, only legitimate daughter of his late uncle, Henry Frederick, Duke of Cumberland," and to give orders that she should have found for her a suitable residence until a permanent one could be fixed upon, and that pecuniary means, sufficient to enable her to keep up her dignity, should be at once placed at her command. She was then living in Alfred Place, Bedford Square; and even by her own statement the information does not appear to have been sent to her officially.

The Dukes of Sussex, Clarence, and Kent, it appears, were not slow in acknowledging their new cousin, being satisfied that the documents with their father's signature, "George R.," were genuine; and although the Duke of Cambridge did not acknowledge her till a far more recent date (1844), and the Duke of York refused to follow suit altogether, she maintains that the Duke of Kent had long previously gone so far as not only to make a will bequeathing to her £10,000, and to assign to her and her child a yearly income of £400 under his hand and seal, promising solemnly to see his "cousin reinstated in her Royal birthright at his father's demise," but absolutely to nominate her as the future guardian of his infant daughter, her Majesty Queen Victoria.

In the Session of 1822 or 1823 her case was introduced to the [illegible] Parliament by Sir Gerard Noel. He moved [illegible] Select Committee to inquire into the truth of statements made in her petition, which he had presented three months before. It seems he was very earnest in her cause, thoroughly believed in the genuineness of her case, and persisted in announcing that he "had it in command from this Royal personage" to do so and so—"for Royal personage he would continue to believe her" until she was proved and declared to be an impostor by a Select Committee of the House of Commons. The petition of that day seemed to aim not only at the declaration of Mrs. Ryves's legitimacy and Royal descent, but also to the acquisition of a grant from the Civil List. Sir Gerard Noel declared that he "had always believed that every member of the Royal family was upon the Civil List, but here was a member of the Royal family quite unprovided for."

The motion was seconded by no less a person than Joseph Hume; but Sir Robert Peel, in a most convincing speech, showed the fallacy of the statements, the hollowness of the claim, as well as the injudicious character of the documents used to support it. After sporting the Royal liberties for a time, after dining in State at the Guildhall in 1820, her husband died in 1824; and ten years later this Warwickshire Princess died of broken heart in poverty, if not within the rules of the King's

Bench, and was buried in [illegible]rd of St. James's, Piccadilly, and is entered [illegible]gister of deaths as a Princess of the blood Royal.

Though the Princess Olive was dead and buried, her claims survived. Her daughter, Lavinia Janetta Horton Serres, married a Mr. Ryves, a Dorsetshire gentleman, from whom she afterwards separated. Mrs. Ryves did not let the claims of her mother rest. On the death of George IV. she filed a bill in Chancery against the Duke of Wellington as the King's executor for money due to her mother from the estate of George III., but was defeated by a legal technicality. No other course was open to her until the passing of the "Legitimacy Declaration Act, 1858," when she brought forward a suit to establish her own birth as "the lawful daughter of John Thomas Serres, and Olive his wife." In 1865, she filed the petition to declare the legitimacy of her grandmother's marriage with the Duke of Cumberland. On the 13th of June, 1866, the Court for divorce and matrimonial causes declared that Olive Serres was not the legitimate daughter of the Duke of Cumberland, and that there was no valid marriage between the said Duke and Olive Wilmot. Against this decision Mrs. Ryves appealed to the House of Lords as a last resource. She failed, and the failure broke her heart. She died in poverty in lodgings in Queen's Crescent, Haverstock Hill, at Christmas, 1871, like her mother before her, and is buried in the humblest of humble graves in the cemetery at Highgate.

Her husband died the year before his ambitious wife. Three daughters and two sons yet survive, the heirs only of disappointed hopes and of vain ambition.

The Wager of Battle.

On a dim November day in the early part of the present century an unwonted crowd gathered round the avenues of the Court of Queen's Bench at Westminster with a view to obtain admission to witness a young man, the son of a Warwickshire farmer, record his plea in answer to an appeal for murder. The 17th of November, 1817, will long be memorable in the annals of criminal jurisprudence for this plea; for when the prisoner, Abraham Thornton, was placed at the bar, the record was read, and when he was asked if he was "guilty or not guilty of the said felony and murder whereof you stand appealed," the young man took a slip of paper from the hands of his counsel, and said distinctly, "Not guilty! and I am ready to defend the same with my body;" and with these words he threw down a large gauntlet or glove, the fellow of one he wore.

There was silence in the Court. For the first time for many long years a prisoner had demanded to be tried by "Wager of Battle," and that for a cruel and brutal murder committed in Warwickshire. It was not a matter of wonder that the Court, over which Lord Ellenborough presided, should willingly grant time to those who had to consider what counter plea could be adduced in answer to this challenge.

The circumstances of the case were peculiar, and had become the theme of the county side for many months. The evidence forthcoming on the question was voluminous, but the facts themselves were but brief.

On the 27th of May, 1817, a young woman named Mary Ashford, who does not appear to have had a stain upon her character, left her uncle's house at Langley to attend a dance at an inn, known as Tyburn House, near Castle Bromwich. She was accompanied by a friend named Hannah Cox, and at the dance they met with Abraham Thornton, who appears to have paid great attention to Mary Ashford, and ultimately left the house with her, at twelve o'clock, with the intention of going home. They were seen together shortly after this time, and again at three o'clock. At four o'clock Mary Ashford went to Mrs. Butler's house at Erdington Green to change her dress and put on the clothes she had worn the evening before. Her friend, Hannah Cox, let her in, and there was nothing to lead to the supposition that at that time Mary Ashford was not in her usual health and spirits. She left the house between four and five o'clock, and at half-past six o'clock her shoes, bonnet, and the bundle containing her dancing dress she had with her were seen by the side of a pit on the road to Langley, and in that pit the body of Mary Ashford was found, and there was no doubt she had been abused, violated, and murdered. On the road between Erdington Green and Langley there were the marks of a man and woman's footsteps on the surface of a recently harrowed field, apparently made by persons who had been running. There were marks of a struggle, some signs of blood, and the mark of a man's footstep near the pit itself. Thornton admitted being with the deceased until four o'clock, and that they had been on terms of undue familiarity together, and his clothes were stained with blood. Evidence was given to show that Thornton had been seen walking slowly some distance away from the scene of the murder within so short a time as to prohibit the idea that he could have traversed the distance in the time which had elapsed.

On the 8th of August, 1817, Warwick was the scene of great excitement. As early as six o'clock in the morning crowds assembled round the County Hall doors, anxious, by coaxing, interest, or entreaties, to be admitted. At eight o'clock the press was so great that the javelin men of the Honourable Henry Verney, High Sheriff, could hardly make way for the entrance of the witnesses and other persons engaged on the trial. The doors were not thrown open for the admission of the public till after nine, though Mr. Justice Holroyd had taken his seat on the bench and had begun the trial soon after eight o'clock. The trial lasted twelve hours; and at the end, after a deliberation of only six minutes, Mr. George Hues, of Kenilworth, the foreman of the jury, announced the verdict of "Not Guilty," and Thornton was discharged. We are told by an eyewitness that his acquittal at the trial produced a sensation never equalled by any similar event. The *Lichfield Mercury*, then a paper of some importance, distinguished itself by issuing a map of the locality and publishing the portraits of the accused and the girl. Opinions have always been divided respecting the guilt or innocence of Thornton; and the case would have been forgotten, like many other similar stories of sin and crime, but for the subsequent proceedings.

On Thursday, the 9th of October, 1817, John Hackney, a sheriff's officer, of Birmingham, went to Castle Bromwich, armed with a writ from the Sheriff, and arrested Abraham Thornton, to answer the suit of William Ashford, the eldest brother and heir of Mary Ashford, on an appeal of murder. In the beginning of November a writ of Habeas Corpus was directed to the High Sheriff and the Keeper of the Warwick Gaol to bring the body of Abraham Thornton to the Court of Queen's Bench, and on the 6th of November he was brought before the Court. The writ of appeal and the subsequent proceedings were read, and at the request of Mr. Reader, the prisoner's counsel, the 17th of November was appointed to receive the prisoner's plea.

The proceedings had been taken under an old and obsolete law, which had come from Celt to Saxon times, and had found favour with Norman lawgivers. Even as far back as 1600 the law had been denounced as barbarous, cruel, and unjust, when Ralph Claxton petitioned the House of Lords * that they would interfere against such a plea for the avoiding of the shedding of blood, or otherwise by battle.

When Thornton threw down his glove as his "wage of battle," it was not taken up, but was ordered to be kept in the custody of the officers of the Court. The counter plea came before the Court on November 22, 1817, and the replication on January 24, 1818, and during this period Thornton was kept a prisoner in the King's Bench as a State prisoner. On January 29, issue was joined on the general demurrer, and on the 6th of February the argument commenced. It continued on February 7th, and on April 16th, 1818, the Court of Queen's Bench decided unanimously that, by the law of England, Abraham Thornton was entitled to his wager of battle. William Ashford declined the combat, by reason of his extreme youth, and Thornton was discharged from custody. This law was repealed (59 George III., c. 46) June 22, 1819; but Thornton, whose

* Lords' Journal, iv. 208.

father was a builder at Castle Bromwich, found public opinion so strong against him—for the whole county side believed him guilty—that he emigrated to America, and nothing more was heard of him.

William Ashford, who thus declined the combat, lived till February 18, 1866, when he died in Birmingham, whilst his sister, and the sister of the murdered young woman, Mrs. Lovett, lived till April, 1875, when she died at Erdington, not far from the spot where the murder was committed.

www.ingramcontent.com/pod-product-compliance
Lightning Source LLC
Chambersburg PA
CBHW020534300426
44111CB00008B/663

* 9 7 8 3 3 3 7 0 2 1 4 1 2 *